Human Rights and Environmental Sustainability in State-Owned Enterprises

This book presents case studies on the human rights performance of state-owned enterprises from four Latin American and three European countries, as well as foreign investments by Chinese state-owned enterprises on these continents. State-owned enterprises are considered among some of the worst perpetrators of contamination and corporate human rights violations around the globe, both domestically and abroad. This volume examines whether companies implement the UN Guiding Principles on Business and Human Rights and how their state owners regulate or incentivize their human rights compliance. Studies cover different sectors ranging from finance to extractives and air transport in Brazil, Chile, China, Ecuador, Finland, France, Germany, and Mexico and allow contrasts between companies from countries with different degrees of human rights regulation, including due diligence and supply chain laws. The work shows that states are rather hesitant to implement the UN Guiding Principles "leading by example." The book will be essential reading for academics, researchers, and policy-makers working in the areas of international human rights law, comparative administrative law, and corporate social responsibility.

Judith Schönsteiner is a full professor at the Universidad Diego Portales, Chile.

Markus Krajewski is a professor at the University of Erlangen-Nürnberg and holds the chair in public law and public international law.

Human Rights and International Law
Series Editor: Professor Surya P. Subedi, OBE, QC (Hon), DCL.

This series will explore human right law's place within the international legal order, offering much-needed interdisciplinary and global perspectives on human rights' increasingly central role in the development and implementation of international law and policy.

Human Rights and International Law is committed to providing critical and contextual accounts of human rights' relationship with international law theory and practice. To achieve this, volumes in the series will take a thematic approach that focuses on major debates in the field, looking at how human rights impacts on areas as diverse and divisive as security, terrorism, climate change, refugee law, migration, bioethics, natural resources and international trade.

Exploring the interaction, interrelationship and potential conflicts between human rights and other branches of international law, books in the series will address both historical development and contemporary contexts, before outlining the most urgent questions facing scholars and policy makers today

Available titles:

The Incoherence of Human Rights in International Law
Absence, Emergence and Limitations
Edited by Louisa Ashley and Nicolette Butler

Human Rights and Environmental Sustainability in State-Owned Enterprises
Edited by Judith Schönsteiner and Markus Krajewski

About the Series Editor

Professor Surya P. Subedi, OBE, QC (Hon) is Professor of International Law, University of Leeds, member of the Institut de Droit International and former UN Special Rapporteur for human rights in Cambodia.
www.routledge.com/Human-Rights-and-International-Law/book-series/HRIL

Human Rights and Environmental Sustainability in State-Owned Enterprises

Edited by Judith Schönsteiner
and Markus Krajewski

Routledge
Taylor & Francis Group
LONDON AND NEW YORK

First published 2025
by Routledge
4 Park Square, Milton Park, Abingdon, Oxon OX14 4RN

and by Routledge
605 Third Avenue, New York, NY 10158

Routledge is an imprint of the Taylor & Francis Group, an informa business

British Library Cataloguing-in-Publication Data
A catalogue record for this book is available from the British Library

ISBN: 978-1-032-27115-6 (hbk)
ISBN: 978-1-032-27116-3 (pbk)
ISBN: 978-1-003-29142-8 (ebk)

DOI: 10.4324/9781003291428

Typeset in Galliard
by Apex CoVantage, LLC

Contents

List of contributors *vii*

1 Introduction 1
JUDITH SCHÖNSTEINER AND MARKUS KRAJEWSKI

2 PEMEX and human rights: A case study of Mexico's largest state-owned enterprise 11
HUMBERTO CANTÚ RIVERA

3 Human rights and environmental sustainability in the Ecuadorian National Mining Company ENAMI EP 27
MARÍA JOSÉ LUQUE MACÍAS

4 Regulation of state-owned enterprises (SOE) in Brazil in relation to human rights 44
VICTÓRIA VITTI DE LAURENTIZ AND DANIELLE ANNE PAMPLONA

5 Chile: Due diligence and financial inclusion policies in the state-owned Banco Estado 62
MACARENA CONTRERAS SOTO, FRANCISCO SÁNCHEZ LAY AND JUDITH SCHÖNSTEINER

6 State-owned enterprises and human rights in Finland 84
MIKKO RAJAVUORI AND JUHO SALORANTA

7 Human rights responsibilities of state-owned companies in Germany: Development cooperation and sustainability financing as case studies 106
MARKUS KRAJEWSKI AND TINA BROSI

8 A review of the regulatory framework relating to human rights and environmental concerns for state-owned enterprises in France 129
MIHAELA MARIA BARNES

9 Chinese state-owned companies and investment in Latin America and Europe 147
LARRY CATÁ BACKER (白 轲)

10 Preliminary conclusions and prospects for further research 192
JUDITH SCHÖNSTEINER AND MARKUS KRAJEWSKI

Index *201*

Contributors

Editors

Markus Krajewski PhD, is a professor at the University of Erlangen-Nürnberg and holds the chair in public law and public international law. Professor Krajewski is one of the programme directors of the MA in Human Rights and chairperson of the Interdisciplinary Research Centre for Human Rights Erlangen-Nürnberg (CHREN). He also holds a MS in international affairs from Florida State University. His research focuses on international economic law, human rights, European external relations and the law of public services. Professor Krajewski is co-editor of the European Yearbook of International Economic Law (EYIEL), and Secretary General of the German branch of the International Law Association.

Judith Schönsteiner is a full Professor at the Universidad Diego Portales, Chile. She earned her PhD in law and an LLM in international human rights law from the University of Essex and an MA in political sciences from Johannes Gutenberg Universität Mainz, Germany. She was the director of the UDP's Human Rights Centre from 2012 through 2017 and Leibniz fellow of the Max Planck Institute of Public Comparative Law and International law in 2021. Professor Schönsteiner teaches business and human rights and is the director of Latin America's first Diplomado sobre Derechos Humanos y Empresas and an associate member of the Centre for Human Rights Erlangen Nürnberg (CHREN).

Authors

Larry Catá Backer (白 轲) is a W. Richard and Mary Eshelman Faculty Scholar and professor of law and international affairs at Pennsylvania State University and holds a BA from Brandeis University, a MPP from Harvard University's Kennedy School of Government, and a JD from Columbia University. Professor Backer focuses his research on governance-related issues of globalization and the constitutional theories of public and private governance, with an emphasis on institutional frameworks for public-private law governance systems. Recent work centres on issues of corporate social responsibility, mixed regulatory systems, and regulatory governance, especially touching on SOEs and SWFs. He has published widely on business and human rights issues.

Mihaela Maria Barnes is the Founder of Nomos Strategy. She advises on matters of public international law, international economic law, business and human rights, sustainability and corporate governance. Dr. Barnes earned her Ph.D. in International Law from the Graduate Institute of International and Development Studies, Geneva and her LL.M. in International and European Law (specialization: International Trade and Investment Law) from the University of Amsterdam. Dr. Barnes was a Visiting Fellow at the Lauterpacht Centre for International Law, University of Cambridge and a member of the Coordinating Committee of the European Society of International Law Interest Group on Business and Human Rights. She has published extensively in peer-reviewed journals and lectured at universities, research institutes and industry bodies around the world. A revised version of her Ph.D. dissertation (State-Owned Entities and Human Rights: The Role of International Law) was published by Cambridge University Press in 2022.

Tina Brosi is a PhD researcher and research assistant at Friedrich-Alexander-University Erlangen-Nürnberg. She studied law from 2016 until 2022 with a focus on international and European law. During her studies, she participated in the Philip C. Jessup International Law Moot Court Competition, coached one team, and was bailiff coordinator of the German National Round at the FAU. She also participated in the FAU's Model UN project. Her research focuses on corporate responsibilities for human rights and the human rights implications of the war on terror.

Humberto Cantú Rivera is a professor at the School of Law and Social Sciences of Universidad de Monterrey (Mexico) and Director of its Human Rights and Business Institute. He holds a PhD from Université Panthéon-Assas Paris II. He is the founding director of the Latin American Academy on Human Rights and Business and is a member of the steering committee of the Teaching Business and Human Rights Forum. He has published widely on business and human rights and has advised governments, international organizations, and business and civil society organizations on the topic, including as Expert Advisor to the government of Mexico in relation to the business and human rights treaty negotiations in the UN Human Rights Council.

Macarena Contreras Soto is a Chilean lawyer and a graduate in legal and social sciences from Universidad Diego Portales, with a diploma in business and human rights from the same university. She works as an analyst at the Inter-American Human Rights System of the Ministry of Foreign Affairs of Chile. Previously, she was a legal consultant in the Social Development Division at the Economic Commission for Latin America and the Caribbean of

United Nations (ECLAC), after having interned and worked at the Special Rapporteurship on Economic, Social, Cultural, and Environmental Rights at the Inter-American Commission on Human Rights. Between 2020 and 2023, she was a professor and coach of the human rights moot court team at the Universidad Diego Portales.

Victória Vitti de Laurentiz is a Brazilian lawyer with a PhD focusing on Human Rights Due Diligence from USP Law School (2022) and a bachelor's degree from Ribeirão Preto Law School-USP (2016). She was a visiting researcher at Yale University in 2018 and a member of the Yale-USP Food Law Clinic, coordinated by Professor Dr. Eduardo Saad-Diniz, responsible for the "private sector and collaborative governance" guideline. She worked as a research assistant at the University of Montréal (2016) and as a fellow at the DAAD-Winterkurs in Freiburg-Germany (2015). She is a collaborator of the USP Business and Human Rights Working Group founded in 2020.

María José Luque Macías is a Marie Sklodowska-Curie Postdoctoral (MSCA) Fellow, at Ghent University. She earned her Dr. Jur. from the FAU Erlangen-Nürnberg and an LLM from Potsdam University and is an Ecuadorian lawyer (UCSG) with research interests in international investment law, human rights law, and the business and human rights debate. Since the publication of her dissertation with Springer in 2021, her post-doctoral research has focused on analysing the nexus between human rights and the environment. At present, her project NGOsteertIACtHR empirically explores the influence of NGOs' agenda-setting power on IACtHR's case law relating to environmental matters.

Danielle Anne Pamplona is the Coordinator of the law graduate program at Pontíficia Universidade Católica do Parana (PUCPR-Brazil) and a full professor at PUCPR. She has a PhD from Universidade Federal de Santa Catarina UFPR, Brazil and was a Martin Flynn global law professor at the University of Connecticut and an international visiting scholar at the Bonavero Institute of Human Rights (2022) and the Max Planck Institute for Comparative Public Law and International Law, Heidelberg (2019). She was a postdoctoral student at the Washington College of Law at American University, Washington, DC (2015–2016) and is Director of the Human Rights Clinic at PUCPR and Co-President of the Global Business and Human Rights Scholars Association.

Mikko Rajavuori is Assistant Professor of Law at the Faculty of Law, University of Turku. Before his appointment, Rajavuori worked as an Academy of Finland post-doctoral fellow at the Center for Climate Change, Energy, and Environmental law (CCEEL), University of Eastern Finland. Dr. Rajavuori specializes in economic law and sustainability governance at the national, international, and transnational levels. In addition to his academic work, Rajavuori advises companies, NGOs, and the government on issues as varied as corporate governance, foreign investment, and business and human rights.

Juho Saloranta is a doctoral researcher and lecturer in business and human rights at the University of Eastern Finland, specializing in corporate sustainability issues from the legal perspective. His doctoral studies focus on due diligence/duty of care in operations and supply chains, corporate governance, and access to remedy. Previously, he worked as a legal advisor at the European Parliament and as a legal intern at the Business and Human Rights Resource Centre. Saloranta is also the founder of the Finnish Corporate Responsibility Law Association.

Francisco Sánchez Lay graduated from University of Chile Law School and obtained a master's degree in international human rights law at Universidad Diego Portales, with a dissertation on the human rights policies of Banco Estado. Since 2018, he has worked as governance senior Advisor at the United Nations Development Programme country office in Chile. Mr. Sánchez previously worked as a legal analyst at the Transparency and Integrity Commission of the General Secretariat of Presidency of Chile, where he also served as Chile's official point of contact for the Open Government Partnership (2014–2018) and as director of legal affairs at the Chilean National Chapter of Transparency International (2011–2014). Mr. Sánchez has also been an activist for LGBTI human rights at Fundación Iguales (2012–2018).

1 Introduction

Judith Schönsteiner and Markus Krajewski

The special role and responsibilities of state-owned enterprises (SOEs) with regards to human rights and sustainability have long been recognised in the relevant international normative standards and by international human rights bodies. The 2011 United Nations Guiding Principles on Business and Human Rights (UNGPs) urge states to "take additional steps to protect against human rights abuses by business enterprises that are owned or controlled by the State". In 2016, the United Nations Working Group on Business and Human Rights called on states to use SOEs to "lead by example".[1] Despite this normative recognition of the functions of SOEs, there is not enough empirical evidence and relevant data with regards to the human rights performance of SOEs. While there is a growing but still limited body of scholarship concerning theoretical, conceptual and normative issues,[2] case studies and concrete country examples remain scarce even though SOEs are active in high-impact sectors and

1 UN Working Group on Business and Human Rights, Report to the Human Rights Council, Leading by Example – The State, State-owned Enterprises and Human Rights 2016, A/HRC/32/45. CERALC, Liderando con el ejemplo en América Latina y el Caribe: Estado, Empresas de propiedad estatal y derechos humanos. Nota informativa del Grupo de Trabajo de la ONU sobre Empresas y Derechos Humanos, 2023.

2 See Rajavuori, Mikko (2015): "How Should States Own? Heinisch v Germany and the Emergence of Human Rights Sensitive State Ownership", *The European Journal of International Law*, Vol. 26, No. 3: pp. 727–746. Backer, Larry Catá (2017): "The Human Rights Obligations of State-Owned Enterprises (SOEs): Emerging Conceptual Structures and Principles in National and International Law and Policy", *Vanderbilt Journal of Transnational Law*, Vol. 50, No. 4: pp. 827–888; Mayer, Benoit, Mikko Rajavuori and Mandy Meng Fang (2017): "The Contribution of State-Owned Enterprises to Climate Change Mitigation in China", *Climate Law*, Vol. 7, No. 2–3: pp. 97–124. Barnes, Mihaela (2018): "The United Nations Guiding Principles on Business and Human Rights, the State Duty to Protect Human Rights and the State-Business Nexus", *Revista de Direito Internacional, Brasilia*, Vol. 15: p. 41. Rajavuori, Mikko (2018): "Governing the Good State Shareholder: The Case of the OECD Guidelines on Corporate Governance of State-Owned Enterprises", *European Business Law Review*, Vol. 29, No. 1: pp. 103–142. Schönsteiner, Judith (2022): "Inter-American Elements for a Systemic Approach to State-Owned Enterprises", *Human Rights Obligations, Business and Human Rights Journal*, Vol. 7, No. 3: pp. 397–417. Barnes, Mihaela (2022): *State-Owned Entities and Human Rights. The Role of International Law* (Cambridge: Cambridge University Press), reviewed by Uvarova, Olena (2023): "Mihaela Maria Barnes, State-Owned Entities and Human

DOI: 10.4324/9781003291428-1

responsible for contamination and corporate human rights violations in many countries both domestically and in respect of their investments abroad. The impact is often due to the sectors in which they are operating, such as mining, oil and gas, and infrastructure, and services such as finance and air transport but can also be due to lack of enforcement of regulation or absence of accountability mechanisms. In these contexts, the question of whether SOEs take measures for respecting human rights becomes more important.

The present book seeks to fill the lacuna of systematic information and evaluation of SOE performance towards international human rights standards. To this end, the various chapters explore the human rights and environmental sustainability performance of European and Latin American SOEs in different countries and sectors according to a common framework of analysis. It contains reports on four Latin American countries (Brazil, Chile, Ecuador and Mexico) and three European countries (Finland, France and Germany). The two regions were chosen to enable comparisons among legal and political systems of a certain proximity. In addition, SOEs of the People's Republic of China is studied with regards to its investments in Europe and Latin America. Based on the UNGPs of 2011 and OECD Guidance of 2017, the country studies provide a concept-driven description and analysis of human rights policies as well as regulatory and governance-based accountability mechanisms of SOEs that are considered to enhance environmental sustainability and respect for human rights.

In this introduction, we define the core concepts addressed in the book, in particular the notion of SOEs, human rights due diligence and state responsibility for actions and omissions of SOEs in international human rights law. Subsequently, we provide an overview of the chapters of the book, identifying common themes and questions and drawing comparisons between the different country studies.

1 Conceptual framework

State-owned enterprises (SOEs) are companies that have at least a 10% of state ownership, be that at the federal, regional or local level, regardless of the legal form of the SOE. SOEs worldwide show a great variety of governance structures and regulation and oversight models, as well as ownership structures.[3] Their functions reach from sector regulation or administration and execution of economic or social policies, including monopolies, to the provision of essential services and ordinary business, where SOEs are equal competitors to private companies. While the OECD shows a preference for

Rights. The Role of International Law (Cambridge: Cambridge University Press, 2022)", *Business and Human Rights Journal*, Vol. 8, No. 2: pp. 301–303. doi:10.1017/bhj.2023.18.

3 OECD (2021): Ownership and Governance of State-Owned Enterprises: A Compendium of National Practices, available at www.oecd.org/corporate/ownership-and-governance-of-state-owned-enterprises-a-compendiumof-national-practices.htm.

this last type of SOEs and recommends states moving towards this model, realities are much more complex even among OECD members and associate members and become even more variable on a global level.

Human rights obligations with regards to SOEs can be established on two grounds: First, SOEs must respect the human rights, by virtue of international human rights treaties ratified by their state owners,[4] in the UN Guiding Principles on Business and Human Rights, and the OECD Guidelines on Governance of State-Owned Enterprises. Second, state organs must protect against negative human rights impact caused by SOEs. In its 2016 report, the Working Group on Business and Human Rights recommends that states should go beyond policy recommendations like those included in national action plans and amend national legislation in order to bring SOE governance and policies in line with the UNGPs.[5] That report, however, did not define legal obligations regarding SOEs and human rights but turned around "policy rationales" that would bring states to "lead by example".[6] Questions of legal obligations and responsibilities entered the discussion on SOEs and human rights through regional human rights systems.[7]

Quite obviously, there are different conceptions about SOE human rights responsibilities and obligations, distinguishing basically between the state responsibility to protect and guarantee and the business responsibility that can be understood, under certain conditions, as a state obligation to respect. On the one hand, Barnes follows the distinction between Pillar I obligations of the state and Pillar II responsibilities of the SOE,[8] a position that seems to be mainly reflected in European countries; the United States, Canada and Australia; the OECD, with its ideal-type distinction between SOE activity and public functions; and the European Court of Human Rights. In the Americas, on the other hand, the law recognizes that SOEs are not ideal-type institutions and very often either carry out public functions or are closely controlled by the state, and the corresponding responsibilities can be either of respect, protection and guarantee.[9] Backer, for his part, proposes leaving behind the Euro-centrist model of SOEs reflected in the OECD and approach human rights obligations of state-owned enterprises more holistically.[10]

4 Barnes 2022 and Schönsteiner 2022 with slightly different viewpoints on the issue of state responsibility, mainly due to a regional focus on Latin America in the second study.

5 UN Working Group on Business and Human Rights, Report to the Human Rights Council, Leading by Example – The State, State-owned Enterprises and Human Rights 2016, A/HRC/32/45, para. 26.

6 Ibid., paras. 12 and 23.

7 Inter-American Commission of Human Rights, Business and Human Rights: Inter-American Standards, OEA/Ser.L/V/II, CIDH/REDESCA/INF.1/19 (1 November 2019), paras. 50 and 312. For a debate, see Schönsteiner 2022.

8 Barnes 2018.

9 Schönsteiner 2022.

10 Backer 2017, 877.

In international law, there are several unresolved issues around SOEs.[11] One of them is immunities of state-owned enterprises in foreign courts and jurisdictions;[12] another one is attribution of actions and omissions of SOEs to their owners. Schönsteiner considers that even the business responsibility to respect can and should be attributed to the state in certain situations, following both recent arbitral jurisprudence and inter-American case-law.[13] Barnes, in turn, considers that attribution in general international law is based on a very limited view of direct attribution and rather construed around the concept of state due diligence regarding its enterprises.[14] The CERALC project led by the Office of the High Commissioner on Human Rights in collaboration with the ILO, the OECD and the Working Group on Business and Human Rights published a report in 2023 in which it follows the idea of direct attribution in certain cases.[15] The Inter-American Commission and Court of Human Rights presumed complete attribution implicitly until the judgment in Muelle Flores,[16] where, for the first time, attribution was at least in principle dissociated from the ownership stake. In that sense, the Inter-American Court took a functional criterion into account,[17] based on which SOE actions and omissions should be attributed to the state.

This volume adopts a pragmatic and systemic[18] approach of analysing the implementation and compliance of SOEs with UN and OECD standards, as well as international human rights treaty law. The studies do not ask who exactly is responsible for ensuring that a SOE "leads by example" but whether *any* actor pushes the SOE, through legal or policy or governance incentives, to do just that. Therefore, the normative framework of this book is based on the UN Guiding Principles on Business and Human Rights and the OECD Guidelines for Multinational Enterprises, as well as the OECD Guidelines on Governance of SOEs, complementing the human rights and environmental obligations that derive from the international treaties the respective states have

11 Barnes 2022. Earlier, Dereje, Jonas (2016): *Staatsnahe Unternehmen. Die Zurechnungsproblematik im Internationalen Investitionsrecht und weiteren Bereichen des Völkerrechts* (Baden-Baden: Nomos); Lee, Jaemin (2015): "State Responsibility and Government Affiliated Entities in International Economic Law", *Journal of World Trade*, Vol. 49: p. 117. Badia, Albert (2014): *Piercing the Veil of State Enterprises in International Arbitration* (Alphen aan den Rijn: Wolters Kluwer).

12 Backer, Larry (2021): 'Un Somaro Piumato' – Rethinking the Scope and Nature of State Liability for Acts of Their Commercial Instrumentalities: State Owned Enterprises and State-Owner Liability in the Post-Global, draft available at https://ssrn.com/abstract=3878303 (accessed 23 March 2024).

13 Schönsteiner, Judith (2019): "Attribution of State Responsibility for Actions or Omissions of State-Owned Enterprises in Human Rights Matters", *University of Pennsylvania Journal of International Law*, Vol. 40: p. 895.

14 Barnes 2022, 264.

15 UNWG 2023, 24.

16 Muelle Flores v Peru, IACtHR Series C 375 (2019).

17 Schönsteiner 2019.

18 Schönsteiner 2022.

ratified. If pertinent for the relevant sector and state, authors include reference to the Paris Agreement of 2015 on climate change. The chapters of this book identify specific risks and pitfalls of accountability in SOEs that derive from the oversight and/or governance structure of the respective companies. Overall, it can be shown that SOEs, with very few exceptions in specific aspects of their performance, do not lead by example in human rights issues.

While Principle 4 of the UNGPs establishes state obligations with regards to SOEs, the respective duties are not just grounded in Principle 4; rather, as Backer rightly observes, "[T]he second pillar matters [for SOEs], . . . its scope of responsibility is autonomous of the state duty, and . . . it applies in equal measure to both private and public enterprises".[19] Questions of state responsibility and attribution aside, state due diligence and corporate due diligence are, from a functional viewpoint, quite similar.[20] Thus, Pillar II spells out how due diligence obligations of a state boil down to concrete mechanisms in a business structure – in this case, a state-owned enterprise.

Today, a trend has emerged to require human rights due diligence from all companies of a certain size; nevertheless, there seems to be no reason according to the UNGPs that would justify why a SOE would not have to carry out human rights due diligence. The OECD Guidance makes no difference either.

Human rights treaty bodies understand that states have several (specific and direct) obligations in relation to SOEs. For example, the Committee on ESCR has considered that the state has an obligation to respect human rights in the context of the SOE's activities: for example, in relation to water diminution or contamination through "waste from state-owned facilities"[21] and in relation to harm to health through "unlawfully polluting air, water and soil, e.g. through industrial waste from State-owned facilities".[22] Furthermore, "where the State has direct influence over rates of remuneration",[23] equitable working conditions should be achieved "as rapidly as possible".[24]

The question whether SOEs have obligations beyond the duty to respect human rights and might be responsible for guaranteeing or protecting them takes us to re-considering the means through which a state complies with its obligations. Whenever a SOE carries out functions that correspond to guaranteeing, for example, social rights or protecting inhabitants from human rights violations carried out by other private actors, the SOE would have the

19 Backer 2017, 864.

20 Schönsteiner 2022.

21 Committee on Economic, Social and Cultural Rights, General Comment 15, The right to water (Twenty-ninth session, 2003), U.N. Doc. E/C. 12/2002/11 (2002), para. 21.

22 Committee on Economic, Social and Cultural Rights, General Comment No. 14: The right to the highest attainable standard of health (art. 12), U.N. Doc. E/C.12/2000/4 (11 August 2000), paras. 43–45.

23 Committee on Economic, Social and Cultural Rights, General Comment No. 23, The right to just and favourable conditions of work (article 7 of the International Covenant on Economic, Social and Cultural Rights), U.N. Doc. E/C.12/GC/23 (26 April 2016), para. 14.

24 Ibid.

corresponding obligations. *Heinisch vs Germany* in the European Court of Human Rights was identified years ago as the exception to this European trend, which, despite some inconsistencies,[25] is construed upon reasoning on standing and attribution.[26] The source of these obligations is the delegation of functions; had the state delegated the guarantee of the right to water to a private company, the same duty to guarantee would arise as well.[27] If the state decided to entrust matters of policing to a SOE, the duty to protect would arise.[28]

2 Overview of the country studies

Based on the standards and obligations summarised here, the country studies in this book address issues of the three pillars of the UN Guiding Principles with regards to SOEs. In particular, the chapters contain factual information covering both regulation and governance mechanisms that might incentivize SOEs' human rights performance. On the one hand, regulation may cover general issues such as corporate law, environmental law or sectorial regulation for specific business sectors such as mining, banking, and oil and gas concessions; it may also refer to specific due diligence regulation as in France or Germany and specific regulation for SOEs in Latin American countries. On the other hand, governance measures may include human rights policies; due diligence procedures; risk and impact assessment; compliance and transparency mechanisms; access to remedies; and, eventually, civil, administrative or criminal liability schemes for board members, CEOs or responsible public officials. Finally, studies document concrete human rights impacts of SOEs, highlighting whether information is easily accessible or not. Studies in this book analyse publicly available documentation and do not incorporate interviews with key actors. Rather, the chapters of this book embed their analyses in historical and systematic overview of SOE structures, governance and accountability models. Sector-specific risks and issues are not addressed explicitly, but authors identify regulatory or policy-implementing functions in several countries, such as Ecuador, China and Chile.

25 Barnes, Mihaela (2022): "The European Court of Human Rights and State-Owned Entities: Engagement and Development of a Jurisprudence Constante", *The Law & Practice of International Courts and Tribunals*, Vol. 21, No. 2: pp. 369–415. doi:10.1163/15718034-12341478.

26 Rajavuori 2015, 727. Schönsteiner 2019.

27 *Ximenes Lópes v Brazil*, IACtHR Series C 149 (2006).

28 For a critical approach to the limited view on the responsibility to protect found in the UNGPs, see Bilchitz, David (2016): "A Chasm Between Is and Ought? A Critique of the Normative Foundations of the SRSG's Framework and the Guiding Principles", in: Deva, Surya and David Bilchitz (eds), *Human Rights Obligations of Business. Beyond the Corporate Responsibility to Respect?* (Cambridge: Cambridge University Press), p. 131 and 135; McCorquodale, Robert and Jonathan Bonnitcha (2017): "The Concept of Due Diligence in the UN Guiding Principles on Business and Human Rights", *European Journal of International Law*, Vol. 28, No. 3: p. 899.

The country studies were chosen to reflect different conceptions of SOEs, sectors, ownership structures and regulation. However, we attempted to cover the same sector(s) in at least two studies, provided state-ownership was relevant. Thus, the book includes studies on extractives, services and infrastructure – in particular, electricity – and banking. The Finnish study in addition realises a cross-sectorial overview. In general, countries have had considerable state ownership in past decades; thus, from Latin America, we included (from North to South), Mexico, Ecuador, Brazil and Chile; in Europe, again from North to South, Finland, Germany and France. Finally, considering the important investment by Chinese SOEs in both Europe and Latin America, we included a chapter on the impact of their foreign activities.

At the same time, the issue of the legal status of SOEs and the attribution of their actions or omissions to states under international (human rights) law is still a contested aspect in international law and in flux also in the Inter-American Human Rights System.[29] As of yet, no country in Latin America has a due diligence law, although a draft bill has been introduced in the Brazilian Congress, and in Chile, the competent ministry is attempting to draft such a bill.[30]

Overall, Latin American SOEs, if reaching the turnover threshold of the 100 largest companies to be evaluated by the Corporate Human Rights Benchmark, show medium scores just as their European counterparts. For example, the Colombian Ecopetrol scores 37.9 out of 100.[31] Thus, it is running close to the state-owned extractives company with the best score worldwide, the Norwegian Equinor with 38.8. This is a surprising result, considering that generally, European companies are considered world's best in human rights terms. The Brazilian state-owned Petrobras received 28.7 points. Vale's score is at 25.8 – the Brazilian state is a minority shareholder through a state-owned bank, and the government holds 12 golden shares. Latin American companies analysed in this book – including PEMEX – do not reach the CHRB threshold of the 100 largest companies and, therefore, do not have CHRB scores. Eletrobras is not evaluated by CHRB because the benchmark does not include energy companies. These limitations could, in future research, be overcome if smaller SOEs were systematically analysed against the criteria of the CHRB, either by the World Benchmarking Alliance itself or by other researchers.

For both Mexico and Ecuador, authors chose to study SOEs from the extractives sectors. Humberto Cantú Rivera examines Mexico's oil and gas giant PEMEX, asking whether regulation, governance and access to justice can enhance a human rights approach to its activities. The chapter discusses the domestic regulation of SOEs in light of the international and inter-American human rights frameworks, looking specifically into legal liability

29 Schönsteiner 2022.

30 In Peru, there is a draft elaborated by civil society and, in Colombia, a governmental initiative.

31 All data in this paragraph is taken from World Benchmarking Alliance, 2023 Corporate Human Rights Benchmark, available at www.worldbenchmarkingalliance.org/publication/chrb/.

under domestic law to evaluate whether access to justice is achieved in relation to the damage the SOE causes.

In Ecuador, ENAMI, the state-owned mining company, administers the country's mining concessions and operates some of them. María José Luque Macías studies the extent to which human rights are considered in the different regulatory and governance mechanisms and asks in relation to two concrete mining projects, the Llurimagua and Los Cedros mines, whether the company has managed to respect human rights: in particular, environmental and indigenous rights.

Danielle Anne Pamplona and Victória Vitti de Laurentiz, in turn, analyse Eletrobras, Latin America's largest energy company, owned by the Brazilian state. Revising the template of state regulation, governance and access to justice and studying the Belomonte hydroelectric project that was brought before the Inter-American Commission of Human Rights, they discuss in particular whether the company's policy and behaviour can be considered "leading by example" in relation to other Brazilian SOEs and energy companies.

In the Chilean case study, Macarena Contreras Soto, Francisco Sánchez Lay and Judith Schönsteiner chose the state-owned enterprise that is most remote from executive control (in comparison to the rest of Chilean SOEs): the consumer bank Banco Estado. The case study examines whether, in such a setting, respect for human rights is only based on governance mechanisms or also responds to specific policy-making or regulatory intervention by the state. The chapter addresses respect for human rights in client relations, policy definitions and investment conditioning.

In Europe, SOEs are usually more distant to the state. After massive privatisation during the 1980s and 1990s, the number and relevance of SOEs in Europe decreased significantly. The European – or better EU – conception of SOEs is illustrated by the rules on public enterprises enshrined in Article 106 of the Treaty on the Functioning of the European Union (TFEU), which requires EU member states to submit SOEs to the general disciplines of competition law and internal market regulations. In this model, SOEs are allowed to exist side by side with private entities, but any privilege or support given exclusively to SOEs can only be justified in exceptional circumstances. This approach aligns with the OECD framework on SOEs, which also sees them as competitors to private enterprises. The EU also claims to be "a frontrunner in implementing the UN Guiding Principles on Business and Human Rights"[32] but has not addressed SOEs specifically in this context. None of the numerous EU legal instruments, including the EU Corporate Sustainability Due Diligence Directive (EU CSDDD),[33] contains specific regulations for SOEs.

32 European Union External Action Service, Business and Human Rights, available at www.eeas.europa.eu/eeas/business-and-human-rights_en.

33 See Council of the European Union, Proposal for a DIRECTIVE OF THE EUROPEAN PARLIAMENT AND OF THE COUNCIL on Corporate Sustainability Due Diligence and amending Directive (EU) 2019/1937 – Letter to the Chair of the JURI Committee of the

The EU CSDDD, however, will also have an impact on SOEs in EU member states as it will apply to enterprises regardless of their ownership structure. However, the actual implementation requires legislative activities in the member states and may therefore only become legally relevant in the coming years. The country studies in the volume therefore do not take the impact of the EU CSDDD on SOEs into account.

Just as Latin American SOEs, European state-owned companies are not the largest worldwide, and therefore, only two European state-owned companies are evaluated by the CHRB: the Norwegian Equinor (see earlier in this chapter) and the Italian ENI, in which the Italian State holds a 30% golden share. ENI scores 55.9, the best result of a SOE in the CHRB sample. The case studies selected for this volume shed some light on the range of different regulatory and governance models that European states have implemented. It seems surprising that European companies do not have considerably better scores throughout than Latin American ones, which do not have to respond to due diligence regulation and mostly not even to non-financial reporting in the home country.

Mikko Rajavuori and Juho Saloranta take a cross-sectoral approach on Finnish SOEs, with a focus on six companies, covering some in which the government is a direct shareholder (these include, e.g., Finnair and energy companies Fortum and Neste); a company the state operates through a holding company (logging company Stora Enso); the holding company itself, Solidium; and the Finnish export credit agency Finnvera. They ask to what extent the companies have to respond to human rights requirements by the state and to what extent the Finnish ownership entity implements human rights policies in the companies. In that context, they take into account sector-related differences and differences related to the type of ownership.

In Germany, enterprises owned by public entities exist at federal, state and communal levels, but most of them are enterprises of local governments entrusted with the provision of public services. Due to their size, many of them are not subject to the 2021 Supply Chain Due Diligence Law (*Lieferkettensorgfaltspflichtengesetz*). After describing how German SOEs are constituted and structured in administrative law and how, in general, their accountability mechanisms work, Markus Krajewski and Tina Brosi's chapter looks at two federally owned enterprises: the state-owned bank KfW and the GIZ, the German agency for international cooperation, specialising in "sustainable development" and technical counterpart of the government's foreign development policies. For the purposes of examining the implementation of human rights obligations, the two companies are especially interesting as they both have significant extraterritorial activities, either through their investment (KfW) or their main activities (GIZ). Both enterprises are also subject to the Supply Chain Due Diligence Law.

European Parliament, available at https://data.consilium.europa.eu/doc/document/ST-6145-2024-INIT/en/pdf. Final approval pending when closing this chapter.

Mihaela Maria Barnes's analysis of two French SOEs also looks at two companies which are regulated by an explicit legal due diligence framework. The Loi de Vigilance (Due Diligence Law) adopted in 2017 applies to both Electricité de France (EDF, 84.5% state-ownership) and Air France-KLM (28.6% French state ownership). Furthermore, as for all EU countries, several directives on business respect for human rights need to be taken into consideration. In France, all companies in which the state has majority ownership, majority votes or decision-making power are considered public. The chapter examines the companies' understanding of specific governance and regulatory initiatives on respect for human rights and discusses whether they effectively "lead by example".

Against the macroeconomic backdrop of Chinese foreign economic policy, the chapter by Larry Catá Backer studies the extent to which human rights and environmental sustainability issues are relevant in the Belt and Road Initiative that drives foreign investments by Chinese SOEs. The case study discusses whether Chinese SOEs can be analysed under a liberal framework of international human rights law and, rather than examining a single SOE, examines the submissions by the Chinese state and Latin American and European civil society actors to the Committee on Economic Social and Cultural Rights that was reviewing Chinese treaty commitments in 2021. Backer posits that Chinese SOEs present an anomaly in liberal democratic internationalism, as they operate under government and party control and pursue interests different to those defined by companies in liberal economies.

Despite the differences of the legal, political, economic and regulatory contexts of SOEs in the Latin America and European countries studied in this volume, two things seem clear: First, the lack of empirical data and factual information as well as the complexity of SOE systems render clear and concise assessments of the performance of SOEs vis-à-vis human rights obligations difficult and require further research. Second, in all case studies, the role of the state remains of significant relevance. The normative and doctrinal framework of state obligations under human rights law with regards to SOEs therefore need to be studied and discussed further. In the final chapter of this volume, we offer further preliminary conclusions.

2 PEMEX and human rights

A case study of Mexico's largest state-owned enterprise

Humberto Cantú Rivera[1]

1 Introduction

The year 1911 was an important year for the oil industry in Mexico as it was during this time the country became the fourth largest oil producer in the world: it exported more than 900,000 barrels of oil, with more than 90% of its oil production controlled by American and British corporations Doheny and British Pearson, respectively. However, it wasn't until the First World War that Mexico became an important player in the oil world market. The higher demand for oil encouraged the country to increase its oil production and eventually allowed the country to become the second largest oil exporter worldwide. The increasing interest in guaranteeing oil production was at its peak during this period, when several countries, especially those greatly dependent on the Mexican reserve (such as the United States), even tried influencing Mexico's domestic situation during its revolutionary war in order to maintain their oil supplies. Oil became such an important product for the Mexican economy that in 1921, it represented one third of the federal income. However, soon after, there was a worldwide decline in oil production, and by 1930, Mexico's production was only 30% of what it had been in 1921. Nonetheless, the national economy began to grow, with industrial production becoming its major source of income.

A deep sense of nationalism was instilled in the country during the post-revolutionary era. Mexican authorities wanted to keep the oil industry's income, which belonged to foreign investors in the country. This led to the approval of initiatives such as an increase in taxes on exported oil products and subsidies for kerosene and gas, amongst others. Due to the high importance that oil and its derivatives represented for the national economy and with the aim of controlling its supply and prices in order to promote industrialisation, Petróleos de México (PETROMEX, now PEMEX), a national oil company, was founded.[2]

1 The author would like to acknowledge the research assistance provided by Ms. Alejandra Benavides, research assistant at the Human Rights and Business Institute of the University of Monterrey, for the preparation of this chapter.

2 Uhthoff López, Luz María (2010): "La industria del petróleo en México, 1911–1938: del auge exportador al abastecimiento del mercado interno. Una aproximación a su estudio", *América*

DOI: 10.4324/9781003291428-2

The expropriation of foreign oil companies in 1938 by President Lázaro Cárdenas became part of what is known today as the Cárdenas Doctrine. Based on the persistence of this rooted nationalism and the need for independence and sovereignty, Cárdenas "freed" Mexico from the external political and economic pressure exerted on the country by foreign oil companies by no longer granting privileges to foreign investors and their investments, instead equalizing nationals to foreigners and forcing foreign investors to adapt to Mexico's laws.[3]

This historical background[4] sets an important basis to understand the particularly sensitive character of oil production in Mexico as well as its economic and political importance for the federal government. However, it also serves as a platform to analyse the extent to which this public company has been able to evolve and respond to contemporary demands, especially in relation to its potential involvement in environmental degradation and human rights abuses. As it is known, the UN Guiding Principles on Business and Human Rights[5] (UNGPs) stipulate that one of the key contexts in which governments can play a role in protecting against human rights abuses is precisely through the adequate regulation of enterprises they own or control.[6] Specifically, the interpretation provided by the UN Working Group on Business and Human Rights in this regard highlights the need to "lead by example", notably through the adoption of human rights policies and due diligence processes that allow state-owned enterprises (SOEs) to identify, prevent, mitigate and redress any actual or potential risks their activities may pose to human rights.[7] Thus, the level of proximity between the government and the SOE and the extent to which the former controls the latter would constitute reasons to consider the existence of a state duty to adopt measures and to ensure that the SOE respects human rights. Whether PEMEX currently integrates human rights considerations into its policies and practices is the main subject of the following paragraphs.

This chapter aims to address several specific questions to review the level of alignment of PEMEX with international responsible business conduct standards twelve years after the adoption of the UNGPs and the last review of the OECD Guidelines for Multinational Enterprises in 2023. Thus, the chapter

---

Latina en la Historia Económica, Vol. 33: pp. 5–30, available at https://www.scielo.org.mx/scielo.php?pid=S1405-22532010000100001&script=sci_abstract.

3 Torres, Blanca (1991): *México y el mundo: Historia de sus relaciones exteriores. Tomo VII: De la guerra al mundo bipolar* (México: Senado de la República).

4 See also Baker, George (2015): "Mexico's Upstream Business Model", *Mexican Law Review*, Vol. VIII, No. 1: pp. 123–125.

5 Human Rights Council, Guiding Principles on Business and Human Rights: Implementing the United Nations "Protect, Respect and Remedy" Framework, A/HRC/17/31 (21 March 2011).

6 *Ibid.*, principle 4.

7 Human Rights Council, Report of the Working Group on the Issue of Human Rights and Transnational Corporations and Other Business Enterprises, A/HRC/32/45 (4 May 2016), pars. 74–77.

will first look at the governance of PEMEX, considering both Mexico's Constitution and the company's regulatory framework (2), prior to analysing the extent to which its legislation and policies facilitate the inclusion and consideration of human rights standards (3). These elements will be completed with an analysis on the feasibility of holding PEMEX accountable, through judicial and non-judicial mechanisms, for its involvement in human rights abuses and environmental degradation (4), followed by some concluding remarks (5).

2 The governance of PEMEX

As it was explained before, understanding the functioning and role of PEMEX requires insight into the historical relevance of the constitutional control of oil activities, which undeniably ties the company to Mexico's post-revolutionary past (A).[8] But the reforms to its legal framework also point to a clearer understanding of the economic impact and opportunities brought by globalisation, especially the need to establish an effective corporate governance model (B) as an effort to become a reliable partner within its engagement in transnational business activities (C). The coexistence of sovereignty and transnationality in a single entity underscores the complexity of PEMEX, which translates into a difficult governance framework.

2.1 *The constitutional control over oil activities and the role of PEMEX*

While article 27 of Mexico's Constitution is key to understanding the country's position over the use of its natural resources, article 25 is also relevant to grasp how PEMEX works and how it influences Mexico's economy. Article 25 sets the foundation for state-owned enterprises by stating that the federal government will have complete ownership and control over its SOEs, specifically when it comes to the exploration and extraction of oil and other hydrocarbons, an activity considered "strategic" for the country's development. Therefore, its control is an exclusive attribution of the public sector.[9] In terms of the type of SOE, both the PEMEX Law and the Constitution refer to it as a "productive enterprise of the State", exclusive property of the federal government, with a separate legal personality and technical, operative and management autonomy.

The understanding of the key aspects of article 27 is important for two reasons. First, it establishes that the nation has direct control over all natural resources, including petroleum and all hydrogen carbides in any state (solid, liquid or gas). Such control is inalienable as well as imprescriptible, and the use

8 Baker, George, *op. cit.*, p. 135, describes this as a "populist" regime, explaining that it is populist "in that it consciously follows the contours of the government's petroleum narrative that has circulated since 1938, which is that a dimension of Mexico's national identity is associated with the exclusivity of the ownership of the country's hydrocarbon endowment".

9 Constitución Política de los Estados Unidos Mexicanos, art. 25.

and/or exploitation of such resources may only be carried out through concessions granted by the federal government.[10] However, concessions *cannot* be granted when it comes to the oil industry since, according to the Constitution, maintaining control over it will allow the country to achieve its purpose of obtaining income for the Federation that will contribute to the country's long-term development. Likewise, article 27 refers to the state's regulatory power and its right to impose on private property the modalities required by public interest as well as the management of the use of natural resources susceptible to appropriation, such as oil, in order to make an equitable distribution of public wealth and achieve a balanced development of the country.

These elements, as well as the possibility for the state to expropriate private property for public purposes, reflect a historical concern with the use – and abuse – of natural resources by private parties, particularly foreign investors. However, a 2013 constitutional reform of article 27 made an effort to modernise the hydrocarbons sector, with the aim of facilitating domestic and foreign investment and fostering collaboration and competition between private parties and PEMEX.[11] Beyond the prohibition to grant concessions and the explicit statement that hydrocarbons will remain national property, paragraph 7 of article 27 stipulates that the state will undertake oil exploration and extraction activities through SOEs or contracts of SOEs with private parties. This constitutional reform therefore allowed the participation of the private sector in this area in an effort to modernise one of Mexico's major sources of revenue. While the current administration has taken different steps to reinforce the role of PEMEX in the energy sector, to the detriment of other companies participating in the area, the 2013 constitutional reform not only affected the absolute monopoly of the state in the sector but also gave way to a new understanding of how PEMEX should be governed, to which we turn next.

2.2 *The corporate governance approach of PEMEX*

While, for practical matters, PEMEX has traditionally been managed as a parastatal entity[12] by the federal government (notably aligned to the different desires and focuses of every single administration), its legal framework

10 Constitución Política de los Estados Unidos Mexicanos, art. 27.

11 See Márquez, García, Lauren Astrid and Mendoza Noriega, Isidro Andrés (2020): "Análisis del control gubernamental en las empresas productivas del Estado a raíz de la reforma energética en México de 2013", *Boletín Mexicano de Derecho Comparado*, No. 127: pp. 142–145.

12 A "parastatal entity", while not clearly defined, refers to those entities that are classified as such by the Organic Law of the Federal Public Administration (*Ley Orgánica de la Administración Pública Federal*). Article 3.II of the Organic Law refers to enterprises with state participation, including productive companies of the State. PEMEX falls under such a category. For the purpose of this chapter, reference to a "parastatal entity" shall be understood as meaning an entity that is owned and controlled by the state, despite having a commercial or productive nature in its activities, with its own legal personality and benefitting from technical, operative and management autonomy.

has slowly evolved to include some explicit characteristics and elements of corporate governance in an effort to transform it into a reliable and modern player in the global and regional energy sectors. This is particularly important considering that corporate governance in Mexico is not mandatory by law for commercial societies.

The legal framework regulating PEMEX's activities and operations[13] sets forth that the company will be operated and administered by a board of directors and a general director, whose main functions are to define the policies, guidelines and strategic goals of PEMEX and its subsidiaries as well as to carry out the management, operation, and execution of PEMEX'S strategic goals and objectives, respectively. Furthermore, it is the responsibility of the board to develop PEMEX's business plan with a five-year perspective, in which the business opportunities; main commercial, financial and investment strategies; an assessment of the company's operative and financial situation; results and performance indicators; and a strategic and commercial risk assessment must be included.[14]

PEMEX's director is appointed by the president of Mexico and may be removed at the discretion of the Federal Executive or through a decision adopted by at least seven of the ten members of the board. The board of directors, on the other hand, has ten members, including the Ministers of Energy and Finance; three members from the federal government appointed by the president; and five independent board members, also appointed by the president and ratified by the Senate.[15] Article 18 sets forth a fiduciary duty imposed on the board members, who are expected to act impartially and to the benefit and best interest of PEMEX,[16] a duty that is completed by references to diligence and loyalty (including different anti-corruption measures) in articles 33 and 34.

Furthermore, article 40 sets forth that the board will have committees of audit;[17] human resources and remuneration;[18] strategy and investment;[19] and purchases, leases, works and services.[20] All the committees will be able to request from the director any information necessary for the fulfilment of their functions,[21] thereby creating a structure aimed at facilitating informed decision-making. The law also creates a special regime on subsidiary companies,[22] foreseeing that PEMEX will have subsidiaries that will bear the same legal personality and affiliates (*filiales* in Spanish) that, despite ownership of over 50%

13 Ley de Petróleos Mexicanos.
14 Ley de Petróleos Mexicanos, art. 14.
15 Ibid., art. 15.
16 Ibid., art. 18.
17 Ibid., art. 42.
18 Ibid., art. 43.
19 Ibid., art. 44.
20 Ibid., art. 45.
21 Ibid., art. 41.
22 Ibid., arts. 59–71.

by PEMEX, will not be considered SOEs and will be regulated by the private law of their place of incorporation. As will be explored later in this chapter, the creation of foreign affiliates has transformed PEMEX into a transnational conglomerate, as has been the case with other Latin American oil SOEs.

Finally, as part of its corporate governance strategies, article 95 of the law sets forth that the board of directors of PEMEX shall issue a Code of Ethics[23] that will be applicable to its personnel, subsidiaries and affiliates as well as establishing the principles and guidelines that will be applicable to them. In addition, it has the responsibility to determine which organs will be in charge of monitoring compliance with the Code of Ethics and of establishing sanctions.

2.3 PEMEX as a transnational conglomerate?

One of PEMEX's outstanding characteristics is the fact that, for all its political use as a manifestation of Mexico's sovereignty, it has at least partially adapted to the logic of market economy and globalisation. As a result, it has slowly transformed itself into a transnational conglomerate under the direct control of the state.

As explained before, the constitutional reform of 2013 and the adoption of secondary legislation in the hydrocarbons sector led to a renewed understanding of the role that PEMEX had to play to compete with other public and private oil companies as well as to take advantage of its position in order to obtain better results in oil extraction and refinement. Article 61 of the law is instrumental in that regard as it foresees that companies in which PEMEX holds a controlling interest (that is, over 50% of its ownership stake) will be considered affiliates but not parastatal entities, as PEMEX was in the past. As a result, they will be considered private companies, regulated by the applicable law of their place of incorporation.

This change in the legal nature produces an important effect as it facilitates the indirect participation of the state in transnational oil markets, with PEMEX as an intermediary. But it also means that as an economic actor, the state (and PEMEX) enter into a dynamic in which sovereignty becomes blurry. When considered from an international legal perspective,[24] the not-so-evident effects of this situation go from the characterisation of the SOE as a fully private actor (with its consequences in terms of legal liability) to the inability of the State to claim sovereignty (and immunity) as a result of its activities *de jure gestionis*.

23 *Código de Ética de Petróleos Mexicanos, sus Empresas Productivas Subsidiarias y Empresas Filiales* (2019). The current version is available in Spanish at www.dof.gob.mx/2019/PEMEX/codigo_de_etica_122019.pdf.

24 See generally Sandoval Cervantes, Daniel (2020): "Lex Petrolea, transnacionalización de la regulación de los hidrocarburos y geopolítica de la energía", *Anuario Mexicano de Derecho Internacional*, vol. XX.

While most of its foreign activities relate to oil commercialisation, its transformation into a transnational conglomerate raises important questions regarding its accountability, not just from the perspective of transnational litigation but also from the perspective of international arbitration.[25] The law establishes in article 115 that PEMEX and its subsidiaries (but not its affiliates) may agree to engage in alternative dispute resolution mechanisms, including arbitration, and they may subject themselves to the application of foreign law, to the jurisdiction of foreign commercial courts and to arbitration agreements when convenient.

Additionally, as a transnational group of companies, this transformation raises the question of how and whether PEMEX and its conglomerate can adapt to comply with relevant applicable norms in the areas of sustainability, including in social and environmental risk management, and human rights as is currently the case for many other competitors in the oil market.

****

Despite the inherent political tensions regarding the role of PEMEX, both as a symbol of Mexico's sovereignty and as an economic entity that is the main contributor to Mexico's GDP (and therefore called to adhere to market practices), the constitutional reform and adoption of secondary legislation in 2013 have led to important efforts to convert it into a competitive player in the global oil markets. This change can be more clearly observed in PEMEX's corporate governance as the law has set forth important elements that would be more characteristic of a private oil company than of a state-owned enterprise. However, such a transformation has also led to the adoption (at least on paper) of a series of procedural requirements and safeguards to instill modern practices regarding transparency and accountability as a means to inspire trust from other parties. This is an important element because its effort to expand to foreign markets, even if only to ameliorate its standing and commercialization in Mexico, puts PEMEX and its transnational conglomerate in a complex position, considering the growing calls and demands for companies, especially in the extractive sector, to take measures to address human rights, environmental protection and climate change as part of their risk management process.

3 Human rights considerations in PEMEX's legal framework and policies

As incipient research shows, the human rights obligations of SOEs are still unclear and insufficiently developed in international law.[26] That, however,

25 For a general discussion on arbitration in relation to the energetic reform in Mexico, see Arredondo, Dante L. (2019): "The Mexican Limbo for International Investment Arbitration: Mexico and the Transnational Model. Investment Arbitration Under the Energetic Reform and the Latest Political Changeover", *Revista de Investigaciones Jurídicas*, No. 43: pp. 317–359.

26 Schönsteiner, Judith (2022): "Inter-American Elements for a Systemic Approach to State-Owned Enterprises' Human Rights Obligations", *Business and Human Rights Journal*, Vol. 7,

does not bear any particular relevance for the domestic human rights obligations of publicly owned companies, particularly when they have been explicitly transposed into the legislative and regulatory frameworks. Regardless, and as the following lines will show, the recent focus, recommendations and policy guidelines of different international organizations or expert bodies on the topic have yet to make a serious impact in the governance and behavior of SOEs, including PEMEX.

To begin with, an analysis of PEMEX's Law[27] and Regulation[28] shows only an indirect and brief reference to the issues that are normally considered as pertaining to human rights. For example, article 4 of the PEMEX Law alludes to social and environmental responsibility as part of the company's purpose and behaviour but fails to make any explicit reference to human rights or responsible business conduct. The law's regulation does not even make reference to such elements. The only exception can be found in articles 82 and 83, providing that in the context of contract for purchases, leases, works and services, the company and its subsidiaries shall have mechanisms to prevent, identify, correct and sanction irregular, illicit or negligent acts or omissions that could affect PEMEX's operations.[29] This legal approach to risk management could constitute a basis on which to expand the company's approach to human rights; however, as it can be observed, the focus is particularly aligned to modern corporate compliance approaches. While not mentioning such issues at the normative level may be troubling from a legal and management perspective, human rights are at least partially addressed at the corporate policy level.

Since 2019, PEMEX has issued several policies that touch on human rights from different angles. For example, in its Code of Ethics,[30] the company highlights respect, equality and non-discrimination as "ethical principles" and relations with third parties, personal relationships, community and environment and human rights as "Corporate ethical guidelines". In the section on relations with third parties, the company commits to avoiding procurement from people or companies that engage in any practices that are not in compliance with the Code of Ethics; on personal relationships, it expressly rejects any type of

---

No. 3: pp. 397–417; Cubides Sánchez, María Isabel (2022); "Empresas públicas: Cerrando la brecha de impunidad entre el deber de proteger y el deber de respetar los derechos humanos", in: Cantú Rivera, Humberto (ed.), *El tratado sobre empresas y derechos humanos: Perspectivas latinoamericanas* (Mexico: Tirant Lo Blanch); Prieto Ríos, Enrique y Pontón Serra and Juan Pablo (2022): "¿El Estado colombiano está liderando desde el ejemplo? La implementación de los Principios Rectores por las empresas estatales en Colombia", in Cantú Rivera, Humberto and Danielle Anne Pamplona (eds), *A una década de los Principios Rectores sobre las empresas y los derechos humanos* (Mexico: Tirant Lo Blanch).

27 Ley de Petróleos Mexicanos, art. 4.

28 Reglamento de la Ley de Petróleos Mexicanos.

29 Ley de Petróleos Mexicanos, art. 83.

30 *Código de Ética de Petróleos Mexicanos, sus Empresas Productivas Subsidiarias y Empresas Filiales*, 2019. Available in Spanish at www.dof.gob.mx/2019/PEMEX/codigo_de_etica_122019.pdf.

discrimination or harassment or any type of conduct or violence that affects dignity and human rights. But beyond these elements, it is in the sections on community and environment and human rights that the Code of Ethics makes a clearer pronouncement on what it considers to be the guidelines to follow. In the first, PEMEX commits to preventing risks to people, communities and the environment; however, it fails to make reference to the rights of indigenous peoples per se, an important omission considering the type of work the company performs and the geographical areas where it operates. In its section on human rights, beyond a general statement on the commitment to promote, respect, ensure and protect human rights (a clear reference to Mexico's constitutional mandate on human rights in art. 1), it makes a curious selection of the rights the company supports (adequate conditions at work, freedom of thought, conscience and religion and equal pay) and the violations it "rejects" (slavery and human trafficking and child labour), which, of course, entails the risk of ignoring other rights that must be respected or other adverse impacts that may arise.

The Code of Ethics is complemented by a Code of Conduct,[31] also adopted in 2019, that in several instances touches on human rights issues. In a section on personal relationships, the Code of Conduct sets forth the obligation of all its employees to respect human rights and comply with any PEMEX policy on the matter. In a separate section on community relations, the Code of Conduct declares that the company is socially responsible; it respects the customs, human rights and traditions of the communities where it operates, ultimately seeking to contribute to their sustainable development. Furthermore, it highlights several obligations: to treat with dignity and respect the members of the communities where the company operates, respecting their customs and traditions; to respect the environment; and to support and promote human rights in the communities. In addition to those sections, there are other references to conditions of work, including the prohibition of sexual and labor harassment or abuse.

While the adoption of an Organic Statute[32] by PEMEX's board in 2019 provided another important opportunity to have a better focus on its human rights obligations, the only serious contribution was the creation of a management position regarding social responsibility. Most of the focus of that function revolves around providing support and donations to communities, but article 91 of the statute identifies two relevant functions that have important human rights implications: 1) to participate and follow up on the procedures of free, prior and informed consultation that the Ministry of Energy undertakes in relation to PEMEX's projects and 2) to provide its opinion on the content of social impact assessments that PEMEX or its subsidiaries elaborate to

31 *Código de Conducta de Petróleos Mexicanos, sus Empresas Productivas Subsidiarias y, en su caso, Empresas Filiales*, 2019. Available in Spanish at www.dof.gob.mx/2019/PEMEX/codigo_de_conducta_102019.pdf.

32 *Estatuto Orgánico de Petróleos Mexicanos*, 2019.

comply with legal requirements, notably Mexico's Hydrocarbon Law. Beyond those references, however, the Organic Statute of the company fails to address human rights generally or human rights due diligence specifically.

The previous policies were completed by a 2018 document entitled "Policies and Guidelines for the Development of Due Diligence in PEMEX, its subsidiaries and affiliates, in the fields of corporate ethics and integrity" (Due Diligence Policies and Guidelines).[33] This document focused on the undertaking of commercial due diligence and the assessment and mitigation of risks of corruption. However, it was updated in 2021, with the supposed inclusion of human rights, equality and non-discrimination as elements introduced in the due diligence process.[34] Upon closer review, however, what the company does is present a questionnaire to "third parties" – defined as any natural or legal person that wishes to engage in a commercial relationship with PEMEX – to explain how they promote and protect human rights, particularly the elimination of forced labor, the eradication of child labor, the abolition of discrimination in the workplace and the promotion of a preventive approach to the environment. In terms of mitigation measures when "red flags" have been detected in relation to human rights, social responsibility, inclusion, equality and non-discrimination, PEMEX may request the third party to commit in writing to develop and promote a preventive program and to ensure a positive social and environmental impact as well as to adopt an internal policy on the matter. Furthermore, the policies and guidelines set forth a model confidentiality agreement, in which the parties declare they know the International Bill of Human Rights and the ILO Declaration on Fundamental Principles and Rights at Work and agree to be guided by "high standards of human rights protection". Finally, the model confidentiality agreement includes an operative clause that requires the parties involved to commit to respecting human rights during the execution of the agreement. However, there is no reference at all to PEMEX's own responsibility to undertake human rights due diligence processes in line with international responsible business conduct standards.

A final element of PEMEX policies is a "Human Rights Declaration",[35] adopted in 2019, in which the company commits to promote, respect, ensure and protect the human rights of its personnel, suppliers, investors, commercial partners, communities and the society. The declaration stipulates the rights it specifically aims to respect in relation to each type of stakeholder, and it particularly specifies its commitment to promote its personnel and contractors

33 *Políticas y lineamientos para el desarrollo de la debida diligencia en Petróleos Mexicanos, sus Empresas Productivas Subsidiarias y, en su caso, Empresas Filiales, en materia de Ética e Integridad Corporativa*, 2018.

34 *Políticas y lineamientos para el desarrollo de la debida diligencia en Petróleos Mexicanos, sus Empresas Productivas Subsidiarias y, en su caso, Empresas Filiales, en materia de Ética e Integridad Corporativa*, 2021.

35 *Declaración de Pemex para promover, respetar, proteger y garantizar los Derechos Humanos*, 2019, available at www.pemex.com/etica_y_transparencia/etica/Paginas/declaratoria-dh.aspx.

adopting preventive, mitigation and remediation measures for any negative human rights impacts that may affect the communities with which they interact. It completes its declaration with a compilation of the policies and mechanisms available to report any failure in their implementation, including an ethical line, an email and an internal telephone number.

As it can be observed, the human rights considerations in PEMEX's policies fall particularly short of the focus adopted in international policy guidelines, including the UNGPs and the OECD Guidelines for Multinational Enterprises on Responsible Business Conduct,[36] by failing to address all internationally recognised human rights. Of note is the fact that, despite referring to the OECD Guidance on Due Diligence for Responsible Business Conduct as one of the documents that were reviewed for the renovation of its Due Diligence Policies and Guidelines, the company also fails to clearly distinguish between commercial due diligence and human rights due diligence, including the differences in their implementation. This is reiterated in its most recent sustainability report (2020), in which no analysis is declared to have been undertaken in relation to PEMEX's own activities,[37] focusing instead on third parties and particularly on certain rights or violations, instead of all human rights.[38] Such failure may well be connected to the political landscape of the country, where fossil fuels have again become a central element of Mexico's economy and political discourse and where issues that may affect or disrupt PEMEX's operations could be in conflict with the government's position on the topic.

Despite the limitations in the understanding of the concept of human rights due diligence and its inadequate translation into the company's policies, the existing approach does provide a basis to support a more explicit inclusion of human rights and environmental standards into the procurement practices and business relationships of the company, since the Due Diligence Policies and Guidelines already provide for the inclusion of some requirements by any third party wishing to do business with PEMEX. Of course, to align closer to the standards set forth by the UN Guiding Principles, it would be desirable to focus on the full scope of human rights and to ensure that all governance entities, suppliers, contractors and affiliates undertake risk-based due diligence processes. This, in turn, could entail the need for PEMEX to go beyond exclusively establishing specific performance requirements into contractual clauses and instead focus on overseeing the manner in which its suppliers and

36 *OECD Guidelines for Multinational Enterprises on Responsible Business Conduct*, 2023.

37 PEMEX, *Informe de Sustentabilidad 2020*, p. 115. As per the report, most of the focus revolves around capacity building on inclusion, equality and non-discrimination.

38 Certainly, the focus on some rights linked to the environment, such as water or the environment itself, are included within different sections, highlighting the need to ensure a thorough understanding of the content of human rights. It is important to note, however, that the most recent sustainability reports have started to include references to the company's impact on climate change, which may imply at least some level of recognition of the issues posed by such a global threat and the role of the company in combating it.

contractors put into place a system that allows them to identify, prevent and mitigate human rights and environmental risks.[39]

4 Can PEMEX be held liable for environmental and human rights violations?

One of the most frequently recurring situations regarding oil operations has been the potential risks that such activities entail for human rights and the environment, especially the complexity of holding those companies accountable if they fail to prevent oil spills.[40] That complexity can be further exacerbated by the state ownership or control of said companies, particularly considering that the economic interests of the state itself may be deeply interrelated with those of the company. As a result, legal liability and reparations may be difficult to ensure.[41]

In the case of PEMEX, its liability regime is determined partially by its own constitutive law and partially by the general legal regimes on civil and environmental liability. To begin with, article 115 of PEMEX's Law only provides that any "national controversies" involving PEMEX and its subsidiary companies will be subject to the jurisdiction of federal courts and that the company may agree to participate in non-judicial dispute resolution procedures. However, there are no further references to its liability in cases of environmental degradation or human rights violations, with article 3 merely stipulating that the company will also be subject to commercial and civil law. Nevertheless, the Federal Law on Environmental Liability provides in article 12.I that any action or omission related to hazardous materials or waste leading to environmental damage will result in the objective (strict) liability of its perpetrator. In addition, article 25 of the law stipulates that environmental liability will be attributed to the natural or legal person that fails to prevent the damage, if it had a legal duty to do so. Furthermore, articles 68 and 69 of the General Law for

39 Sherman III, John (2021): No Need to Reinvent Wheels: Drafting Meaningful Human Rights Due Diligence Through Model Suggested Supply Chain Contract Clauses, March, available at https://shiftproject.org/aba-contract-clauses/.

40 See Lambooy, Tineke, Aikaterini Argyrou and Mary Varner (2013): "An Analysis and Practical Application of the Guiding Principles on Providing Remedies with Special Reference to Case Studies Related to Oil Companies", in Deva, Surya and David Bilchitz (eds), *Human Rights Obligations of Business: Beyond the Corporate Responsibility to Respect?* (Cambridge: Cambridge University Press). See also Lindsay, Rae, et al. (2013): "Human Rights Responsibilities in the Oil and Gas Sector: Applying the UN Guiding Principles", *The Journal of World Energy Law & Business*, Vol. 6, No. 1; Meeran, Richard and Jahan Meeran (eds) (2021): *Human Rights Litigation against Multinationals in Practice* (Oxford: Oxford University Press).

41 See generally Barnes, Michaela Maria (2022): *State-Owned Entities and Human Rights: The Role of International Law* (Cambridge: Cambridge University Press); see also Cubides Sánchez, María Isabel (2022): "Empresas públicas: Cerrando la brecha de impunidad entre el deber de proteger y el deber de respetar los derechos humanos", in Cantú Rivera, Humberto (ed.), *El tratado sobre empresas y derechos humanos: Perspectivas latinoamericanas* (Mexico: Tirant Lo Blanch).

the Prevention and Integral Management of Waste set forth the liability of any natural or legal person responsible for the pollution, as well as for any resulting health damage, establishing a duty to repair, compensate and remediate the environmental degradation.

This has led to an interesting judicial analysis on the liability regimes applicable to PEMEX for its involvement in negative impacts on the environment, particularly through the lens of a recent decision in a criminal court.[42] In the *cas d'espèce*,[43] PEMEX presented a criminal complaint for the third-party sabotage of its oil pipelines in Guanajuato, a state in central Mexico, in December 2013. The environmental regulatory authority initiated an administrative procedure against PEMEX, determining its administrative liability for violating several environmental laws and for failing to remediate the environmental damage caused by the sabotage. PEMEX appealed the ruling on the basis that it cannot be held liable for oil spills resulting from illicit acts, acts of God or force majeure. However, the appellate court found that even if the oil spill was the result of third-party sabotage, PEMEX had hazardous waste management obligations of an objective (strict) nature due to the type of economic activity it undertook. The appeal was upheld by the Federal Tribunal of Administrative Justice (FTAJ) in 2015. However, PEMEX filed an *amparo* claim[44] against the decision in 2016, arguing that several of its "fundamental rights" recognized by the Constitution and by article 8 of the American Convention on Human Rights had been violated by the judgment of the FTAJ. The case was heard by the specialized chamber of the Eighteenth Administrative Tribunal of the First Circuit, based in Mexico City.

On the issue of environmental liability for sabotage, the tribunal analysed whether illicit acts limited PEMEX's liability under the different – and allegedly contradictory – applicable laws. To that end, the tribunal highlighted the existence of a special environmental liability regime deriving from the constitutional recognition of the right to a healthy environment, which is of a different nature than the ordinary administrative liability regime. However, it also recognised that it would have to make a systemic interpretation between several applicable and complementary laws, including the Federal Law on Environmental Liability and the General Law for the Prevention and Integral Management of Waste, on the one hand and the applicable regulations for the oil industry, which also derived from article 27 of the Constitution, on

42 It must be noted, however, that very few judgments regarding PEMEX's liability for non-labor-related issues have been identified.

43 Decimoctavo Tribunal Colegiado en Materia Administrativa del Primer Circuito, *PEMEX Refinación (ahora PEMEX Logística) vs. Sala Especializada en Materia Ambiental y de Regulación del Tribunal Federal de Justicia Administrativa*, Amparo directo 474/2016 (24/08/2017).

44 The *amparo* procedure is used, among others, to challenge the conformity of a judgment with constitutional provisions, normally before federal courts. An *amparo directo en revisión* is a type of amparo whereby the Supreme Court may exceptionally and discretionally review a case in which the direct interpretation of a constitutional provision (including regarding human rights aspects) is the subject matter.

the other. In its analysis, the tribunal reasoned that because the environmental liability regime derives from the constitutional recognition of the right to a healthy environment (which was a recent addition to the Constitution), the inferior normative hierarchy of the regulatory framework that establishes PEMEX's limited liability for illicit acts would have to be disregarded in order to ensure the necessary environmental remediation. To arrive at such a conclusion, the tribunal relied on international environmental principles, such as the "polluter pays" principle and other elements of the Rio Declaration on the Environment and Development.[45]

But probably the most important part of the judgment was the determination that PEMEX's environmental liability derived from the nature of its activities – that is, the management of hazardous materials and waste – and from the duty of care arising from it.[46] The tribunal argued that the scope of PEMEX's duty of care included taking reasonable measures against foreseeable or reasonably avoidable situations of environmental damage, including the illegal sabotage of its oil pipelines. Thus, in the opinion of the court, the focus of PEMEX should be in taking measures to prevent such situations from happening, especially since it was in a better position to understand the functioning and risks of its activities.

Furthermore, the tribunal considered that because the company was using the area where the oil leaks happened, it had a joint and several liability to ensure the environmental remediation. As a result, PEMEX was found liable for its inherently dangerous activities and for its failure to take adequate preventive measures to avoid the sabotage of its oil pipelines.[47] While the judgment only referred to environmental liability, it would be feasible for a court to consider following a similar approach in cases related to human rights, especially considering the judicial doctrine of their "transversal" effect[48] vis-à-vis other legislative or regulatory frameworks.

Beyond the few judicial decisions on PEMEX's liability for environmental impacts, one specific non-judicial mechanism stands out for its potential to

45 Decimoctavo Tribunal Colegiado en Materia Administrativa del Primer Circuito, *PEMEX Refinación (ahora PEMEX Logística) vs. Sala Especializada en Materia Ambiental y de Regulación del Tribunal Federal de Justicia Administrativa*, Amparo directo 474/2016 (24/08/2017), p. 41.

46 *Ibid.*, p. 80.

47 As it can be observed, such a decision mirrors similar conclusions reached by courts in Colombia and The Netherlands regarding corporate liability for environmental damage. For the Colombian case (OCENSA), see Supreme Court of Justice, Civil Cassation Chamber, SC5686–2018 (19 December 2018); for the Dutch case (*Akpan et al v. Royal Dutch Shell PLC et al*), see The Hague District Court, Case C/09/337050/HA ZA 09–1580 (30 January 2013).

48 SCJN, First Chamber, *Amparo directo en revisión 5505/2017* (13 January 2021). For a short interpretation of the judgment and the "transversal effect" doctrine, see Cantú Rivera, Humberto and Barboza López, Miguel (2022): "Corporate Liability for Human Rights Abuses in Latin American Courts: Some Recent Developments", *Business and Human Rights Journal*, Vol. 7, No. 3: pp. 481–486.

establish liability for the company's involvement in human rights violations: Mexico's National Human Rights Commission (CNDH). The CNDH is a national human rights institution with a complaints-handling mechanism that allows it to issue non-binding recommendations to administrative authorities for human rights violations.[49] While it does not have the competence to issue recommendations to private companies directly, in a recent commentary, it determined that it did have a direct competence over actions or omissions of state-owned enterprises that constitute human rights violations.[50] As a result, the CNDH can issue recommendations to PEMEX for cases in which its behavior directly or indirectly harms human rights or the environment and establish reparatory measures, as well as filing administrative or criminal complaints against it. The potential relevance of such a mechanism lies in its political visibility and moral and social impact, which could be complemented by other administrative or judicial measures. However, no cases have been resolved yet regarding PEMEX's human rights impacts as a result of its oil operations.[51] The aforementioned examples highlight some of the limitations of holding PEMEX liable for environmental or human rights violations through both judicial and non-judicial mechanisms. However, they also provide some clarity on the judicial interpretation of the applicable liability regime for environmental impacts in a context where different laws provide for varying standards, as well as the possibilities for the national human rights institution to have a more active role in this matter.

5 Conclusion

This chapter sought to analyse the level of alignment of PEMEX's governance and activities with international responsible business conduct standards, particularly the UN Guiding Principles on Business and Human Rights. As it has been addressed in the preceding paragraphs, the regulatory framework of PEMEX fails to clearly and unequivocally declare the responsibility of the company to respect human rights; however, in its internal policies and guidelines, that commitment is at least partially referred to in different instruments, providing for a partial integration of international standards and practices into

49 Cantú Rivera, Humberto (2020): "National Human Rights Institutions and Their (Extended) Role in the Business and Human Rights Field", in: Deva, Surya and David Birchall (eds), *Research Handbook on Human Rights and Business* (Cheltenham: Edward Elgar).

50 CNDH, *Recomendación General 37 sobre el respeto y observancia de los derechos humanos en las actividades de las empresas*, 2019, pars. 138–139.

51 PEMEX has received several recommendations over the years, but many of them derive from the inadequate health services and medical malpractice in its own hospitals. One relative exception is a case involving the sabotage of oil pipelines, where PEMEX's security management team may have detained and held several persons in its facilities as a result of their probable involvement; the CNDH ordered it to stop holding people in its facilities as well as to take different trainings on human rights, the use of force and other relevant issues. See CNDH, *Recomendación No. 12VG/2018* (17 September 2018).

its day-to-day operations. In terms of implementation, PEMEX follows an approach more akin to compliance processes, asking of its contractors and suppliers whether they respect human rights; nevertheless, little evidence has been found of actual efforts by the company to undertake serious human rights and environmental due diligence processes.

A similar situation arises in relation to its own operational-level grievance mechanism, which doesn't appear to be aligned with the effectiveness criteria set forth by Guiding Principle 31, despite being complemented by a legal framework, as access to (judicial or non-judicial) remedy for environmental degradation or adverse human rights impacts caused or contributed to by PEMEX is far from evident. However, some judicial decisions shine light on the possibility of holding PEMEX accountable for failing to adopt preventive, mitigation or remediation measures that should have been foreseeable.

In general terms, this chapter has provided evidence of the insufficient efforts by PEMEX, as the largest Mexican SOE, to walk the talk of human rights; it also offers a glimpse into several measures that could be potentially adopted at the legislative, regulatory and policy levels to facilitate further alignment with international responsible business conduct standards.

3 Human rights and environmental sustainability in the Ecuadorian National Mining Company ENAMI EP

María José Luque Macías[1]

1 Introduction

Traditionally, the discussion of human rights and environmental sustainability of Ecuadorian companies, if any, has been framed as an issue of corporate social responsibility (CSR).[2] In fact, although the Ecuadorian state has been one of the pioneers in promoting the negotiation of an internationally legally binding instrument on transnational corporations and human rights (UN Treaty),[3] this negotiation process has not received much attention in the public debate.[4] However, two recent developments suggest that this state is intending to reverse this trend by endorsing international accountability standards that are likely to steer the conduct of business actors.

On one hand, in October 2020, Ecuador adhered to the Extractive Industries Transparency Initiative (EITI), under which it committed to regularly disclosing information along its extractive industry value chain.[5] To achieve this end, this country shall establish a multi-stakeholder group to oversee this

1 The author is indebted to Danilo Icaza and Stevie Gamboa for their insights on the domestic regulatory framework governing ENAMI EP and to the editors for their helpful comments on earlier versions of this chapter. All views expressed in this chapter are my own.

2 Escobar Freire, Verónica et al. (2019) "The Ecuadorian Business Sector in Front of the Agenda 2030: Challenges and Opportunities." *14th Iberian Conference on Information Systems and Technologies (CISTI)*, pp. 1–6. https://doi.org/10.23919/CISTI.2019.8760799.

3 Following the adoption of the Resolution 26/9 by the UN Human Rights Council, the Permanent Mission of Ecuador to the UN has been one of the members of the open-ended intergovernmental working group on transnational corporations and other business enterprises with respect to human rights. See UN Human Rights Council, Seventh Session, available at www.ohchr.org/EN/HRBodies/HRC/WGTransCorp/Session7/Pages/Session7.aspx#history.

4 Originally, only civil society promoted discussion forums on this initiative. To illustrate, INREDH, 'Foro público: "Instrumento Internacional Vinculante sobre Empresas Transnacionales y Derechos humanos"' (14 agosto 2017) and available at https://inredh.org/foro-publico-instrumento-internacional-vinculante-sobre-empresas-transnacionales-y-derechos-humanos/.

5 Ecuador became member of the EITI initiative on 15 October 2020, prompted by several organizations promoting the open government initiative. GK, EITI: ¿Transparencia o lavado de imagen? (24 Octubre 2021), available at https://gk.city/2021/10/24/que-es-eiti/.

DOI: 10.4324/9781003291428-3

disclosure process on all required areas,[6] notably on social and environmental expenditures by companies and the environmental impact of extractive activities.[7] On the other, the executive branch is currently elaborating a national action plan (NAP) on business and human rights to facilitate the application of the UN Guiding Principles on Business and Human Rights (UNGP) in the domestic business context.[8] With this measure, this country not only abandons its previous stance that the UN Treaty was the only adequate internationally promoted mechanism to protect against corporate abuses of human rights[9] but also commits to upholding its international duty to protect against adverse human rights impacts by business enterprises.[10]

One means of discharging this international legal duty consists in encouraging business enterprises domiciled in its territory to respect human rights throughout their operations.[11] This responsibility constitutes a standard of expected conduct for companies that entails avoiding infringing the rights of others and addressing human rights impacts they can cause or contribute to through their own activities.[12] Thus, mindful of this state duty and corporate responsibility, Ecuador should urge, in particular, the 13 state-owned enterprises (SOEs) that are still active in its current planning structure[13] to explicitly

6 Information shall be provided, at least, over the management of the extractive sector (laws, procedures and award of exploration and production licenses), exploration activities and production/export data, as well as revenue collection, allocation and management. EITI, EITI Standard 2019, Requirements 1–6, available at https://eiti.org/document/eiti-standard-2019#r7-1.

7 Ibid., Requirements 6.2 and 6.4, respectively.

8 During the last presidential term of Lenin Moreno (2020–2021), the process of elaboration of the NAP was implemented in 2020 and, nowadays, its content is periodically reviewed based on the input of and exchange with different stakeholders. See Secretaria Nacional de Planificacion, Ecuador Lanzo Oficialmente el Proceso de Elaboracion del "Plan de Accion Nacional sobre Empresas y Derechos Humanos (PAN)" (15 Octubre 2020), available at www.planificacion.gob.ec/ecuador-lanzo-oficialmente-el-proceso-de-elaboracion-del-plan-de-accion-nacional-sobre-empresas-y-derechos-humanos-pan/, and Ministerio de Relaciones Exteriores y Movilidad Humana, Noticias, Ecuador avanza en la elaboración de Plan de Acción Nacional sobre Empresas y Derechos Humanos (18 Julio 2023), available at www.cancilleria.gob.ec/2023/07/18/ecuador-avanza-en-la-elaboracion-de-plan-de-accion-nacional-sobre-empresas-y-derechos-humanos/.

9 During the government of Rafael Correa, the development of a NAP was not considered essential because the Ecuadorian legal system, together with governmental multi-sectorial programmes and plans, were already deemed to promote and protect human rights in the business context. UNGA, "Report of the Working Group on the Universal Periodic Review, Ecuador", Res. A/HRC/36/4 (20 July 2017) paras 120.4 and 124.

10 UN Human Rights Council, 'Guiding Principles on Business and Human Rights: Implementing the United Nations' "Protect, Respect and Remedy" Framework' (21 March 2011) UN Doc A/HRC/17/31 (UNGP) principle 1.

11 Ibid., principle 2.

12 UNGP n 9 principles 11 and 13; Comisión Inter-Americana de Derechos Humanos, REDESCA, Empresas y Derechos Humanos: Estandares Inter-Americanos (1 Noviembre 2019) (Inter-American report) para 415.

13 Ministerio de Economia y Finanzas, Informacion Estadistica de Empresas Publicas, Reporte Trimestral No. 1 Año 2023, slide 4, available at: www.finanzas.gob.ec/empresas-publicas/.

adhere to its international and inter-American human rights obligations.[14] Otherwise, human rights abuses linked to these companies could be attributed to them and may constitute a breach of their *own* human rights obligations.[15]

As the Ecuadorian SOE operating in the mining sector, the Empresa Nacional Minera (ENAMI EP) is well advised to respect human rights[16] because the exploration of mineral deposits, which it does through its contractors,[17] could pose a risk to various legal entitlements.[18] First, ENAMI EP's exploration activities may severely pollute water resources by harmful substances and pathogenic microbes. This reduces the ability to enjoy the rights to water and health[19] as it may affect the quality of water required for personal and domestic use,[20] as well as the essential environmental hygiene necessary to prevent threats to health from unsafe and toxic water conditions, respectively.[21] In the same way, this pollution may also undermine the enjoyment of the right to a healthy environment (RTHE)[22] since it may considerably alter the ecosystem and other environmental components that are essential conditions for individuals' enjoyment of human rights[23] and environmental assets in their own value.[24]

14 UNGP n 9 principle 4; Inter-American report n 11 paras 108 and 414.

15 UNGP n 9 principles 4, Commentary; Inter-American report n 11 paras 306 and 308.

16 The ENAMI EP was created by the executive in 2010 to manage the sustainable use of minerals in conformity with the mining law. See Executive Decree 203, R.O. No. 108 (14 de Enero de 2010) art 2.

17 Lacking operational capacity, ENAMI EP generally resorts to contractors to carry out the mining activities conferred by the mining concessions' title. To illustrate, ENAMI EP carried out the exploration of copper mines granted within the Llurimagua project, in association with the Chilean state-owned copper company, Codelco. n 50, 52, 108.

18 All mining concessions of ENAMI EP are in the exploration phase, with the exception of those stemming from illegal mining, which are in the exploitation phase, and the state has transferred to it for its formalization. Agencia de Regulación y Control de Energía y Recursos Naturales no Renovables, Catastro Minero Nacional, available at https://gis-sigde.maps.arcgis.com/apps/webappviewer/index.html?id=8b53f9388c034b5e8e3147f03583d7ec.

19 International Covenant on Economic, Social and Cultural Rights (adopted 16 December 1966, entered into force 3 January 1976) 993 UNTS 3 arts 11 and 12; American Convention on Human Rights (adopted 22 November 1969, entered into force 18 July 1978) 1144 UNTS 123 (ACHR) art 26.

20 CESCR, General Comment No. 15: The Right to Water (Arts. 11 and 12 of the Covenant) (20 January 2003) UN Doc. E/C.12/2002/11 para 12 lit. b; *Caso Comunidades Indígenas Miembros de la Asociación Lhaka Honhat (Nuestra Tierra) v. Argentina*, Judgment, IACoHR Series C No. 400 (6 February 2020) (Lhaka Honhat v Argentina) paras 222, 223, 227.

21 CESCR, General Comment No. 14: The Right to the Highest Attainable Standard of Health (Art. 12) (11 August 2000) UN Doc. E/C.12/2000/4 (General Comment No. 14) para 5.

22 ACHR n 18 art 26; Additional Protocol to the American Convention on Human Rights in the Area of Economic, Social and Cultural Rights "Protocol of San Salvador" (signed on 17 November 1988, entered into force on 16 November 1999) (1989) 28 ILM 156 art 11.

23 *Lhaka Honhat v Argentina* n 19 para 203; *Obligaciones Estatales en Relación con el Medio Ambiente en el Marco de la Protección y Garantía de los Derechos a la Vida y a la Integridad Personal – Interpretación y Alcance de los Artículos 4.1 y 5.1, en Relación con los Artículos 1.1 y 2 de la Convención Americana Sobre Derechos Humanos Solicitada por la República de Colombia*, Opinión Consultiva OC-23/17 Serie A No. 23 (15 de Noviembre 2017) (*Advisory Opinion on Human Rights and the Environment*) paras 64, 66.

24 *Advisory Opinion on Human Rights and the Environment* n 22 paras 62 and 63.

In addition, ENAMI EP's incomplete or inaccurate disclosure of information about its mining projects' impacts on water quality and environmental components could initially interfere with the right to seek, receive and impart information about health and water issues as legal entitlements of several substantive human rights.[25] Furthermore, this corporate misconduct could also compromise the enjoyment of procedural rights, such as the rights to freedom of expression and association, by limiting individuals' access to environmental information and association for the promotion and defense of environmental preservation.[26] Finally, corporate infringement on the procedural environmental rights proclaimed in the Escazú Agreement can also contribute to adverse impacts on these human rights, especially those enjoyed by human rights defenders.[27]

Thus, noting the great potential for attribution of human rights abuses to the Ecuadorian state, this chapter analyzes the human rights and environmental sustainability of ENAMI EP in three different steps. Initially, the first section explains the legal framework in which ENAMI EP operates, including its role in the Ecuadorian mining sector, to better understand how the Ecuadorian state may bear responsibility under international human rights law (IHRL) in case of adverse human rights impacts.[28] This means discussing whether attribution arises due to the exercise of a public function or due to the control that the state exercises over this SOE. Informed by these findings, it then outlines the regulatory means through which the state controls the daily business and decision-making of this SOE to identify which social and environmental concerns, if any, are included into these structures. Next, the second section briefly evaluates the governance tools by which ENAMI EP accounts for environmental-related human rights impacts. It examines whether its corporate policies reflect some features of the policy statement this SOE should express to commit to fulfilling this responsibility and whether its processes were conducive to identifying, assessing and preventing human

25 Concerning the right to water, General Comment No. 14 n 20 para 12 lit. b as well as *Lhaka Honhat v Argentina* n 19 para 227. In relation to the right to health, General Comment No. 15 n 19 para 12, lit. c, iii.

26 Concerning the right to freedom of expression, ACHR n 18 art 13; *Caso Claude Reyes y otros v Chile*, Judgment IACoHR Serie C No. 151 (19 September 2006) (Claude Reyes v Chile) paras 76, 77. Regarding the right to freedom of association, ACHR n 18 art 16; *Case of Kawas-Fernández v. Honduras*, Judgment IACoHR Serie C No. 196 (3 April 2009) (Kawas Fernandey v Honduras) paras 143–149; *Caso Escaleras Mejía y Otros v. Honduras*, Judgment IACoHR Serie C 361 (26 September 2018) (Escaleras Mejia v Honduras) para 63.

27 Regional Agreement on Access to Information, Public Participation and Justice in Environmental Matters in Latin America and the Caribbean (signed 4 March 2018, entered into force 22 April 2021) I-56654 UNTS 7 (Escazu Agreement) art 9 paras 1 and 2.

28 To this end, the author strongly relies on the direct attribution's criteria systematized by Schönsteiner. Schönsteiner, Judith (2019): "Attribution of State Responsibility for Actions or Omissions of State-Owned Enterprises in Human Rights Matters", *University of Pennsylvania Journal of International Law*, Vol. 40, No. 4: pp. 895–936.

rights risks.[29] To conclude, the third section discusses the human rights record of ENAMI EP, based on reports of the General Comptroller's Office (Contraloría) and legal proceedings brought by or against ENAMI EP, as well as investigative journalism.

2 The regulatory-based accountability mechanism applicable to ENAMI EP

2.1 Typology, sectors and governance of Ecuadorian SOEs

Within the Ecuadorian legal framework, SOEs belong to the public sector and are legal entities under public law that have their own assets and are endowed with budgetary, financial, economic, administrative and management autonomy.[30] There are two main types of SOEs: those created by the executive through decree[31] and those constituted by normative acts legally issued by the autonomous decentralized governments.[32] Both types of companies may carry out their activities at the local, provincial, regional, national or international level, and their denomination shall contain the indication 'EMPRESA PUBLICA' or the acronym 'EP'.[33]

Ecuadorian SOEs are created for the management of the strategic sectors, the provision of public services, the sustainable use of natural resources or public goods and, in general, the development of economic activities that correspond to the state.[34] To fulfil their corporate objectives, these companies have capacity to form associations, strategic alliances, joint ventures and mixed economy companies with the (national or international) public or private sector.[35] However, there are two economic sectors in which the state (through its SOEs) may only delegate its participation to mixed companies, provided that they have a majority shareholding.[36] The first sector concerns the management

29 This means that ENAMI EP's policies and processes will be reviewed against principles 16–19 of the UNGP. UNGP n 9. Besides, its accountability reports from 2015 to 2022 provided the material to assess ENAMI EP's processes and were retrieved from: ENAMI EP, Rendicion de Cuentas, available at www.enamiep.gob.ec/?page_id=3161.

30 Constitucion de la Republica del Ecuador, R.O. No. 449 (20 Octubre 2008) (Constitution of the Republic of Ecuador) (Constitution) art 315 paras 1 and 2; Ley Orgánica de Empresas Públicas (Organic Law of Public Enterprises), Suplemento del R.O. No. 48 (16 de Octubre 2009), amended through Suplemento del R.O. No. 118 (10 Enero 2020) (LOEP) art 4 para 1.

31 Constitution n 29 art 225 para 3; LOEP n 29 art 5 para 1. In addition, the executive can form a public enterprise, together with the autonomous decentralized governments, by means of public deed. LOEP n 29 art 5 para 3.

32 Constitution n 29 art 225 para 4; LOEP n 29 art 5 para 2. Autonomous decentralized governments are composed of rural parish boards, municipal councils, metropolitan councils, provincial councils and regional councils. Constitution n 29 art 238 para 2.

33 LOEP n 29 art 5 paras 6 and 7, respectively.

34 Constitution n 29 art 315 paras 1 and 2; LOEP n 29 art 4 para 1.

35 Constitution n 29 art 35 para 1.

36 Constitution n 29 art 315 para 4 and 316 para 1; LOEP n 29 art 35 para 2.

of strategic sectors such as non-renewable natural resources[37] because the state reserves to itself the right to administer, regulate, control and manage them[38] as its inalienable, imprescriptible and unseizable property.[39] The second relates to the provision of public services as the exclusive responsibility of the state,[40] which shall establish the control and regulation of their prices and tariffs.[41] This being said, SOEs operating in both economic sectors are also entitled to contract the administration and management of the mixed company.[42]

Finally, the composition of the board of directors (BOD) of SOEs varies according to their type. If the public enterprise is created by the executive, its BOD must be presided over by the chairman of the BOD of the public enterprise coordinating company, known as 'Empresa Coordinadora de Empresas Públicas – EMCO EP'.[43] In addition, the BOD shall be composed of the head of the pertinent ministry and a delegate of the president of the Republic (president).[44] By contrast, if the company is constituted by decentralized autonomous governments, the BOD will be formed by the members established in its normative act of creation, who must not exceed five in number.[45]

2.2 *The role of ENAMI EP in the Ecuadorian mining sector*

Created by the executive in 2010, the ENAMI EP is the Ecuadorian SOE responsible for the management of mining activity in all its phases for the sustainable use of minerals in conformity with the Mining Law.[46] It belongs to the institutional structure of the Ecuadorian mining sector[47] by being the mining activities' executor of the state.[48] In this capacity, the ENAMI EP has two special mining rights

37 Other strategic sectors comprise energy in all its forms, telecommunications, transport, and hydrocarbon transport and refining of hydrocarbons, biodiversity and genetic heritage, the radioelectric spectrum, water, and any others determined by law. Constitution n 29 art 313 para 3.
38 Constitution n 29 art 313 paras 1 and 2.
39 Constitution n 29 art 408.
40 Public services are those relating to drinking water and irrigation, sanitation, electricity, telecommunications, roads, port and airport infrastructures. Constitution n 29 art 314 para 1.
41 Constitution n 29 art 314 para 2.
42 LOEP n 29 art 35 para 2.
43 LOEP n 29 art 7, lit. a, numeral 1. With the arrival to power of President Noboa in November 2023, the BOD's composition for this type of SOEs is expected to change following his information request on the corresponding procedure to extinguish and liquidate EMCO EP. Executive Decree 37 (28 November 2023), available at https://minka.presidencia.gob.ec/portal/usuarios_externos.jsf. After completion of this operational liquidation process, a reform of the LOEP should follow to adjust the composition of their BOD. Gamboa n 1.
44 LOEP n 29 art 7 lit. a, numerals 2 and 3, respectively.
45 The same composition also applies to those companies constituted by the executive and the decentralized autonomous governments. LOEP n 29 art 7 lit. b.
46 Ley de Minería (Mining Law), Ley 45, R.O. Suplemento No. 517 (29 Enero 2009) art 12 para 1.
47 Ibid., art 5, lit. d.
48 In addition, the ENAMI EP is responsible for the utilization of seabed minerals, for which it could conclude contracts for the supply of services with natural and legal persons in accordance with special regulation issued by the president. n 45 arts 21 and 146.

that other national mining activities' developers do not enjoy in the process of public auction for awarding mining concessions, convened by the Ministry of Energy and Mining (Sectoral Ministry):[49] a preferential right to apply for mining concessions in the so-called special mining areas and a right of first option if a third party applies for a mining concession in such area.[50] Also, although this SOE can freely opt for any associative contractual modality,[51] as a SOE, its procurement of goods, works and services, including consulting services, shall be aligned with the national development plan (NDP)[52] and subject to the provisions of the Organic Law of the National Public Procurement System.[53]

Yet just like any other holder of mining rights,[54] their obtainment and exercise by ENAMI EP is, on one hand, under the regulation and control of the sectoral ministry endowed with the competence to, *inter alia*, declare the expiration of its mining rights for non-compliance with environmental obligations[55] or for breaches of human rights,[56] as well as the Agency for Regulation and Control of Energy and Non-Renewable Natural Resources (Agency), which exercises technical control and applies these sanctions.[57] On the other,

49 National mining activities can also be developed by mixed or private companies, the community, associative and family companies, self-managed companies and natural persons. n 45 arts 21 and 29 para 1.

50 These are non-concessioned areas declared by the president in which there is potential for mining development. n 45 art 24 paras 1 and 2.

51 ENAMI EP can celebrate partnerships, joint ventures, strategic alliances and, in general, any act or contract permitted by national laws. n 45 art 12 para 2. Icaza, Danilo (2020): "Mecanismos Asociativos, de Expansión y Desarrollo de las Empresas Públicas en el Ecuador", *Revista Carácter*, Vol. 8, No. 1: pp. 1–26 (e-ISSN: 2602-8476).

52 The national development plan is the instrument to which 1) public policies, programs and projects; 2) the programming and execution of the state's budget; and 3) the investment and allocation of public resources shall be subject. Constitution n 29 art 280.

53 LOEP n 29 art 34. Pursuant to the Constitution, public procurement shall comply with social and environmental responsibility benchmarks. Yet existing laws and manuals adopted for its implementation only address transparency as one of their main guiding benchmarks. Constitution n 29 art 288; Organic Law on Public Procurement art 9 para 7; Organic Law of the National System for Public Procurement art 4; Manual of Good Practices in Public Procurement for the Development of Ecuador (2015).

54 ENAMI EP retains all the rights that mining concessions' titles grant to any mining concessionaire, which include the exclusive right to prospect, explore, exploit, benefit, smelt, refine, commercialize and dispose of all mineral substances that may exist and be obtained in the concession area, becoming beneficiary of the economic revenues obtained from such processes. This type of concessions is granted for a period up to 25 years (renewable for an equal term) and are divided into exploration (in turn, divided into initial and advanced exploration, as well as the integral economic evaluation of the deposit) and an exploitation phase. n 45 arts 18, 30, 31, 36 paras 1 and 3.

55 n 45 arts 5, lit. a, 86 para 3 and 115. Although the expiration would extinguish the mining rights conferred by the state to this SOE, this sanction would not remove its responsibility as former holder for environmental damage, ecosystems' restoration and full reparation to individuals and communities, if applicable. n 45 art 109.

56 n 45 arts 69 and 116.

57 It exercises the state power of oversight, auditing, intervention and control of the phases of the mining activity. Ley de Minera n 38 arts 5, lit. b; 8 para 1; 9 lit. l. Moreover, the Agency registers the contracts entered into by this SOE in the mining registry. Ibid., art 124.

the Ministry of Environment,[58] together with the Sole Water Authority,[59] oversee ENAMI EP's compliance with the environmental obligations.[60] In addition, this Ministry receives popular actions on social, cultural or environmental impacts caused by its mining exploration work.[61]

Hence, this brief description of the role of ENAMI EP suggests that this SOE does not exercise any governmental function in the Ecuadorian mining sector. Said otherwise, it is not legally endowed with any public power to develop, execute or apply the state mining policy that derives from its sovereign to administer, regulate, control and manage the development of the mining industry.[62] On the contrary, as already outlined, the conduct of this SOE is under the control of state-based mining entities that do enjoy this public power,[63] leading to the conclusion that its actions and omissions are not directly attributable to the Ecuadorian state under this criterion.[64]

2.3 *Limited integration of non-economic concerns into state-based control structures*

Although the executive governs ENAMI EP through its BOD, it also controls this SOE, albeit indirectly, through the National Planning Secretariat (NPS), which coordinates the National Planning Council chaired by the president. This is argued because, as an entity of the public sector, ENAMI EP shall align its investment projects with the NDP to obtain the NPS's approval of public resources' allocation.[65] Thus, at least in principle, the NPS could integrate social and environmental impacts into the daily business and decision-making of this SOE since the state planning of the country's development shall be

58 To preserve the ecological balance, the Ministry establishes the environmental control policies that all SOEs shall comply with by designing environmental management to prevent, mitigate, control, rehabilitate and compensate the environmental impacts caused by its activities. LOEP n 29 Disposiciones Generales, Tercera.

59 It grants the reasoned and favourable act on the possible impact on surface and/or subway water bodies. n 45 art 26 para 1.

60 n 45 art 86.

61 n 45 art 91.

62 *Competencia* (public power) is the extent to which the *Constitution and the law enable a body to act and fulfill its purposes*, by reason of the subject matter, territory, time and degree. Código Orgánico Administrativo, R. O Suplemento (31 Julio 2017) art 65 (emphasis added). n 45 art 4 paras 2 and 3.

63 The state develops, executes and applies the mining policy (defined and directed by the president) through, among others, the Sectoral Ministry and the Agency. The Ministry governs and plans the mining sector while the Agency exercises the state power of oversight, auditing, intervention and control of the phases of the mining activity. Ley de Minera arts, 4, 6–9.

64 International Law Commission, 'Draft Articles on Responsibility of States for Internationally Wrongful Acts' (2001) Supplement No. 10 (A/56/10), chp.IV.E.1, arts 4 and 5 and Schönsteiner n 27.

65 This council dictates the guidelines and policies that will orient the national development system as well as approving the NDP. Constitution n 29 art 279 para 1 and n 51.

designed to guarantee the exercise of rights.[66] Hence, the NPS, together with the composition of BOD, are the sole legal mechanisms through which the executive directly intervenes in the daily business of ENAMI EP and that satisfy the control criterion to directly attribute the acts and omission of this SOE to the Ecuadorian state.[67] This being said, the environmental, social and human rights–based regulation of the mining sector does not treat this SOE differently from other private holders of mining rights.[68]

To preserve the environment and thus the enjoyment of substantive human rights, this SOE shall initially observe environmental control policies conducive to executing environmental management plans (EMPs) through elaboration and submission of environmental studies to obtain an environmental license[69] and an audit that allows environmental authorities to monitor, supervise and verify compliance with EMP and applicable environmental regulations.[70] Both studies and EMPs shall contain information about the species of flora and fauna existing in the area as well as carry out monitoring studies and the respective impact mitigation measures on them.[71] Once obtained, this SOE shall then comply with the environmental obligations; non-compliance may result in the expiration of its mining concessions.[72] They include returning water used for its works and processes to the original river or lake from which it was taken, free of contamination so as not to affect the rights of people and nature[73] and taking[74] and undertaking revegetation and reforestation activities as established in EMPs if its mining activities require the removal of vegetation layers and the felling.[75]

Moreover, the state intends to reduce adverse impacts on procedural human rights by ENAMI EP through its obligation to respect people's right to have access to information, participation and consultation in the environmental management of mining activities, in a context in which only the state is obliged to implement these rights.[76] Intended to respect the environment and social engagement of stakeholders in environmental matters,[77] participation and consultation processes shall consider and incorporate people's views into the social and environmental management of the mining activity in all its

66 Constitution n 29 art 275 para 2.
67 n 42, 43, 83, 84 and Schönsteiner n 27.
68 n 45 art 18.
69 n 45 art 78 para 1.
70 For the initial and advanced exploration periods, it shall obtain the approval of environmental files and environmental declaration. n 45 art 78 paras 4 and 6.
71 n 45 art 82.
72 n 54.
73 n 45 art 79.
74 n 45 art 81.
75 n 45 art 80.
76 The fulfilment of this state's obligation cannot be delegated to private entities. n 45 art 87 paras 2 and 4.
77 n 45 art 87 para 2.

phases.[78] In fact, ENAMI EP shall particularly observe this process in relation to indigenous people, when mining exploration or exploitation activities are carried out on their ancestral lands and territories and may affect their interests.[79] Moreover, this SOE shall adequately inform, through the state and during all stages of the mining concession, about potential impacts of its mining activity by considering communities and entities representing social, environmental or trade union as information recipients whilst understanding environmental and social studies formally requested, as well as reports and technical resolutions issued by the competent authority as objects of information.[80]

Finally, human rights' abuses by ENAMI EP will unequivocally lead to the expiration of its mining concessions.[81] Examples of misconduct include resorting to children or adolescents' labour to carry out any mining activity[82] and those previously determined through an enforceable judgment issued by a competent judge.[83]

3 The governance-based accountability mechanism of ENAMI EP

3.1 Policies embedding non-economic concerns into its management systems

The BOD of ENAMI EP establishes its policies and goals in conformity with the guidelines formulated by the president (and implemented by the Sectoral Ministry),[84] as well as approving applicable CSR schemes.[85] To date, the BOD has issued three corporate policies.

The first consists in a policy on health, safety and environmental issues (HSE policy) that aims to provide adequate labour conditions to its personnel, develop a culture of security and health and constantly review mining safety risks and workplace health assessments.[86] The second seeks to comprehensively implement a good practice in public procurement (PP policy) in line with applicable laws.[87] Despite not being explicitly interrelated, these policies

78 n 45 art 89.
79 n 45 art 90.
80 n 45 art 88.
81 Human rights are here understood as the rights and guarantees established in the Constitution and international human rights instruments. Constitution n 29 art 11 para 3 and n 55.
82 n 45 art 69.
83 n 45 art 117.
84 LOEP n 29 art 9 paras 1, and n 45 arts 4 and 6.
85 LOEP n 29 art 9 para 4.
86 ENAMI EP, Política Empresarial de Salud, Seguridad y Ambiente de la ENAMI EP (HSE policy), available at www.enamiep.gob.ec/wp-content/uploads/downloads/2017/05/POL%C3%8DTICA-EMPRESARIAL-DE-SALUD-SEGURIDAD-Y-AMBIENTE-DE-LA-ENAMI-EP.pdf.
87 ENAMI EP, Política De Buenas Prácticas En La Contratación Pública En La Empresa Nacional Minera ENAMI EP, Res. No. ENAMI-ENAMI-2020–0013-RLS (3 Junio 2020) (PP

converge in that they should be directed to benefit communities and contribute to social welfare: the HSE policy embodies ENAMI EP's commitment to adopt the best mining practices in benefit of the environment and communities and to allocate necessary resources to prevent impacts to HSE and communities whilst the PP policy provides that all public contracting processes shall observe aspects relating to ecological impact and environmental responsibility, safeguarding social welfare and its participation.[88]

Moreover, the corporate social responsibility (CSR) policy, initially adopted in 2020, was reformed in 2021 to fulfil the social purpose of ENAMI EP, in line with international CSR guidelines and through the implementation of prevention, mitigation and reparation mechanisms by means of management plans, intervention strategies and community relations programs.[89] This reform sought to align this policy with the national action plan (NAP) for the mining sector issued by the former president, Guillermo Lasso, to open up new mining concessions and streamline environmental procedures to attract socially and environmentally responsible investment in the mining sector.[90]

Whilst none of these corporate policies explicitly express the commitment of ENAMI EP to respect human rights, they have a few characteristics in common with those of the policy statement whose adoption is encouraged by the UNGP.[91] To illustrate, all corporate policies proclaim ENAMI EP's non-economic expectations of its personnel and workers[92] and are publicly available on its institutional website (even though its restructuring would be necessary to improve their accessibility to external audience).[93] Yet, unlike the other policies,[94] the HSE policy clearly prescribes that ENAMI EP's implementation of management systems should be founded on the continuous improvement of its operations, working conditions and environmental responsibility for the benefit of its personnel, the environment and communities.[95] Thus, this operational

policy) art 1, available at www.enamiep.gob.ec/wp-content/uploads/downloads/2020/07/ENAMI-ENAMI-2020-0013-RLS.pdf and n 52.

88 HSE policy n 85; PP policy n 86 art 20, lit. a.

89 More specifically, the CSR policy of the ENAMI EP is consistent with the International Standard ISO 26000 on Social Responsibility Management System. See ENAMI EP, Política de responsabilidad social de la Empresa Nacional Minera ENAMI EP (ENAMI-ENAMI-2021–0035-RLS), 29 de diciembre de 2021 (replacing Res. ENAMI-ENAMI-2020–0038-RLS, 29 de septiembre de 2020) (CSR policy), preamble and single article, numeral 7, available at www.enamiep.gob.ec/wp-content/uploads/downloads/2022/01/ENAMI-ENAMI-2021-0035-RLS_Politica-responsabilidad-social.pdf#.

90 Presidencia de la Republica del Ecuador, Decreto No. 151 (5 Agosto 2021), available at www.fielweb.com/App_Themes/InformacionInteres/de151fw.pdf.

91 n 9 principle 16.

92 HSE policy n 85 and PP policy n 86 art 2. In addition, the CSR policy extends this expectation to operators and strategic partners. See CSR policy n 88, Disposición Final Primera.

93 Only the HSE policy is easily accessible in the ENAMI EP website's library.

94 To illustrate, the CSR policy only defines its content. n 88 single article, numerals 1–12.

95 This corporate commitment can be observed, for instance, in its 2015–2019 corporate strategic plan, 2019 management report and 2018 accountability report n 28.

policy establishes the continuous improvement of its activities as a key parameter of its management systems' implementation, echoing, albeit indirectly, one of the guiding parameters of the human rights due diligence process.[96]

3.2 (Limited) implementation of a due diligence process

Like its policies, the due diligence processes carried out by ENAMI EP did not intend to assess and prevent human rights impacts. On the contrary, they only covered labour matters, thereby seeking to tackle the identified risks of discriminatory treatment of its employees as well as poor working conditions and personal safety, common in the mining sector, through two actions.[97] The first concerned this SOE's implementation of equality policies in recruitment to prevent discriminatory practices through the integration of intercultural, gender, disability and generational criteria,[98] which complemented existing policies aimed at increasing health and occupational safety standards by 80% to make them consistent with international norms.[99] The second dealt more with its undertaking of regular occupational health inspections and continuous capacity building of the occupational and safety delegates, as well as the development of components of health-related trainings for its personnel in accordance with its integral health and safety plan.[100]

Moreover, the non–human rights focus of ENAMI EP's due diligence processes is also observable in its engagement with those likely to be affected by its exploration activities as this neither led to understanding their concerns about actual or potential human rights impacts[101] nor integrated them across its internal corporate processes.[102] To explain, several accountability reports indicate that this SOE generally resorts to the "socialization" of environmental impact studies' results.[103] This communicative process may take the form of organization of dialogue tables as well as community groups and health committees,[104] and it usually goes on to determine which material commitments it must assume in favour of neighbouring communities.[105] Yet with this

96 n 9 principle 17 lit. c.
97 UNGP n 9 principle 18.
98 See Accountability Report 2020; Accountability Report 2019, both n 28.
99 Accountability Report 2018 n 28.
100 Accountability Report 2016 n 28.
101 UNGP n 9 principle 18, lit. b, Commentary.
102 UNGP n 9 principle 19.
103 2022 Accountability Report (Unacota project); 2020 and 2019 Accountability Reports (Muyuyacu project); 2017 Accountability Report (Telimbela/Tornado project), both n 28.
104 In connection with the Llurimagua project, activities to promote ENAMI EP's social responsibility with communities range from social and cultural events to community integration, both agreed with the representative of those communities. Accountability Report 2016 n 28.
105 ENAMI EP's commitments have ranged from carrying out a geological study for the construction of an educational unit in the zone and cooperating in the improvement of access roads for neighbouring communities (Telimbela/Tornado projects) to promoting the agro-productive capacities of socialization's participants (Llurimagua/Unacota projects). 2017

strict focus on responding to material demands, ENAMI EP fails to evaluate the adverse human rights impacts associated with its activities, justifying itself exclusively on the grounds that the state alone is responsible for designing and carrying out participation mechanisms in the formulation of environmental plans and policies.[106] By doing so, this SOE fails to meet its responsibility to respect human rights, which exists independently of the state's ability and willingness to satisfy its own human rights obligations.[107]

4 The environmental-related human rights record of ENAMI EP

4.1 Abuses of human rights through non-compliance with domestic environmental obligations

The first set of human rights abuses by ENAMI EP relates to the irregularities found by the Contraloría while it was obtaining environmental permits and compliance with the EMP for the initial exploration stage of the Llurimagua project.[108] As a result of this special examination, this regulatory entity formulated some recommendations for immediate and mandatory implementation by ENAMI EP.[109]

According to the Contraloría, this SOE initially failed to implement mitigation measures according to the realities of the explored mining zone because the EMP from which they were developed was based on the EIA submitted by ENAMI EP that denied the presence of measurable dissolved elements in water[110] but that, according to Contraloría's auditors, had high concentrations of lead and zinc, which severely affect human health and aquatic fauna.[111]

Accountability Report, Accountability Report 2018, Accountability Report 2022 n 28, respectively.

106 Ibid., and n 75.

107 UNGP n 9 principle 11, Commentary.

108 This state entity performs *ex-post* and external administrative control of all public companies. Contraloría General del Estado, DNA6 Dirección Nacional de Auditoría de Recursos Naturales, DNA6-0001-2019 'Examen Especial al Proyecto Minero Llurimagua en la provincia de Imbabura, a cargo de la Empresa Nacional Minera, ENAMI EP, Ministerio de Minería, Ministerio del Ambiente, Agencia de Regulación y Control Minero, y entidades relacionadas, ubicado en la ciudad de Quito, cantón Quito, provincia de Pichincha, por el período comprendido entre el 1 de enero de 2012 y el 31 de diciembre de 2017', (2019 Contraloría report) available at www.contraloria.gob.ec/Consultas/InformesAprobados/DNA6-0001-2019 and LOEP n 29 art 47.

109 The Contraloría also established a lack of compliance with contractual obligations by ENAMI EP and its contractual partner Codelco. While ENAMI EP failed to establish a joint venture with Codelco for the advanced exploration phase, meaning rights, competencies and obligations between the parties were not established, Codelco's subsidiary carried out an advanced mineral exploration without supporting contractual documents and failed to disclose information on the characteristics of the deposit that would allow them to know, identify and quantify the types of materials found in the project. 2019 Contraloría report n 107 pp. 7–10.

110 n 68; 2019 Contraloría report n 107 pp. 10–21.

111 2019 Contraloría report n 107 pp. 26–31.

The Contraloría determined that these environmental studies were not subject to communities' consultation.[112] From an IHRL perspective, this withholding of information by ENAMI EP considerably diminished the ability of those potentially affected individuals and communities to be aware of the actual environmental and health risks associated with its exploration of copper mines, and thus the accessibility dimension was protected under the rights to water and health.[113] In fact, ENAMI EP's tolerance of the state's omitting to carry out consultation processes certainly limited the possibility of these communities making their positions known as guaranteed by the right to freedom of expression.[114]

Similarly, the exploration activities commenced by this SOE also reduced the availability of flora and aquatic fauna that were essential to the effective realization of the right to health[115] through the removal of native trees and the lack of a micro-watershed conservation plan, in clear violation of the implementation and mitigation measures established in the EMP.[116] Besides, its alleged use of water from unauthorized sources, combined with the lack of guidelines to control its quality,[117] affected the quality of water sources not only as an individual entitlement of the right to water[118] but also as an environmental component protected under the RTHE.[119]

4.2 *Abuses of human rights defenders' rights by means of criminal proceedings*

In 2015, ENAMI EP initiated a criminal complaint against Darwin Ramirez Piedra for his 'alleged' attack against the operators of the Llurimagua copper site.[120] Although Ecuador does not top the list of Latin American countries where this type of threat generally occurs,[121] this case provides another example of the judicial harassment human rights defenders increasingly face in the region.[122]

112 2019 Contraloría report n 107, pp. 22–25.
113 n 24.
114 n 25.
115 n 20.
116 2019 Contraloría report, n 107, pp. 32–43.
117 2019 Contraloría report, n 107 pp. 44–55.
118 n 19.
119 See n 23.
120 Front Line Defenders, Case History: Darwin Javier Ramirez Piedra (2015), available at www.frontlinedefenders.org/en/case/case-history-darwin-javier-ramirez-piedra.
121 Honduras, Guatemala, Mexico and Peru are at the top of the ranking. Business & Human Rights Resource Centre, 'SLAPPs in Latin America, Strategic Lawsuits against Public Participation in the Context of Business and Human Rights' (February 2022), available at https://media.business-humanrights.org/media/documents/2022_SLAPPs_in_LatAm_EN_v7.pdf.
122 Other forms of criminalization against human rights defenders may include, *inter alia*, misuse of counterterrorism relating to national security, illegal and arbitrary detentions and misuse of precautionary measures. IACommHR, "Criminalization of the Work Human Rights Defenders" (OEA/Ser.L/V/II.Doc. 49/15–31 December 2015), pp. 45–106.

According to NGOs' reports, Ramirez Piedra, as the president of the Junin community, actively campaigned against ENAMI EP's activities in the northern region of Intag due to their negative impact on the environment, including water resources.[123] Under these circumstances, he was associated with the attack suffered by ENAMI EP's workers in April 2014,[124] despite testimony that he was at home at the time of the attacks. He was detained for 12 months on charges of rebellion.[125] Although the sentence in first instance was reduced on appeal to 10 months, granting him immediate release on account of the imprisonment period he had already served. This was subsequently overturned by the Imbabura court of appeals in May 2015, reinstating the original sentence and leading to Ramirez's detention for two further months.[126] Nevertheless, the National Court of Quito overturned this later sentence, putting an end to ENAMI EP's efforts to imprison Ramirez Piedra.[127]

To sum up, the criminal complaint faced by Darwin Ramirez Piedra interfered with the accessibility dimension of his rights to water and health because his imprisonment prevented him from imparting information about water and health issues directly linked to this SOE's operation.[128] In particular, this complaint could be framed as an abusive use of judicial mechanisms against a human rights defender that limited his exercise of the human rights to freedom of expression and association[129] and procedural environmental rights[130] as it prevented him from freely participating in associations engaged in human rights monitoring and reporting about ENAMI EP's activities.[131]

4.3 *Abuses of human rights through inobservance of constitutional and mining provisions*

The *Los Cedros* case concerns the decision of the Constitutional Court (CC), which reviewed the protective action initiated in favour of Los Cedros

123 Amnesty International, "Ecuador: Further Information: Environmental Activist Sentenced to Jail" (6 May 2015), available at www.amnesty.org/en/documents/amr28/1604/2015/en/.

124 Unidad Judicial Competente con Sede en el Canton Cotacachi, Valenzuela Carlos (Procurador Judicial de ENAMI-EP) *et al* v Darwin Ramirez Piedra and Victor Hugo Ramirez Piedra, No. de Proceso 1033220140364 (10 April 2014).

125 n 119.

126 Sala Multicompetente de la Corte Provincial de Imbabura, Ramos Gómez, María Gabriela Procuradora Judicial del Gerente General y Representante Legal de la Empresa Nacional Minera EP et al v Ramirez Piedra Darwin et al, No. de Proceso 1010320140501 (5 de Mayo 2015).

127 Corte Nacional de Justicia, Sala Especializada de lo Penal, Penal Militar, Penal Policial, Transito, Corrupción y Crimen Organizado, *Loor Sojos Marcelo, Gerente General Estado Ecuatoriano Empresa Nacional Minera ENAMI EP v Ramírez Piedra Darwin Javier*, Proceso No. 17721-2015-0633 (30 de Septiembre 2015).

128 n 24.

129 n 25.

130 Escazu Agreement n 26.

131 Ibid.

protective forest by the local government of Cotacachi and partially accepted on appeal by the second instance court of the Provincial Court of Imbabura.[132] The CC established breaches of the rights of nature, to water and the RTHE through the Ministry of Environment's provision of a '*registro ambiental*' (*registro*) to ENAMI EP for the commencement of exploration activities without requiring initial environmental studies.[133] For the CC, this Ministry's approval failed to apply the precautionary principle because it merely presumed a low environmental impact from these mining activities, based on the lack of categorization of Los Cedros Forest as a 'protected area', where extractive activities are explicitly banned.[134] In addition, the CC also found violations of the right to environmental consultation because the Ministry's environmental authorization was not preceded by an environmental consultation of neighbouring communities, again an action merely based on ministerial accords that relieved it from the obligation to implement participatory processes for development projects of low impact.[135]

In this context, ENAMI EP indirectly compromised the right to water and the RTHE because its non-submission of environmental studies prior to requesting the *registro* hindered the Ministry of Environment's application of the precautionary principle. It precluded this regulatory entity from having actual information about the intrinsic characteristics of the environmental components of Los Cedros protective park (such as its endemic species, biodiversity, natural cycles and water sources) and the function it performs as a buffer zone that preserves Cotacachi-Cayapas Park as a protected area.[136] Hence, the Ministry was initially prevented from adequately assessing the real risk of major and irreversible damage on Los Cedros protective forest by its mining exploration.[137] In fact, according to the CC, this information would have led the Ministry to establish that there was no scientific certainty about the type and magnitude of impact or damage that could result from metallic mining in this forest, due to the excessive complexity of relating cause and effect of metallic mining activity with the impact on all the aforementioned

132 Corte Constitucional del Ecuador, Judgment No. 1149-19-JP/21 (10 November 2021) (*Los Cedros* case), available at http://esacc.corteconstitucional.gob.ec/storage/api/v1/10_DWL_FL/e2NhcnBldGE6J3RyYW1pdGUnLCB1dWlkOic2MmE3MmIxNy1hM-zE4LTQyZmMtYjJkOS1mYzYzNWE5ZTAwNGYucGRmJ30=.

133 Environmental laws distinguish between *registro ambiental* and an environmental license. While the former is an environmental permit granted for activities or projects of low environmental impact and risk, the latter is required for those of higher character. In addition, the CC found that the Ministry's approval of the EMP made by this SOE was another cause of breaches of these rights. Los Cedros case n 131 paras 218–252.

134 Ibid.

135 *Los Cedros* case n 131 paras 274–278, 281, 320.

136 *Los Cedros* case n 131 paras 218–235 and 112–164, in connection with 236–252.

137 For the realization of the human rights laid down in the ACHR, states shall comply with environmental principles such as the precautionary principle. *Advisory Opinion on Human Rights and the Environment* n 22 paras 125, 175–180.

environmental components of this protective forest and on the Cotacachi-Cayapas National Park alike.[138]

Moreover, this SOE undermined neighbouring communities' exercise of their right to freedom of expression by carrying out socialization of its mining project after obtaining the *registro* because this process did not satisfy the criteria required for the implementation of environmental consultation.[139] To explain, this socialization process was not impartial since it was carried out by an interested party, thereby contradicting the non-delegable character of consultation processes.[140] Besides, this corporate "socialization" prevented these groups from expressing their views about a state regulation likely to affect the environment because it was made *after* its awarding, and its provision of information did not clearly and fully convey the nature, scope and reversibility of the environmental authorization issued through the *registro*.[141]

5 Outlook

The brief description of the environmental and social impacts caused by ENAMI EP's exploration activities shows that accountability mechanisms, especially those related to its governance, need to be strengthened. Its existing policies do not explicitly commit to meeting its responsibility to respect human rights, nor do its processes seek to identify and prevent human rights impacts. Given these shortcomings, there is an urgent need that this SOE design and implement a human rights due diligence process that conforms to the parameters and components listed in the UNGP and is applicable to both employees and contractors alike. Until this happens and the Ecuadorian state adopts an NAP that articulates the behaviour expected of companies operating in its territory, this SOE can become a member of the UN Global Compact-Network Ecuador or other private reporting and certification mechanism in order to integrate the environmental and human rights principles of the UN Global Compact into its governance.[142] This would initially help their corporate policies and due diligence processes become consistent with these benchmarks and allow external stakeholders to monitor their implementation through progress reports the company is required to publish as a member. To achieve this end, the Sectoral Ministry could and should encourage its adherence to the Global Reporting Initiative (GRI) standards for the mining sector to better understand and report about its impacts on the environment and people.[143]

138 *Los Cedros* case n 131 para 146.

139 The protection of this right also requires corporate observance of the procedural environmental right to participation in environmental decision-making. *Advisory Opinion on Human Rights and the Environment* n 22 paras 125, 226–232.

140 *Los Cedros* case n 131 paras 281, 284, 323.

141 *Los Cedros* case n 131 paras 325, 327, 328.

142 So far, ENAMI EP has not adhered to this initiative. n 1.

143 n 62.

4 Regulation of state-owned enterprises (SOE) in Brazil in relation to human rights

Victória Vitti de Laurentiz and Danielle Anne Pamplona

1 Introduction

The aim of this chapter is to assess the extent of regulation of state-owned enterprises (SOE) in Brazil compared to private ones: specifically, how the regulations relate to conduct that may impact human rights.

In Brazil, despite the provision in the constitutional text then in force[1] stating that direct state action in economic activities should occur only to supplement private initiatives, there was a proliferation of state companies in the 1960s and 1970s. The military governments created state companies to develop sectors of the economy considered to be of national interest.[2]

In the 1990s, a movement towards privatization and market regulation began in Brazil. The state, until then directly active in the economy, surrendered certain economic activities to private entities, allowing the public administration to concentrate its efforts on the activities in which the state's presence was essential to the achievement of national priorities.[3] The withdrawal of the state from the exercise of economic activities was accompanied by the exercise of a new regulatory role. Thus, regulation ceased to happen through direct involvement in economic activities and instead became normative, implemented by decentralized and technical bodies, the so-called regulatory agencies.

In this context, the Access to Information Law (12.527/2011), the Criminal Organisations Law (12.850/2013) and the Electoral Mini Reform of 2015 (13.165/2015) stand out for their normative impact with regard to the creation of ceilings for the financing of election campaigns, coupled with the decision of the Supreme Federal Tribunal (STF) (ADI 4650), also in 2015, to adopt a constitutional interpretation that prohibits donations from companies to parties or candidates' campaigns. With specific reference to

1 Brazilian Federal Constitution 1967, art. 163, par. 1.

2 COUTINHO, Diogo; MESQUITA, Clarissa; NASSER, Maria Virgínia. Empresas estatais entre serviços públicos e atividades econômicas. Rev. Direito GV 15 (1) 2019; BARRUCHO, Luis. 50 anos do AI-5: Os números por trás do 'milagre econômico' da ditadura no Brasil, 13 dez 2018 BBC News Brasil, available at www.bbc.com/portuguese/brasil-45960213

3 Law 9491/97, art. 1, item V.

DOI: 10.4324/9781003291428-4

state-owned enterprises, two main innovations comprise the Anti-Corruption Law (12.846/2013) and the State-Owned Companies Law (13.303/2016).

State-owned enterprises are legal entities governed by private law which are controlled directly or indirectly by state entity or entities and by the society. They can be created both to act in the economic realm and to provide public services.[4] In the Brazilian legal system, a state-owned company can be either a public company[5] or a mixed-capital company.[6]

The UN Guiding Principles on Business and Human Rights recognize that there are different instruments available to the state to fulfil its obligation to protect human rights. The state can use direct intervention in the economy through regulatory instruments, and it can also act directly by exploring economic activities through its state-owned enterprises. Inasmuch as the state must use legislative and executive instruments to adapt the conduct of private activities to the normative human rights framework, with even greater intensity, it must use the companies in which it has more breadth of regulation to establish examples of appropriate conduct as the WG highlights in its 2015 report, which recommends states should 'lead by example' regarding corporate respect for human rights. It is therefore expected that the domestic regulatory frameworks will follow this logic and format the relations of state companies with human rights, setting an example to be followed by the private initiative. In the same way, it would be logical to expect that there would be ample guidance and production of norms capable of promoting a general top-down orientation regarding the protection of human rights, starting with state companies.

2 The rise of SOEs in Brazil

Article 173 of the Brazilian Federal Constitution declares that state-owned enterprises (SOEs) shall directly carry out economic activities due to imperative national security or relevant collective interest. The legal status of these companies is set out in law, clarifying their social function and forms of oversight by the state and society. SOEs are subject to the same legal determinations as privately owned companies, including civil, commercial, labour and taxation duties and rights, as defined in the Constitution (art. 173, § 1o, II).

The 90s were characterized by the absorption of new public management concepts, and, consequently, the regulation of the new corporate governance,[7]

4 Bandeira de Mello, Celso Antônio. *Prestação de serviços públicos e Administração indireta*, p. 101.

5 A public company is a company with its own assets and exclusive voting capital, and its share capital is made up of resources from the public sector.

6 A mixed-economy company has both government and private participation in its capital and administration and is always organized as a joint stock company.

7 According to the governance manual of the Federal Court of Audit, corporate governance is defined as the system by which organizations are directed and controlled, which includes mechanisms for convergence of interests of actors directly and indirectly impacted by the activities

as far as SOEs are concerned, turned to compliance schemes based on codes of ethics and integrity. This reflects concern with corruption and, in practice, generates requirements that associate compliance with anti-corruption measures. In Brazil, this trend has intensified since the Law of State-Owned Companies (Law 13.303/2016), which regulates the control structures of these companies, was approved in the wake of Operation Lava Jato,[8] in which allegations of the action of contractors who corrupted senior executives of Petrobras in order to receive overpriced contracts were presented. The politicians responsible for the appointment of these senior executives were also denounced and convicted. It can be observed, therefore, that the importation of corporate governance criteria into public governance generates the structuring of a system concerned with the avoidance of corruption. Notably, the legislation prohibits the government from appointing to the board of directors of state companies individuals who have served in the previous three years as a member of a political party decision-making body. The law demonstrates a clear concern for governance rules and establishes strict rules for the appointment of administrators of state companies and the prevention of overbilling contracts. There is no provision regarding the liability of the company managers, whose responsibility still derives from previous corporate law that provides for the duty of diligence and loyalty. The legislator did anticipate that the statute may provide for management civil liability insurance for directors as coverage for any liability arising from their management acts, excluding, of course, willful misconduct.

The law also establishes that members of the board of directors must publish an annual governance letter, a sort of commitment to the future, in clear and direct language, with relevant information on the developed activities (operational data), control structure, risk factors, economic and financial data, in addition to comments from the administrators on the performance, policies and practices of corporate governance and a description of the composition and remuneration of the administration. There are, however, no provisions on evaluation and indication of the impacts of the activity of these companies on human rights.

The law of SOEs was received with great euphoria by the market, but it did not deliver a much-needed redefinition of the governance model. Even though the legal framework seeks to consolidate in a single legal statute public companies and mixed economy companies, there is considerable criticism to be made regarding the regulatory strategy and lack of smart regulation. Reproducing superficial and generalist measures on the role of integrity, the

---

of organizations. Such mechanisms protect external investors from expropriation by internal investors, the latter being managers and controlling shareholders. BRASIL. Tribunal de Contas da União (TCU). Governança Pública: referencial básico de governança aplicável a órgãos e entidades da administração pública e ações indutoras de melhoria, p. 19.

8 BRASIL, Ministério Público Federal – MPF. Caso Lava Jato. 2023, available at www.mpf.mp.br/grandes-casos/lava-jato/entenda-o-caso.

law does not go beyond innovating, in a timid manner, on some issues such as public procurement, defining priority and performance rules and defining quality control. In the absence of democratic and transparent public management, the gaps that open space for an attractive market to private companies are multiplying.[9]

Brazil represents a point off course in relation to the participation of state-owned companies in the economy. Research conducted at the OECD in 2017, with 40 different countries as an empirical base, found an average of 62 state-owned enterprises per country.[10] The universe of federal state-owned enterprises in Brazil consists of 132 companies, of which 47 are directly controlled, and 85 are subsidiaries. In 2019, there were 200 state-owned enterprises that held total assets of R$4.8 trillion and a net worth of R$711.4 billion and directly employed about 477,000 workers. Of this total, 144 companies were classified in the productive sector, and 38 were in the state financial sector.[11] The number of state-owned companies on national territory, therefore, is an indication of the relevance of these organizations' activities in the country. Moreover, there are also state-owned companies with a relevant role in the capital market that are listed on the São Paulo Stock Exchange.[12]

This is a broad view of the SOEs present in the Brazilian structure. The question remains how well the state complies with Pillar I of the UN Guiding Principles in making SOEs models of protection and respect for human rights. Furthermore, there is also the question of what the state's role consists of in the adoption by SOEs of conduct that respects human rights. In order to suggest answers, we chose to analyze the relation of a specific company with human rights. The company chosen is Eletrobras. It was created as a

9 In practice, this distancing between the agents fosters an extremely repressive and non-educating model. Faced with this mismatch in the national regulatory policy, private companies see the opportunity to play a role in the wave of privatizations. For a better understanding of the 80s privatization wave, see: BREVIGLIERI, Tatiana. Análise dos efeitos da privatização no Brasil no período de 1980–1990, Revista Iniciativa Econômica, 6 (1/2), 2020; and for an overview of the privatization process, see: MODIANO, Eduardo. Um balanço da privatização nos anos 90, in PINHEIRO, Armando; FUKASAKU, Kiichiro. *A privatização no Brasil – o caso dos serviços de utilidade pública*. BNDES, Biblioteca Digital, s/a, available at https://web.bndes.gov.br/bib/jspui/bitstream/1408/2222/1/2000_A%20privatização%20no%20Brasil_P.pdf.

10 OCDE (2017): *The Size and Sectoral Distribution of SOEs in OECD and Partner Countries* (Paris: OCDE), available at https://read.oecd-ilibrary.org/governance/the-size-and-sectoral-distribution-of-state-owned-enterprises_9789264280663-en (accessed 18 November 2022).

11 DIEESE – Departamento Intersindical de Estatística e Estudos Socioeconômicos. Technical Note n. 253. A panoramic view of federal state enterprises and possibilities for action in the post-pandemic. 24.03.21, available (in Portuguese) at www.dieese.org.br/notatecnica/2021/notaTec253Estatais.pdf.

12 SEST – Secretaria de Coordenação e Governança das Empresas Estatais Boletim das Empresas Estatais Federais, n.5, 2017, available (in Portuguese) at www.gov.br/economia/pt-br/centrais-de-conteudo/publicacoes/boletins/boletim-das-empresas-estatais-federais/arquivos/boletim-das-empresas-estatais-federais-2013-5a-edicao.pdf.

mixed-economy company (that is, it has private and state-owned capital), and the Brazilian government, until May 2022, held more than 50% of the voting shares.[13] It is the largest energy company in Latin America, responsible for almost one third of the energy generation capacity in Brazil, and has around 10,000 employees. In 2021, the company invoiced R$44.4 billion and had a net profit of R$5.7 billion.

We will proceed to indicate the company's conduct related to human rights respect and assess the relevance of existing state regulation in inducing such conduct.

3 Eletrobras's commitments to human rights and at least one controversy

Eletrobras is a holding that controls four big generation and transmission subsidiaries (CGT Eletrosul, Chesf, Eletronorte and Furnas) and recently expanded its business, mainly through joint ventures. All its commitments regarding the environment and human rights spread throughout its operations. From the outset, it must be clarified that in the country, the right to a healthy environment has been considered a human right for years. Thus, conduct that concerns environmental rights will be evaluated, not for its possible impact on human rights but, rather, because environmental rights are considered human rights.[14]

The public commitment of Eletrobras's top management level with respect to human rights is made explicit in two documents, a Social Responsibility Policy and a Code of Ethical Conduct and Integrity.[15] The first is based on guiding documents such as the United Nations Global Compact, the Sustainable Development Goals (SDGs), International Labour Organisation (ILO) treaties and conventions, the Organisation for Economic Cooperation and Development (OECD) Guidelines for Multinational Enterprises and the International Standard ISO 26.000. There is a human rights subcommittee that plans and implements the company's human rights policies and actions

13 In June 2022, the company was partly privatized, and the Brazilian state now holds less than 45% of the voting capital but will maintain its Golden Share. We have chosen to maintain the analysis of this company in this study because of its history of efforts to comply with regulatory frameworks related to human rights.

14 The Constitution establishes that environment protection is one of the foundations of the economic order (Art. 170), and it is the responsibility of everyone, state and collectivity, to defend and protect it (Art. 225). According to art. 225, an ecologically balanced environment is everyone's fundamental right. This guides the interpretation of all other environmental norms. The ecologically balanced environment derives from the principle of dignity of the human person and consists of a healthy environment, free of pollution.

15 Eletrobras. Code of Conduct. 2022, available at https://eletrobras.com/pt/GestaoeGorvernancaCorporativa/Codigo%20de%20Conduta%20da%20Eletrobras.pdf, p. 12; Eletrobras. Política de responsabildiade social das empresas Eletrobras, 2018, available at https://eletrobras.com/pt/ResponsabilidadeSocial/Pol%C3%ADtica%20de%20Responsabilidade%20Social%203.0-%20DEL%20237.2018.pdf, p. 5.

and a corporate sustainability committee that consolidates the relevant data from key areas, such as social responsibility and the environment, for the company's annual report.

The social responsibility policy tackles diversity, labour conditions and rights of the child within its own activities and throughout its supply chain, as well as the assessment of impacts. It also promotes training of employees and sensitization of suppliers to human rights; the company develops courses on the themes of diversity and inclusion, moral harassment and respect for human rights in the energy sector. The company adopts different programs related to the theme, such as the solidary selective collection, which promotes the environmentally adequate disposal of waste, with the participation of collectors of recyclable material; a volunteer program, which encourages the exercise of citizenship by its employees; and a program to combat child labour.

The 2021 Annual Report[16] indicates that the company conducted online consultation with shareholders, investors, board members, customers, employees, partners and suppliers in order to build its materiality matrix from a list of 18 themes related to the main impacts of its various companies, based on benchmarking with relevant actors in the global electricity sector. The final list with 6 relevant themes was approved, and the themes were prioritized according to the intensity of their impact, after consultation with different stakeholders. It is not clear from the report how follow-up mechanisms were defined, but it is clear there is a strong culture of identifying and discussing human rights impacts of the main activity, especially the positive impacts the company might have. Moreover, in its biannual reputation survey geared towards different stakeholders,[17] including workforce and impacted communities, there is a full set of human rights issues on which stakeholders are asked to present their perceptions. In addition, the company has created a questionnaire called human rights due diligence questionnaire that is posed to suppliers and joint ventures as the first step of the company's human rights due diligence. The aim is to know if impacts are identified and prevented; however, responding to the questionnaire is not a requirement for contracting or maintaining a contractual relationship with Eletrobras.[18]

Regarding the third pillar of the principles, the company maintains a channel for complaints with priority procedures for those related to human rights.[19] It has also recently implemented a project to centralize its Talk to Us hotline in order to standardize the procedure for corporate hearing and response. Further, it has applied adapted solutions in most of its major assets, including big

16 Eletrobras, Annual Report (2021): available at https://eletrobras.com/pt/Documents/Eletrobras_RA_2021_Resumo%20Executivo.pdf.

17 The most recent was undertaken in November 2020 and the next one, in November 2022.

18 available at https://eletrobras.com/pt/Fornecedores/Cartilha%20para%20fornecedores%20-%20Passo%20a%20Passo%202021.pdf#search=espaço%20do%20fornecedor.

19 Eletrobras, Code of Conduct, 2022, available at https://eletrobras.com/pt/GestaoeGorvernancaCorporativa/Codigo%20de%20Conduta%20da%20Eletrobras.pdf, p. 48.

hydropower plants, to boost local social communication projects. For example, mailboxes have been installed along river margins to collect opinions and complaints from riverain dwellers.

Only recently, since 2020, has there been a commitment to exercise due diligence on human rights within specific companies created to develop specific projects. Nevertheless, as the initiatives described are contemporaneous with some of the controversies in which the company is involved, it is possible to assess the impact of these initiatives.

Despite the existence of such initiatives, the ethics board of Norway's sovereign fund (Norges Bank) decided to exclude investments in Eletrobras from its portfolio due to a decision linked to human rights issues.[20] Eletrobras was excluded for the "unacceptable risk that the company contributes to serious or systematic human rights violations," especially for its role in the development of the controversial Belo Monte hydroelectric dam in Pará,[21] an asset implemented and operated by Norte Energia, one of Eletrobras' joint ventures.

The Belo Monte power plant was a project initiated in the 1970s with feasibility studies. In 2010, the construction began. That year, the largest city in the region, Altamira, had approximately 100,000 inhabitants. The population doubled with the installation of the plant, putting pressure on the already-deficient infrastructure. But the impacts are much broader and more intense. They are derived from different situations in the phases of assessment and studies, construction and operation of the plant. For example, the environmental impact study distorted the number of people who would be affected by the project;[22] the unsatisfactory categorization of this population between owners and non-owners, hindering the identification of who would be affected; and the delimitation of the area directly affected, excluding various riverine and indigenous populations impacted by the modification of the flow of the Xingu River and its affluents.[23]

20 available (in Portuguese) at https://valor.globo.com/empresas/noticia/2020/05/12/bc-da-noruega-exclui-vale-e-eletrobras-de-investimentos-do-fundo-soberano.ghtml.

21 available at www.infomoney.com.br/onde-investir/fundo-soberano-da-noruega-mantera-acoes-de-petroleo-na-carteira-confira-empresas-excluidas-em-2020/.

22 For example, to establish who belongs to the affected population and, therefore, is entitled to compensation, the study makes a classification of the affected areas. They can be considered 'directly affected', 'of direct influence' and 'of indirect influence'. All residents in municipalities classified as an area of indirect influence are excluded from compensation programs. In areas of direct influence, the analysis was carried out by a faster procedure, whose methodology is not clear. To better understand how the inadequacy of the data used and the classifications made influenced the results, see Magalhães, S., R. A. Marin and E. Castro (2009): "Análise de situações e dados sociais, econômicos e culturais", in: Painel de Especialistas (ed), *Análise Crítica do Estudo de Impacto Ambiental do Aproveitamento Hidrelétrico de Belo Monte* (Oakland: International Rivers), pp. 23–35.

23 Mello, C. (2009): "Elementos para análise do RIMA de Belo Monte à luz das conclusões e recomendações do projeto Avaliação de Equidade Ambiental", in: Painel de Especialistas (ed), *Análise Crítica do Estudo de Impacto Ambiental do Aproveitamento Hidrelétrico de Belo Monte* (Oakland: International Rivers), pp. 43–47.

In one of the various legal disputes involving the power plant, the judiciary recognized the impact of the work 'on the cultural traditions, way of life and use of land by indigenous peoples, causing relevant instability in intra- and inter-ethnic relations'.[24] Damages relate to the precarious health, food and social conditions; to an increase in the consumption of alcoholic beverages, illicit drugs and industrialized products; and to the fragmentation of the indigenous people into many villages since the number of members of each village was a criterion to obtain the sum of R$30,000/month per village.[25] Many of these problems could have been foreseen and prevented if the company had adopted procedures to listen to the indigenous communities involved. Free, prior and informed consent (FPIC) is the right of an indigenous nation, group or community to determine its own development and the right to exercise self-determination in the face of government or corporate decisions concerning its territories. This right has been recognized since 1989 with the adoption of ILO Convention 169. A consequence of a compromise to mediate the repudiation of the self-determination of peoples and the guarantee that no political or legal measures would be taken in their absence, prior consultation represents a middle ground between the denial of the self-determination of peoples and the abandonment of the assimilationist policy applied until then. Brazil ratified the Convention in 2002, 14 years after the Constitution provided for the need to hear affected communities whenever their territory was exploited. In 2005, the National Congress speedily passed a decree authorizing the implementation of the Belo Monte dam and determining that consultation should take place at a later date. The decree was declared void by the Supreme Court[26] because the duty to initially hear the affected indigenous communities is not merely a symbolic hearing; it must be effective and efficient. In the meantime, the dam has caused interference in the indigenous cultural features, way of life and land use, producing relevant instability in their intra- and inter-ethnic relations, especially when in search of land and food in a territory where the flow of water has been drastically reduced.[27]

It is clear, therefore, that the measures adopted by the company and its joint venture were not sufficient to avoid social and environmental impacts. It is certainly a reflection on initiatives that lend themselves to highlighting good practices adopted by the company but are far from tackling the existing negative impacts. In the 1990s, when the Belo Monte project was being discussed,

24 Federal Justice Altamira – PA. Civil Public Action 0003017–82.2015.4.01.3903 Public Prosecutor Office vs Brazil et alli. 05.11.20.

25 In April 2023, this figure would be around US$6,000, available at www.brasildefato.com.br/2020/11/18/justica-reconhece-etnocidio-causado-por-belo-monte-a-indigenas-e-ordena-mudancas.

26 Supreme Court, RE 1.379.751, available at https://portal.stf.jus.br/processos/detalhe.asp?incidente=6390761.

27 Federal Justice Altamira – PA. Civil Public Action 0003017–82.2015.4.01.3903 Public Prosecutor Office vs Brazil et alli. 05.11.20.

there was still no talk of corporate human rights due diligence, and although the environmental licensing legislation was already in force, it did not prevent negative impacts. Choosing to carry out a serious procedure could have led to the identification of potential impacts and provided tools for the company, in good faith, to face them. It remains to be seen whether the most recent developments in mandatory due diligence laws will be able to map the real impacts and whether they will have the strength to influence management decisions in order to provide mitigation and reparation.

It seems correct to conclude, therefore, that at the time of the licensing of the construction of Belo Monte, there were no initiatives regarding human rights concerns. A sample of those will be adopted at a later stage under the social responsibility policy agenda but will not relate to any state demand. Throughout the process, there was no lack of voices denouncing the impacts that were added, and they should have been enough to lead to reflection on the correct way of doing business. The project was part of a national energy generation plan. In this sense, the venture was in the hands of the federal government, which would carry it out using the public company, Eletrobras. This suggests that the lack of diligence in relation to the project's impacts on people and the environment is directly attributable to the state.

On the other hand, more recently, Eletrobras seems to have encouraged discussions on energy transition, combating climate change and conserving the Amazon. An example of this materializes through three commitments that Eletrobras has recently made on the 2023 United Nations Conference on Climate Change (COP28), held in Dubai. The company signed a technical cooperation agreement with the National Bank for Economic and Social Development (BNDES) to build partnerships in projects for the decarbonization of the Amazon and for the recovery of Brazilian river basins.

Eletrobras also announced its role as ambassador of the UN Ambition Net Zero Movement, an acceleration initiative that aims to challenge and support member companies of the UN Global Compact in establishing climate commitments that are ambitious and based on science and to integrate Sustainable Development Goal 13 (Climate Action) and the objectives of the Paris Agreement into their business strategies. Finally, Eletrobras presented a working group conducted in partnership with the UN Global Compact in Brazil.

As the objective of this chapter is to assess the performance of the state in relation to its obligation to ensure that human rights are respected by third parties, it is important to evaluate to what extent the Brazilian state determines the conduct of the companies it owns. International law in general, and the guiding principles in particular, clarify that the state's duty to protect human rights can be fulfilled through the development of appropriate laws and public policies and also through the adoption of consistent conduct among the different organs of the state and in its international relations and manifestations in different fora. The next section will evaluate, therefore, how the Brazilian state is doing in this respect.

4 State legislation and other regulation to protect human rights

4.1 Regulations on human rights and business activity

Brazil has not adopted a national action plan on business and human rights. Two initiatives were underway, one in the Ministry of Economy and the other in the Ministry of Women, Family and Human Rights. The first one was published in December 2022[28] and is called Action Plan in Responsible Business Conduct, although it only gathers information on policies, laws and regulations already implemented and related to the issues addressed in the chapters of the OECD Guidelines for Multinationals Enterprises. The second one did not take off due to the impossibility[29] of hiring people responsible for drawing up a baseline assessment. Nevertheless, Decree 9571/2018 conveys the non-binding national guidelines for business and human rights and establishes measures to foster and implement human rights principles for the state and national and multinational corporations with activities in Brazil, as well as criteria for oversight, accountability and redress in the event of human rights violations.[30]

Although the decree aims to allocate rights and duties to the public and private spheres, the voluntary nature of the norms, which may or may not be implemented by companies, undermines greater expectations regarding the effective prevention of violations. However, there are obligations to be implemented in the axis that refers to the state.[31] Although the normative provisions of the decree indicate a series of requirements for a basic structure of integrity programs, the definitions used present the same vagueness and indeterminacy as soft law instruments.

In parallel, it is important to note that, apart from the decree mentioned earlier, there is still no other regulatory instrument dedicated specifically to the tensions arising from business activities in the face of human rights, establishing standards of conduct expected of companies in terms of preventing and addressing negative impacts.[32]

28 Available (in Portuguese) at www.gov.br/produtividade-e-comercio-exterior/pt-br/assuntos/camex/pcn/PACER2212225.pdf.

29 The budget allocated for this was very low, so contracting was hampered. Information about the call is available at https://vendor.un.org.br/processes/5834.

30 There is also a bill at the National Congress (572/2022) that aims to substitute for Decree 9571/2018, which has been on hold since shortly after being presented.

31 Such as BHR capacity building amongst public officials; to provide for greater approximation between public policy and human rights protection, as well as to implement more public policies on this subject; to improve on transparency and social participation; to foster the adoption of due diligence by companies; to create channels for clear communication regarding the subject between companies and the state; to guarantee work conditions; to fight discrimination and to promote inclusion; and to foster the adoption of codes of conduct on human rights.

32 For a comprehensive study on reparation tools in Brazil: Pamplona, Danielle; Atchabahian, Ana; Santana, Anna. Brasil in Experiencias latinoamericanas sobre reparación en materia de empresas y derechos humanos, Konrad Adenauer Stiftung, 2022, pp. 133–165.

4.2 *State regulations on the theme of human rights in the energy sector*

As Eletrobras is a company in the energy sector, it was created under the aegis of the Ministry of Mines and Energy, which has as its institutional mission to 'formulate and ensure the execution of Public Policies for the sustainable management of energy and mineral resources, contributing to the country's socio-economic development';[33] its current structure was established in 2019.[34] Besides its competence for strategic environmental assessment, there is no mention of the topic of human rights protection, either through preventive activities or responses to negative impacts that may arise from the activities that are overseen by the Ministry. However, Brazilian public law does provide for environmental corporate liability, as mentioned above, and the entirety of the civil regime applies equally to private and public companies.[35] As the objective of this text is to evaluate the supervision of power generation activities as they relate to human rights, upon observing the absence of a framework that could establish guidelines for identifying and evaluating the impacts of this relationship in the ministry responsible for the topic, we sought in its structure some agency that could address these concerns.

Agência Nacional de Energia Elétrica (ANEEL), the regulatory agency for the electric power sector, was created under the Ministry of Energy. It is directly responsible for issuing norms to be followed within the electricity sector by both state-owned and private companies. Brazilian regulatory agencies were created as institutions that are legally independent of executive departments or ministries. The purpose of delegating regulatory powers to independent agencies was to insulate the process of rulemaking and oversight from political influence. Thus, these agencies must be impartial government bodies and regulate all agents with the same rules, regardless of whether they private or state-owned companies.[36]

Among its attributions, there is no mention of the supervision of the impacts of regulated activities on human rights or the promotion of practices that prevent and address such impacts. In its user service charter, ANEEL

33 Available at https://dados.gov.br/organization/about/ministerio-de-minas-e-energia-mme.

34 Decree 9.675/2019.

35 Brazil: Pamplona, Danielle, Ana Atchabahian and Anna Santana (2022): *Brasil in Experiencias latinoamericanas sobre reparación en materia de empresas y derechos humanos* (Bogotá: Konrad Adenauer Stiftung), pp. 133–165.

36 Regulatory agencies are expected to act with greater transparency, autonomy and impartiality. However, even if autonomy is sought for regulatory agencies, one cannot forget that they are part of a government – which was often not the one that appointed its current leaders – and, thus, are subject to political and media pressures.

In this context, it is necessary to mention the political and economic capture of the agency. This capture indicates that the agency becomes a means of protection and benefit of regulated business sectors. It exists when the agency loses its authority condition committed to the realization of the collective interest and instead acts to legitimize the realization of singular interests of certain regulated business sectors. The Constitution provides that the Federal Court of Auditors (part of the legislative branch) will oversee acts carried out by regulatory agencies.

indicates that it makes available to society a communication channel to receive complaints and information related to dam safety.[37] This provision allows any person, without the need to identify themselves, to present communications regarding possible irregularities observed in water storage dams for purposes of electric power generation. However, there is no clarification on the internal procedure adopted to deal with complaints, response times or information on open and closed procedures and outcomes.

The absence of guidelines and procedures regarding human rights compels us to look beyond the ministry responsible for energy generation activities. Despite there being no sectorial provisions on the protection of human rights, there are some general regulations by the Brazilian government pointing to the appropriate prevention and redress actions for all public companies in the country.

4.3 State-owned enterprises regulations on human rights and business

At the global level, a 2016 United Nations report acknowledges a significant absence of attention to human rights impacts and responsibilities in the scope of operations of state-owned enterprises. It further reports that, in many countries, state-owned enterprises have been undermined by issues of corporate governance, regulatory capture, direct subsidies and inefficiencies and lack of transparency and responsiveness.[38] The report notes that policies, guidelines and good practices are lacking at both the national and international levels. We indicate next how the energy sector in Brazil fits into this description.

In the Ministry of Economy, we find a governance indicator (IG-SEST), developed by the Secretariat of Coordination and Governance of State Enterprises (SEST), which is responsible for determining policies and guidelines for state-owned enterprises in the country. It is an instrument for continuous monitoring of the governance of federal state-owned companies under the direct control of the union. The indicator assesses compliance with the requirements of Law No. 13,303/2016, its regulatory decree (Decree 8,945/2016) and the guidelines established in the resolutions of the Interministerial Commission of Corporate Governance and Administration of Corporate Holdings of the Union (CGPAR).[39] The index is ascertained in three dimensions, composed of blocks, which contain evaluation items of: I. Management, Control and Auditing; II. Transparency of Information; and III. Councils, Committees and Board of Directors. These norms were created in the wake of the regulation of state companies, and, therefore, when requiring the supervision of

37 This follows from the provisions of the National Policy on Dam Safety (Law 12.334/2010 art. 5, par. 3)

38 Leading by Example: The State, State-Owned Enterprises and Human Rights (UNITED NATIONS. General Assembly. Human Right Council. Leading by example: the state, state-owned enterprises and human rights: report of the working group on the issue of human rights and transnational corporations and other business enterprises. 2016. (A/HRC/32/45).

39 Decree 6.021/2007.

conduct, they are essentially linked to codes of conduct and integrity, which also do not include provisions related to human rights.

The evaluation of the SEST governance indicator is performed through the application of a questionnaire made available in the state-owned Companies Information System (Siest), whose questions are answered by the participating state-owned companies themselves. The answers that indicate full or partial compliance with the questions must be duly proven by means of documents attached to the system or by the inclusion of links to pages of public access which show the effective existence, in the companies evaluated, of the practices described in the statements.

The IG-SEST instrument currently includes among its objectives the incentive to implement OECD guidelines and good governance practices by federal state-owned companies, including aspects related to the promotion of equity and diversity as well as environmental responsibility. The inclusion of these questions was the result of a partnership between the Ministries of Economy and the Ministry of Women, Family and Human Rights.[40]

In practice, the questions added to the questionnaire aim to encourage companies to create whistleblower channels to receive complaints about the integrity and ethics of public servants in the performance of their functions, in addition to mechanisms that allow for denunciations without retaliation. The new questions also inquire about women's access to leadership positions, racial diversity in hiring and plurality.

This instrument requires a company statement on the promotion of the adoption of conduct in relation to human rights. Although it does not seek to know the content of such conduct, it contributes to transparency in their regard.

Insofar as the actions of companies are evaluated annually in this way, an index of compliance and conformity with the requirements is received, in addition to incentives for innovative practices capable of improving compliance with human rights by the public sector. When we observe the general average over time, the first cycle of evaluated companies resulted in a 4.15 on a scale of 0 to 10, while the fifth cycle showed a significant increase in the average by reaching the level of 8.07.[41] There is little empirical evidence, however, that the increase in this index has, in fact, resulted from a real engagement with new corporate governance[42] standards or from the training of federal

40 MMDHC – Ministério dos Direitos Humanos e da Cidadania. Empresas estatais serão avaliadas a partir das ações em direitos humanos. 2021. Available (in Portuguese) at www.gov.br/mdh/pt-br/assuntos/noticias/2021/junho/empresas-estatais-serao-avaliadas-a-partir-das-acoes-em-direitos-humanos.

41 The elaboration of the averages in each cycle was based on the evaluation of 87 federal state-owned companies, whose individual scores in each cycle are available at www.gov.br/economia/pt-br/assuntos/empresas-estatais-federais/igsest/historico/evolucao-estatais-igsest.

42 The concept of corporate governance proposed by IG-SEST to public agencies is that provided in Decree 9,203 of 2017, which is defined as a 'set of leadership, strategy and control mechanisms put in place to evaluate, direct and monitor management, with a view to conducting public policies and providing services of interest to society.'

state-owned companies to carry out mappings and action plans with human rights indicators.

The SOE statute does not expressly provide for human rights respect, but it indicates sustainability as an element of the social function of public companies (e.g., article 8 creates the obligation to annually disclose an integrated or sustainability report, and article 45 provides for variable remuneration to contractors based on attendance of environmental sustainability criteria). The use of sustainability in this legislation is closely related to the environment, and it is disconnected from the broader meaning that sustainability could potentially assume if regarded as a means of getting SOEs to comply with social and governance criteria. In the same sense, the Brazilian bidding law (14,133/21) states that one of the goals of procurement procedures is to encourage innovation and sustainable national development. All these references to sustainability could be developed into human rights demands in further regulation, but this is not yet the case.

Article 9 of the SOE statute[43] requires SOEs to maintain a whistleblowing channel for employees and individuals outside the company, which should protect whistleblowers against retaliation from corporate officers. SOEs must produce and disclose several documents related to corporate governance, including an annual sustainability report (article 8, IX). Likewise, SOEs must adopt social and environmental sustainability practices compatible with the market in which they operate. In other words, according to this provision, SOEs should adopt environmental and social practices that are of a higher standard than what is required by law if commonly adopted by private competitors. SOEs must publish 'a report on the compliance, within the company's business, with the social and environmental conditions established by environmental bodies' (Article 7, VIII).

It can, however, be argued that the whistleblowing provisions do not go quite far enough: reporting channels and whistleblower protection are provided for, but little is said about the policies and procedures that should be adopted in consequence of the information received or how, in practice, confidence in the efficiency of these channels can be established.[44]

Therefore, it is possible to find regulations on corporate governance essentially as a result of allegations of corruption involving companies. There was no room for the development of regulations that could be aimed at preventing negative impacts on human rights, along the lines of the provisions of the UN Guiding Principles on Business and Human Rights, since they have not been internalized in the domestic legal system. With regard to state-owned enterprises within the scope of the guiding principles, the starting point is Principle 4, which states:

> States should take additional steps to protect against human rights abuses by business enterprises that are owned or controlled by the State,

43 Law no. 13.303/16.

44 OECD (2020): OECD Review of the Corporate Governance of State-Owned Enterprises: Brazil, available at www.oecd.org/corporate/soe-review-brazil.htm, p. 119.

> or that receive substantial support and services from State agencies such as export credit agencies and official investment insurance or guarantee agencies, including, where appropriate, by requiring human rights due diligence.

This principle raises relevant questions about why states are expected to take additional measures to protect human rights in the context of state-owned enterprises and whether it would be sufficient or not for states to take appropriate measures to ensure that both private and state-owned enterprises respect human rights. At this point, it is important to clarify that the need for specific and additional measures when dealing with state-owned enterprises is also based on the principle that states should 'lead by example',[45] serving as models and parameters for the evolution of governance and integrity in other business sectors. Following this reasoning, the state should not demand less from enterprises directly associated with it than it would demand from private enterprises.

The guiding principles, however, do not directly specify what additional steps states should take to ensure that state-owned enterprises respect human rights. The UN Working Group report thus suggests steps ranging from requiring audits on systematic reporting on socio-environmental impact to cooperation with victim redress measures that include remediation of abuses and engagement with board members, which represents a significant vehicle for states to manage their relationships with state-owned enterprises.[46]

It is worth noting that when a human rights violation occurs in the context of the activities of a state-owned enterprise, it can also constitute a direct violation of the international law obligations of the state itself, thus giving rise to international accountability if the acts of the company are directly attributable to the state.[47] Similarly, it should be acknowledged that, after the turbulent scenario of Operation Lava Jato, the involvement of large Brazilian state-owned companies such as Petrobras reflects an additional difficulty in demonstrating a real change of course in its activities.[48]

45 Leading by Example: The State, State-Owned Enterprises and Human Rights (United Nations General Assembly. Human Right Council. Leading by example: the state, state-owned enterprises and human rights: report of the working group on the issue of human rights and transnational corporations and other business enterprises. 2016. (A/HRC/32/45).

46 Available at www.ohchr.org/EN/Issues/Business/Pages/Reports.aspx.

47 At the Inter-American Court of Human Rights [IACtHR] see, among others, Case of Velásquez Rodríguez v Honduras, Merits, 29 July 1988 and Case of Ximenes-Lopes v. Brazil, 4 July 2006.

48 Garcia Lopez reinforces the elements that amplify the risks associated with corruption in state companies: 'It is in the sphere of state companies, the sector least subject to public transparency and the scrutiny of bureaucratic control bodies, that the connection between politics, extraction of public resources and parties is most intense. . . . Although economic motives pervade power struggles in all sectors of the Esplanade, their intensity varies and, in the case of state companies, assumes a relevance that ends up becoming the epicenter of the broadest

At the same time, recent discussions on social and environmental governance (ESG) addressing the growing concerns about carbon emission rates and human rights violations have increasingly entered the realm of state-owned enterprise regulation as well. To avoid reproducing merely superficial incentives, the starting point should focus on risk mapping in order to more accurately define the scope of the socially and/or environmentally harmful activity. It is by starting from the negative impact that one can identify in production chain logics that are reversible or potentially sustainable.

Given the specific nature of state-owned companies, and especially when considering the different levels and natures, the ability to comply with human rights depends on a materiality map that reflects the reality of each public agency. Once the scope of the action plan has been defined, the next challenge is to control and monitor whether what is stated in the social and sustainability reports is effectively fulfilled in practice.

Overall, the revision of regulation and governance shows there is no indication of specific mandatory conduct that should be taken by SOEs in relation to human rights.

4.4 *Regulation applicable to state-owned and private companies*

The lack of specific legislation for SOEs did not prevent some regulation from happening. The regulation came from the body that regulates stock exchanges. Brazil's only stock exchange currently in operation, Brasil Bolsa Balcão (B3), is located in São Paulo. It manages the organised securities and derivatives markets through registration, clearing and settlement services. B3 acts as a central counterparty for all transactions in its trading system and provides centralized deposit service of assets.

Brazil's B3 has four listing tiers. Brazil's New Market (*Novo Mercado*) (NM) provides the highest corporate governance standards and transparency requirements. As the top listing segment, New Market has the most stringent standards and focuses on the protection of investors. In 2005, a sustainability index was created, aiming to be the indicator of the average performance of the asset prices of companies selected for their recognized commitment to corporate sustainability. B3's Corporate Sustainability Index is based on the application of a questionnaire to companies involving five dimensions: human capital, social capital, corporate governance and top management, environment and business model and innovation. Under the human capital dimension, questions are related to compliance with labour legislation, the existence of diversity and inclusion actions and the protection of minority rights and gender equality. Under the social capital dimension, questions are related to companies' commitments regarding human rights, communication with local

records of organized corruption'. Lopez, F. G. (org.) Cargos de confiança no presidencialismo de coalizão brasileiro. Brasília: IPEA 2011, p. 25.

communities and management measures for negative impacts on the local community, among others. These examples indicate that if responses are true to the facts, they may indicate companies adopting conduct that is in line with the guiding principles. The companies that participate in the index perform better on the stock exchange and produce documents that more frequently indicate their concern with ESG criteria and compliance with the SDGs.

Since 2017, the Brazilian Securities Commission (CVM) obliges listed companies to report – based on a 'comply or explain approach' – on the adoption of the good practices set forth in the Brazilian Code of Corporate Governance (Rule 586, amending Rule 480 of 2009). Built on the G20/OECD Principles of Corporate Governance and other international standards, as well as existing Brazilian and Brazilian Institute of Corporate Governance (IBGC) guidance, the code is underpinned by principles of transparency, fairness, accountability and corporate responsibility. The code is broader in scope than B3's listing requirements, providing companies with details in its five chapters on shareholders, boards of directors, executive management, supervisory and control bodies and ethics and conflicts of interest. These indices are established within the framework of financial activities and relate especially to investor risk management. Although it is relevant for sustainability and human rights issues for the company to maintain governance structures that allow its members to discuss those issues, it is also relevant to point out that this is neither a Parliament product nor regulation meant to increase levels of human rights protection and respect in the country.

5 Conclusions

State-owned enterprises occupy a singular space in Brazilian political and economic history and in popular perception as they relate to the promise of economic development. The multiplication and involvement of state-owned enterprises in major corruption schemes in recent decades have certainly had a negative impact on popular perception of the level of capture of these organizations. Hence, the plethora of compliance processes that are more concerned with corruption than with human rights. The relevance of SOEs incidence is due to their size and power of influence. As evaluated in the case of Eletrobras, as the largest energy company in Latin America, its capacity to impact rights and use its power of influence to encourage appropriate conduct cannot be underestimated. This text pointed to several initiatives in the company that refer to sustainable practices and human rights. In fact, it is possible to conclude that the company adopts different measures that end up demonstrating that it is aware of the positive impacts it can have on the communities where its businesses are being implemented and developed. However, SOEs' capacity to respond to the negative impacts it causes is weaker. This is noticeable not only by the impacts caused by the Belo Monte hydroelectric plant but also by the absence of mechanisms that give satisfactory answers to those who are impacted. This is an acceptable scenario if the company has prevention mechanisms so robust as to drastically reduce the negative impacts. As this is not the case, the company must be concerned not only with giving visibility to the positive things it does but also with facing its negative impacts with the same willingness. There is therefore much to be done in relation to Pillar II of the guiding principles, which deals with the company's responsibility to adopt human rights due diligence procedures, and even more needs to be considered under Pillar III, which deals with preparedness measures.

In order for these initiatives to be better developed, state action is necessary. As mentioned, this is what Pillar I requires: the state must promote respect for human rights through all means available to it. Brazil has no binding legislation on business and human rights, generally speaking. It has not even adopted a national action plan. It is a country with a very protective history in terms of labour and environmental legislation. This set of norms, however, does not involve the due diligence that companies should have when engaging in their business activities. From the point of view of the need for prevention and the establishment of the responsibility of companies to adopt human rights due diligence procedures, there are no rules applicable to the public or private sector.

Similarly, when we insert human rights compliance in the context of the ESG debate for state-owned companies, there are still major challenges ahead. Smart regulation necessarily requires creative solutions that also leave aside the 'universal formulas' of decarbonization and human well-being metrics. The use of metrics applied internally to companies in a single sector which establish the risks that situations present for the company itself, its investors and potential investors does not encourage the adoption of conduct that respects the environment and people. There is an urgent need for new metrics and realistic indicators that go beyond common sense and can, based on a complete materiality map, identify reversibility opportunities in production chains.

Scrutiny of state actions for the topic leads to the conclusion that there is no generic guidance on the topic of human rights and business and no specific guidance for SOEs. Examples of initiatives such as those found at Eletrobras should be attributed to other fronts. It may be that participation in international forums that discuss the topic drives internal discussion. The discussion among investors about the need to pay attention to factors other than profit generation may have some resonance. Definitively, this is not a coordinated action of the Brazilian state through the executive and its ministries or the work of Parliament.

5 Chile

Due diligence and financial inclusion policies in the state-owned Banco Estado

Macarena Contreras Soto, Francisco Sánchez Lay and Judith Schönsteiner[1]

1 Introduction

Chilean state-owned enterprises are active in sectors as diverse as drinking water, mining, gambling and maritime transportation.[2] There are mainly two types of corporate structures: state-owned enterprises created by specific laws and others that are grouped under a system of public enterprises (Sistema de Empresas Públicas) (SEP). The level of control state organs exercise over the companies tends to be higher for those enterprises created by specific laws,[3] although, generally, regulation applies in the same way to private and public enterprises. Executive control over the companies' boards of directors was considerably reduced to facilitate the country's inclusion in the OECD in 2010. This does not mean, however, that Banco Estado or other state-owned enterprises (SOEs) cannot carry out public functions.

According to the UN Guiding Principles on Business and Human Rights, state-owned enterprises should "lead by example" regarding the implementation of human rights due diligence and the effective compliance with respect for human rights in their activities and business relationships (see Introduction). Furthermore, the OECD considers that responsible ownership of state-owned enterprises encompasses human rights policies.[4]

The exact scope of human rights standards for state-owned enterprises is still debated; however, the Inter-American System of Human Rights has

1 The authors thank Tomás Novoa López-Hermida for excellent research assistance and Markus Krajewski, Carlos Miranda and Danny Rayman for their observations on earlier drafts. This research received public funding from the National Agency of Research and Development (ANID), Fondecyt de iniciación N° 11150853 and Fondecyt regular N° 1201380. Thanks to Patrick Humpal for proofreading.

2 See *Sistema de Empresas – SEP*, available at https://sepchile.cl (accessed 18 October 2023).

3 See Judith Schönsteiner, Vicente Martínez and Carlos Miranda (2020): "Atribuibilidad al Estado de Chile de Actos y Omisiones de sus Empresas Públicas del Sector Extractivo a la Luz de la Jurisprudencia de Tribunales Regionales de Derechos Humanos", *Revista Chilena de Derecho*, Vol. 47: p. 757.

4 See OECD (2015): *OECD Guidelines on Corporate Governance of State-Owned Enterprises* (Paris: OECD Publishing), p. 60.

DOI: 10.4324/9781003291428-5

developed the standard that state-owned enterprises have to respond to state obligations in human rights matters.[5] Even if this thesis were not accepted, if a SOE carries out a public function, this would make it subject to those standards.[6]

This article focuses on Banco Estado, a state-owned bank, analysing its commitment to human rights. Although Banco Estado declares itself as just another bank in Chile's banking sector, its purpose includes enhancing the accessibility of financial services to persons who would otherwise not meet the market's criteria for bank accounts, debit cards and other financial services. The authors chose the bank for this case study as its design permits examining both the bank's explicit human rights policies and its conformity with human rights in its public policy contribution towards the accessibility of financial services without discrimination. This is why we analyse Banco Estado under the human rights obligations Chile has committed to when ratifying international and regional human rights treaties such as the American Convention on Human Rights or the International Covenant on Economic, Social and Cultural Rights.

In order to answer whether the bank complies with the responsibilities and obligations international human rights law imposes, we will first briefly identify human rights and environmental risks in the Chilean banking sector and describe the regulation of the banking sector and the control state organs exercise over Banco Estado, beyond the oversight mechanisms that exist for private banks. Finally, we will describe and assess the bank's human rights policy and the accessibility of financial services policy, determining whether they are in conformity with international human rights standards.

2 Human rights and environmental risks in the Chilean banking sector

Banks such as Banco Estado face three main areas of human rights and environmental risks: those related to clients and workers, respectively, and risks related to the investments they make: i.e., risks in the investee companies that they should identify, prevent and mitigate through appropriate human rights due diligence of the investment portfolio.[7] Regarding individual clients and

5 See, in particular, Sarayaku v Ecuador, IACtHR Series C 245 (2012) para 76; Trabajadores Cesados de Petroperú et al v Peru, IACtHR Series C 344 (2017), paras 81, 162, 172 and 193; Muelle Flores v Peru, IACtHR Series C 375 (2019) and Inter-American Commission of Human Rights, Business and Human Rights: Inter-American Standards, OEA/Ser.L/V/II, CIDH/REDESCA/INF.1/19 (1. November 2019) para 50.

6 See Judith Schönsteiner (2022): "Inter-American Elements for a Systemic Approach to State-Owned Enterprises' Human Rights Obligations", *Business and Human Rights Journal*, pp. 1–21.

7 UN Human Rights Council, Guiding Principles on Business and Human Rights (2011); OECD (2022): *Responsible Business Conduct Due Diligence for Project and Asset Finance Transactions,*

workers, their responsibilities vary to the extent that they cause or may cause human rights damage. Regarding investee companies, they are usually not directly responsible but are considered to be "directly linked" to their investments. However, if they do not carry out proper due diligence, this makes them responsible for contributing to the harm that their investee companies may cause in their activities.[8]

Concretely, banks in Chile are at risk of discriminating against clients, in particular, on the grounds of discrimination that are systemic in Chilean society, such as racial and ethnic discrimination against migrants and indigenous persons, discrimination on grounds of gender identity, and – most frequently – discrimination on grounds of socio-economic origin, which, in Chile, is based on prejudices regarding certain surnames of "rich" and "poor" families, as well as the neighbourhood in which a person lives.[9] Regarding workers, banks face risks mainly regarding discrimination in the workplace and in hiring processes as legislation, aside from the general Anti-discrimination Law enacted in 2012,[10] a quota for persons with disabilities of 1% in larger enterprises since 2018,[11] does not provide for non-discrimination guarantees before signing a work contract. Additionally, they do not provide explicit guarantees against anti–trade union practices that are widespread in the country because collective labour rights are not sufficiently guaranteed (although generally recognized in art. 1 of Law 19.069) or sexual and workplace harassment. Furthermore, enterprises should address health and safety risks arising from long hours of desk work, compatibility of family and work life and the gender pay gap.

The human rights risks related to the investment portfolio are more difficult to determine as they depend on the sectors and countries where a bank's finance is distributed. As Banco Estado invests mainly in Chile,[12] the main risks involve violations of workers' rights, issues of discrimination and, depending on the industry sector, violations of the right to water, indigenous peoples' rights to land and self-determination and the right to live in a healthy environment. Risks and violations have been documented in different sector-wide[13] or

---

OECD Business and Finance Policy Papers (Paris: OECD Publishing); Shift (2021): ***Financial Institutions and Remedy: Myths and Misconceptions*** (New York: Shift Project, Ltd).

8 OECD, Due Diligence for Responsible Corporate Lending and Securities Underwriting: Key considerations for banks implementing the OECD Guidelines for Multinational Enterprises (2019).

9 INDH report, OR UN committee reports.

10 Law 20.609.

11 Law 21.015, inserts Art. 45 in Law 20.422. Reform of 25 April 2018.

12 Banco Estado, Estados Financieros 2020–2021.

13 See for example, Aylwin, José, Hernando Silva and Rubén Sánchez (2021): *Impacto de la Industria Forestal en los Derechos Humanos del Pueblo Mapuche de la Comuna de Lumaco* (Temuco: Observatorio Ciudadano); Aylwin, José, Marcel Didier and Oriana Mora (2021): *Human Rights Impact Assessment of SQM Against the Rights of the Lickanantay Indigenous People* (Santiago: Observatorio ciudadano); Instituto Nacional de Derechos Humanos (2021):

project-specific human rights impact assessments and in the National Baseline on Business and Human Rights.[14]

3 Regulation and norms in the banking sector

Chile's banking sector is – in comparison to other sectors – heavily regulated. Here, we will focus on the main characteristics and the environmental and human rights norms applicable to the sector.

3.1 Regulation and actors in the banking sector

Oversight in the banking sector is carried out by the Comisión para el Mercado Financiero (Financial Market Commission) (CMF), which was established in its current structure and mandate in 2019.[15] Despite being a state-owned bank, Banco Estado falls fully under the general oversight regime of the CMF.[16] One of the commission's main objectives is to ensure optimal behaviour and stability of the financial market. This is achieved through the oversight of disclosure standards that seek to avoid information asymmetry among actors.[17] Directors' duties in the banking sector follow the general scheme of responsibilities defined in company law. Thus, directors have to employ the "care and diligence" that a person would usually employ in their own business[18] and respond to prejudice against shareholders and owners[19] but not explicitly for prejudice caused to clients, workers or third parties. This responsibility is additionally restricted to intentional and negligent prejudice.[20] The approval of the company's annual reports in the shareholder meeting does not exempt directors from this responsibility. Directors and CEOs must pay compensation for damage caused in this context.[21] The law that created the Banco Estado does not define additional duties for directors, and the scheme of personal liability is the same as for private banks; however, as they are public officials, anti-corruption and integrity measures apply to them.

Industria Salmonera en Chile y Derechos Humanos (Santiago); Contreras, Macarena and Judith Schönsteiner (2017): "Derecho al Agua, Emergencias y Responsabilidades del Estado y de las Empresas Sanitarias", in: Vial, Tomás (ed), *Informe Anual sobre Derechos Humanos en Chile* (Santiago: Ediciones UDP).

14 Schönsteiner, Judith et al. (2016): "Estudio línea base sobre empresas y derechos humanos", Centro de Derechos Humanos, Universidad Diego Portales, available at https://derechoshumanos.udp.cl/publicacion/estudio-linea-base-sobre-empresas-y-derechos-humanos-en-chile/ (accessed 18 October 2023).

15 Library of National Congress. Law 21.000, art. 1. The Financial Market Commission Act.

16 Id., Finance Ministry Decree-Law 3, The Banking Act, art. 2, amended 2019.

17 Id., Law 21.000, art. 1. The Financial Market Commission Act.

18 Id., Law 18.046, art. 41. The Companies Act (Ley de Sociedades Anónimas in Spanish).

19 Ibid., art. 133, reiterated in art. 21 DFL 3.

20 Ibid., art. 41.

21 Ibid., art. 133.

3.2 Human rights and environmental norms for the banking sector

From 2023 onwards, pursuant to General Rule 461, larger companies that must report to the CMF need to include information about human rights, ESG and climate change in their sustainability reports.[22] The standards to be used for reporting on material risks are the ones issued by the Sustainability Accounting Standards Board (SASB).[23] The Human Capital Standard, a general (not sector-specific) document that references human rights and the UN Guiding Principles was adopted in 2020 but has not yet been approved.[24]

General Rule 461 requires governing boards to report on human rights issues, especially related to corporate governance structures, and on compliance with the UN Guiding Principles or comparable standards.[25] A statement on good practices, including how human rights and environmental sustainability are built into business; risk assessment and strategic processes; and how relevant units or individuals are identified is also required.[26]

On risk management policy, governing boards are asked to describe their general guidelines, especially on environmental and human rights issues, noting the guiding national or international recommendations, if any. Organisations are asked to report on risks and opportunities in the businesses of both the parent company and its subsidiaries, including human rights and environmental risks, particularly climate change.[27]

General Rule 461 emphasises the need to report on the mechanisms or processes used to identify risks or how their significance was determined, including whether amending existing policies or introducing new human rights due diligence procedures were considered. Also requested are reports on the role of the board and senior management in detecting, assessing, monitoring and managing social, human rights and environmental risks, notably climate change and how risk is prioritised, mitigated, transferred, accepted or prevented.[28]

Strategic planning has to be reported on in general terms, with explicit mention of environmental, climate and human rights issues and their place in corporate governance. Reports must also include commitments adopted in compliance with UN Sustainable Development Goals or comparable

22 Financial Market Commission, Guide to Implementation and Monitoring of Section 8.2 of General Rule 461.

23 Ibid., p. 5

24 SASB, Human Capital Bulletin, p. 4 and p. 9. Social Capital Standard, p. 4, in 'human rights and community relations', and 'Human Capital Standard' (2020), available at https://sasb.org/wp-content/uploads/2020/12/Human-Capital_Preliminary-Framework_2020-December_FINAL.pdf (accessed 25 October 2023).

25 Ibid., s 2.

26 Ibid., s. 3.

27 Ibid., s 3(iii).

28 Ibid., s 3(iv).

guidelines. Furthermore, reports must also note any policies intended to positively impact the public interest in areas such as human rights, poverty eradication, education, health and food.[29]

Regarding sustainability indicators, General Rule 461 requires reporting on "metrics that are material to the organisation and industry . . . based on the Sustainable Industry Classification System (SICS) considered relevant by the Board or management and the Sustainability Accounting Standards set by the Sustainability Accounting Standards Board (SASB)".[30]

The commission publishes an implementation and monitoring guide[31] designed to assist enterprises in applying the regulations. Complementing voluntary reporting carried out in 2022 by some corporations,[32] incorporation of new sustainability and human rights standards will be noted in 2023 reports.

Non-compliance with disclosure requirements can have legal consequences. Under the Chilean Companies Act, directors or liquidators are held jointly and severally liable for damages caused to the company by non-compliance with general regulations.[33] The Securities Act and the Financial Markets Commission Act both contemplate fines and criminal penalties, noting that providing tendentious or false information, "even if not intended to gain an advantage or benefit for oneself or third parties, shall be punishable by up to 5 years' imprisonment".[34] Liability can be avoided if administrators, managers or intermediaries can successfully prove diligence in attempting to prevent events.[35] It is not yet clear which capacities and training the Commission has in order to carry out stringent oversight of human rights issues that, until now, have never been under the institution's mandate. It is clear, however, that Banco Estado is one of the companies that has to report under General Rule 461 from 2023 onwards.

4 State control over Banco Estado

Banco Estado is an autonomous, duly constituted, state-owned enterprise.[36] Its statutes define providing banking and financial services for the development of national economic activities as its purpose.[37] Its patrimony is independent

29 Ibid., s 4.2.

30 Financial Markets Commission, General Rule 461 (12 November 2021) Section 8.2: Indicators.

31 Financial Market Commission, Guide to Implementation and Monitoring of Section 8.2 of General Rule 461.

32 PUC and ILO, Primer Diagnóstico sobre Empresas y Derechos Humanos Chile 2022 (9 January 2023).

33 Library of Congress. Law 18046, art. 7(3). The Publicly Traded Companies Act.

34 Library of Congress. Law 18045, art. 61. The Securities Act.

35 The Securities Act, arts. 59 and 61.

36 Library of Congress. Ministry of Finance, Decree-Law 2079: Charter of the Banco Estado, Art. 1.

37 Ibid., Art. 3.

from the state budget.[38] Although no minister sits on the board, all board members, except the workers' representative, are appointed by the president of the Republic. Despite the general applicability of banking sector laws and general corporate law, there are several special rules for Banco Estado that constitute the entry point for state control over the enterprise. It is through these specific norms that the state exercises its ownership functions.

4.1 Special rules for Banco Estado

Banco Estado operates under a charter established by organic law (decree law adopted during the dictatorship) 2079, which states that the bank "is governed primarily by its Charter, and, in matters not contemplated therein, by the laws applicable to banking institutions and other provisions governing the private sector. General or special public sector norms shall not apply unless expressly stated otherwise".[39] The charter holds Banco Estado operations, regardless of their nature, to the same obligations, limitations and prohibitions applicable to commercial banks.[40] As a result, Banco Estado is regulated by its own caw and Charter first and by the private sector regime as needed for all other purposes.

Applicable public sector norms are contained in Title I (General Rules) of the Public Sector Act,[41] which notes that state-owned enterprises created by law are part of the public sector, and in Title III on Public Sector Integrity.[42] Law 20880, the Public Sector Integrity and Conflict of Interest Prevention Act, requires directors and management of state-owned enterprises created by law to declare their interests and personal assets.[43] Banco Estado, however, is not subject to the citizen participation requirements that would usually apply to public bodies.[44]

4.2 Board of directors

Banco Estado is governed by a board of directors, comprising seven presidential appointees and one elected staff representative. The bank's chairman and deputy chairman are chosen from among the presidential appointees.[45] Senior management is headed by an executive committee consisting of the chairman, the deputy chairman and the chief executive officer.[46] The CEO,

38 Ibid., Art. 4 and 31, establishing limits of the purchase of shares and debt operations.
39 Ibid., art. 2.
40 Ibid., art. 29.
41 Per art. 1(2) of Law 18575, the General Public Administration Act.
42 Per art. 52 of Law 18575, the General Public Administration Act and art. 37 of Law 18046, the Publicly-Traded Companies Act.
43 Article 4(7) of Law 20.880, the Public Administration Integrity and Conflict of Interest Prevention Act.
44 Per art. 75, Law 18575.
45 Art. 9, Decree-Law 2079: Charter of the Banco Estado.
46 Art. 12, Decree-Law 2079: Charter of the Banco Estado.

who also serves at presidential discretion, is in charge of the day-to-day bank business.[47] All directors and the CEO are nominated and removed at the full discretion of the governing executive. This makes the board of Banco Estado the most dependent on the presidency among all the state-owned enterprises in Chile. Other SOEs have specific procedures and grounds to remove a nominated director.[48] In the last ten years, there have been many changes in the presidency of Banco Estado, mostly because board presidents were named ministers.

4.3 *Active transparency for SOEs*

In relation to disclosure, general corporate law requires companies to provide relevant, true and timely information.[49] The Financial Market Commission determines what is to be considered relevant, essential or material information.[50] However, as a state-owned enterprise, Banco Estado also falls under the Access to Information Law that was enacted in 2008 to comply with the ruling of the Inter-American Court of Human Rights in the Claude Reyes case.[51] Notably, the right to request and obtain information is not legally excluded.[52] The bank's integrated annual report notes that its corporate sustainability policy is based on transparency and information, principles it considers basic to ensuring integrity. Thus, "[p]er the human rights instruments signed by Chile, we incorporate best practices on integrity and transparency into our culture and stakeholder relations".[53]

These practices include disclosing the salaries of board and executive committee members on the Banco Estado website, as required by Law 20.285,[54] and opening 23,015 accounts for candidates to the posts of "president, mayor, councillor, governor, deputy, senator, regional councillor and constituent to receive campaign contributions, thereby contributing to the transparency of electoral processes".[55] In addition to providing information on its website (i.e., active transparency) and because of its public role, Banco Estado must address requests from individuals for information not legally excluded on other relevant content (i.e., passive transparency).

Overall, the implementation of human rights due diligence should considerably improve the conformity of Banco Estado's transparency policy with

47 Art. 25, Decree-Law 2079: Charter of the Banco Estado.

48 For a description of the mechanisms, see Miranda, Martínez, Schönsteiner (2020).

49 Library of National Congress. Law 18.045, art. 9. The Securities Act, and Law 18.046, art. 76. The Publicly-Traded Companies Act.

50 Library of National Congress. Law 21.000, art. 5. The Financial Market Commission Act.

51 Tello, E. C., G. M. Cerna and M. A. Pavón (2009): "Acceso a la información pública: los desafíos del Consejo de la Transparencia", *Anuario De Derechos Humanos*, No. 5: pp. 193–204.

52 BCN. Law 20.285, art. 10.

53 Banco Estado. Memoria Integrada 2021, p. 48.

54 Banco Estado. Memoria Integrada 2021, p. 34.

55 Banco Estado. Memoria Integrada 2021, p. 154.

international human rights standards. “Leading by example”, as the UN Working Group states, in this context would mean that Banco Estado provides insight regarding human rights–related complaints, which can be found in the database of the judiciary[56] but are not explicitly identified in the bank's reporting. The bank does report, however, administrative sanctions in labour and environmental matters.[57] In addition, we would expect information on the measurement of sustainable finance, the prevention of green- and white-washing in these contexts and in particular, information about investments in high-risk sectors and in companies that contribute to fighting climate change but, at the same time, commit or are at risk of committing considerable human rights violations, such as the logging sector with regard to indigenous land rights and the right to water.[58] The bank should also provide information about the segment of population that does not manage to access its services and could include proposals regarding how to extend financial inclusion to those who do not qualify for even the easily accessible products of Banco Estado.

5 Human rights in Banco Estado

Banco Estado, in the past, was not subject to specific norms regarding human rights policies, due diligence or grievance mechanisms. However, article 6 of the Chilean Constitution generally provides for the third-party effect (*Drittwirkung*) of constitutional rights, and article 20 of the Constitution foresees the possibility of filing a constitutional action against private institutions and persons. As all general norms regarding labour rights, environmental protection and other human rights-related issues apply, the bank, indirectly, needs to commit to at least some human and labour rights standards to be compliant with the law. Due to the gaps between national regulation and international human rights standards, however, compliance with national law does not necessarily prevent human rights violations as defined in the international realm. Regarding the bank's investments, Chilean law only provides for human rights reporting standards regarding large enterprises that fall under General Rule 461; this means that until Banco Estado carries out a human rights due diligence also covering its investments and funds, the standard of the UN Guiding Principles and OECD Due Diligence Guidance is not met. In the following, we describe and analyse the corporate human rights policies of Banco Estado as of March 2023.

We wish to highlight that this analysis is only possible because Banco Estado replied to our written questionnaire in great detail and shared documentation with us that is relevant and pertinent to our research. Banco Estado was one

56 For a revision up until 2017, see Sánchez, op. cit.

57 Memoria 2022, Anexo, p. 17.

58 See for example, Aylwin, José et al. (2021): *Impactos de la industria forestal en los derechos humanos del pueblo mapuche en la comuna de Lumaco* (Temuco: Observatorio Ciudadano).

of the very few banks that responded to our questions regarding investment, finance and human rights. The positive evaluation of the transparency rules for state-owned enterprises under Chilean corporate, environmental and access to information laws (see earlier in this chapter) coincides with the readiness to provide this information.

Additionally, we revised the Annual Report 2022, which, for the first time, includes indicators of General Rule 461 on all ESG issues but, surprisingly, not on human rights and human rights due diligence, which are reported but only indexed regarding the GRI.[59]

5.1 Human rights policies and commitments

In 2016 Banco Estado unveiled a corporate sustainability policy setting out guidelines and stakeholder commitments intended to "integrate a sustainable vision throughout the business and explicitly state the elements of shared value that have always been present".[60] The policy applies to all Banco Estado and subsidiary staff, and all stakeholders are encouraged to become familiar with and apply its provisions.[61] The policy is based on the principles of 1) upholding human rights, 2) Compliance with the law, 3) transparency and information, 4) prevention of unlawful acts, 5) risk management, 6) due process of complaints and 7) social and environmental criteria.[62] Today, human rights is considered a sustainability principle.[63]

The policy also emphasises adherence to the international human rights instruments Chile has signed. It advances and upholds these rights as required by "the Universal Declaration of Human Rights, the United Nations Guiding Principles on Business and Human Rights, and other internationally recognised instruments adopted by Chile".[64] This commitment includes the provisions of Chilean and international law on labour rights, freedom of association, forced and child labour, equality and non-discrimination.[65] Banco Estado also adheres to the 17 sustainable development goals contained in the United Nations 2030 Agenda, noting that a number of its initiatives and programmes effectively support 6 of these goals, especially those related to narrowing the equality gap.[66]

This means that the bank does not have an explicit human rights policy but includes a human rights framework in its sustainability policy. This framework not only recognizes that the UN Guiding Principles are a relevant point of

59 Annual Report 2022, published 5 April 2023, p. 58.
60 Memoria 2021, p. 32.
61 Ibid., p. 32.
62 Ibid.
63 Annual Report 2022, p. 166.
64 Banco Estado, 'Memoria Integrada' (2021) p. 72.
65 Ibid.
66 Ibid., p. 33. Eradicating poverty, gender equality, decent work and economic growth, reducing inequality, climate action, partnerships.

reference but also mentions treaty obligations. Further research is needed to establish whether Banco Estado considers these treaty norms binding on the enterprise. Previous research by one of the authors suggests that international human rights law standards should be considered binding on SOEs.[67]

5.2 *Risk and impact assessment, due diligence and human rights*

In the Annual Report 2022, Banco Estado committed to carrying out a human rights due diligence regarding its main operations.[68] Before, Banco Estado had already committed to working with sellers and providers that respect human rights, offer decent working conditions, "prohibit child or unsafe, forced or compulsory teenage labour . . . and utilise fair and transparent practices".[69]

Banco Estado notes that it collaborates with vendors and service providers in encouraging the promotion and respect of key priority issues, such as Chile's economic, social and environmental development.[70] The bank's procurement and sustainability policies require vendors to comply with all applicable social, labour and environmental regulations.[71] Banco Estado further notes that its invitations to bid include sustainability criteria based on a social and environmental scorecard "recognising labour inclusion, gender empowerment, and environmental accountability".[72]

Similarly, large recipients of Banco Estado financing are subject to due diligence procedures introduced in 2021 that include an environmental risk assessment.[73] High- or medium-risk category A and B companies[74] are assessed by independent consultants based on an internal review and a questionnaire.[75] The 2021 Annual Report reveals that "[i]f shortcomings are identified, customers are required to endorse a supplemental compliance plan designed to mitigate risk. The plan is scrutinised on a regular basis by independent consultants and the bank's own Social and Environmental Risk Unit".[76]

While Banco Estado has not yet carried out a human rights due diligence process, there is a mechanism for including environmental issues in the usual due diligence. The bank also includes service providers (regarding labour

67 Schönsteiner, Judith (2022): "Inter-American Elements for a Systemic Approach to State-Owned Enterprises", *Human Rights Obligations, Business and Human Rights Journal*, pp. 1–21.

68 Annual Report (2022) p. 58.

69 Banco Estado, "Memoria Integrada" (2021), p. 72.

70 Banco Estado, "Memoria Integrada" (2021), p. 74.

71 Banco Estado, "Políticas de sostenibilidad, Proveedores", available at https://bancoestado.cl (accessed 25 October 2023). Link does not work.

72 Banco Estado, "Memoria Integrada" (2021), p. 74.

73 Banco Estado, "Anexo Memoria Integrada" (2021), p. 42.

74 Categories similar to Equator Principles.

75 E-mail questionnaire answered by Banco Estado (24 November 2021); Banco Estado. See as well, "Anexo Memoria Integrada" (2021), p. 42.

76 Banco Estado, "Anexo Memoria Integrada" (2021), p. 42.

issues) and clients (regarding environmental aspects) in its evaluation. Even though the bank is not explicit on whether providers are included in due diligence exercises, contractual arrangements extend human rights and labour standards to them, as the UN Guiding Principle 17 requires.

5.3 *Green and sustainable finance*

Human rights standards on investments and finance differ from standards regarding a bank's own activities analysed in the previous section. If a bank carries out adequate human rights due diligence, it will not be considered responsible for an investee company's human rights violations. In this context, we examined whether Banco Estado carries out human rights due diligence regarding its investments and whether it contains initiatives on green and sustainable finance.

Therefore, we analysed the Questionnaire on Social and Environmental Risks that Banco Estado uses for corporations and large enterprises.[77] The questionnaire does not show the ponderation of the indicators or the effects on decision-making that a certain score will have: in particular, whether negative answers will in any case lead to the exclusion as a client, or enhanced credit conditions in the logic of sustainability linked loans. According to information provided by Banco Estado responding to questions by email, a committee analyses the information provided and, in cases of serious deficiencies such as, for example, high environmental fines, decides between three options: not to finance, to finance under conditions, or present an action plan.[78]

The questionnaire clearly identifies the issues that Banco Estado considers relevant, the instruments and certifications it asks its large clients to have and the procedures it considers important to have in place. Thus, for example, the questionnaire asks about codes of conduct; grievance mechanisms; social and environmental impact assessment mechanisms; subcontractor policies; citizen participation or consultation mechanisms; non-discrimination policies and procedures; health and safety policies; energy efficiency policies; climate change policies; water protection and residues policies; natural resources and biodiversity protection programs; and whether the applicant uses land from which people are or could be evicted and, if yes, whether it has compensation mechanisms in place. The questionnaire also asks for the relationship the company has with indigenous communities and what policies it has in place regarding cultural heritage. While it is not clear to us whether this questionnaire is part of a complete due diligence process, it certainly addresses several human rights risks that client companies might face, even though there is no explicit reference in this document to human rights treaties or the UN Guiding Principles, only a reference to the Global Compact. In terms of verification of the

77 Document on file with project leader, ANID Proyecto Fondecyt No. 1201380.

78 Response to follow-up questions (30 November 2021).

information, Banco Estado does not content itself with the mere statement of human rights performance; rather, the bank requires companies to prove the responses to the questionnaire. While this does not constitute the required on-the-ground and independent verification of information, it is a considerable improvement over good-faith credulity.

In its investment decisions regarding specific projects, according to information obtained from the responses of an email questionnaire sent to Banco Estado,[79] the bank uses the Equator Principles and IFC performance standards to evaluate credit risk related to social and environmental factors. These standards refer to environmental and social issues, and the EP additionally mention human rights.[80] Reporting is only required for projects from the highest-risk categories these instruments mention. Banco Estado also assesses risk for the middle category; thus, for risk and impact categories A and B, the bank prepares a social and environmental evaluation report and may additionally request environmental due diligence by an external expert proposed by the client company and approved by the bank. The expert must prove to be free of conflicts of interest. It is possible, under the policies of the bank, to tie credit conditions to ESG action plans. Follow-ups are every four or six months.

In addition to this information obtained directly from the bank, we carried out empirical research to find out whether the bank's green funds or subsidiaries links to stock markets, securities and administration of funds or uses human rights–related indicators or at least fund descriptions. For this purpose, we first revised the information that Banco Estado and its subsidiaries[81] reported to the CMF and checked whether they mentioned human rights, sustainability, inclusion, non-discrimination or environmental issues.[82] We found that among the subsidiaries of Banco Estado, two entities related to the securities market and risk capital, respectively, did not register any hits for the period covered (2016–2021). To the contrary, both the subsidiary in charge of the stock trade and the Administradora General de Fondos (General Asset and Investment Manager Company) mention a definition of sustainability based on an environmental, social and economic pillar.[83] In addition, the self-regulation code commits to non-discrimination on grounds of "race, religion, sex, nationality or others" and prohibits any "abusive conduct", "including sexual solicitation and advances, [and] discrimination on grounds of ethnic

79 Responses obtained on (24 November 2021).

80 Equatorprinciples.org, and Wörsdörfer, Manuel (2015): "The Equator Principles and Human Rights Due Diligence – Towards a Positive and Leverage-based Concept of Corporate Social Responsibility", *Philosophy of Management*, Vol. 14, No. 3: pp. 193–218.

81 Banco del Estado de Chile; Banco Estado Corredores de Seguros; Banco Estado S.A. Administradora General de Fondos; Banco Estado Corredores de Bolsa; Fondo Mutuo Banco Estado N.N. (around 15 funds); Banco Estado Capital de Riesgo S.A.

82 Search terms used: "Derechos humanos", "derechos fundamentales"; "ambient*"; "verde"; "sustentabilidad", "sostenibilidad", "sustentable", "sostenible"; "acceso"; "vivienda", "igualdad", "no-discriminación"; "género".

83 Código de Autorregulación, last amended 18 December 2028, pp. 3–4.

origin, religion, physical [sic] disabilities, political or any other opinions, economic or social position, or grounds of any other nature."[84] Although this is clearly a very broad list, the inclusion of two lists of discriminatory grounds suggests that the second one responds to a later update, when Chilean laws on discrimination and harassment had changed. The limitation to physical disabilities, however, uses language that is not in line with international or national law. Considering the historical use of terms, physical disabilities must be read as including sensorial ones. A debate on the inclusion of persons with intellectual disabilities is pending, not only for Banco Estado but also for general legislation.[85]

Finally, Banco Estado offers one green fund that commits to investing 60% of its capital in instruments

> whose policies, prospectuses, statutes or regulations incorporate principles contributing to the preservation and protection of the environment or actively seek to improve the living conditions of individuals, communities and society at large per the 17 sustainable development goals set out by the United Nations in 2015.[86]

The green fund internal rules do not provide further guidance on indicators to be used but reiterate the commitments in its voting guidelines:

> [T]he General Asset and Investment Manager Company shall endeavour to vote in the best interest of investors, emphasising long-term value creation, the safeguard of investor rights, Board independence and efficiency, alignment of compensation schemes with investor interest, transparency, *and social and environmental accountability*.[87]

Overall, while sustainable finance in Banco Estado is mainly related to the reduction of greenhouse gas emissions rather than the prevention of human rights violations and related damage in projects or companies, the bank has instruments and procedures in place to carry out environmental due diligence and social impact assessment that include relevant human rights issues: in particular, regarding the right to water, the right to live in a clean environment and non-discrimination. A complete human rights due diligence is, however, not part of the bank's policies, either in relation to its own activities or in relation to its clients and investments. The bank does not have any specific

84 Ibid., pp. 16–17.

85 Comisión Asesora Presidencial sobre Inclusión Social de Personas en Situación de Discapacidad, Plan Nacional sobre Inclusión Social de Personas en Situación de Discapacidad. Propuesta (April 2016), available at https://comisiondiscapacidad.cl (accessed 25 October 2023), pp. 52–58.

86 Fondo Mutuo Banco Estado Mi Futuro Verde, Reglamento Interno, p. 1.

87 Ibid., p. 9. Emphasis added.

mechanism to prevent green-washing, or to prevent green finance from funding projects with considerable human rights risk or violations.

5.4 *Gender equality*

Banco Estado gathers gender equity data on both domestic and international partnerships and its own programmes, notably the empowerment initiative for women-led micro-enterprises *Crece Mujer Emprendedora*. Launched in 2015, this initiative seeks to give small businesswomen enhanced access to financial and non-financial services in an effort to help them strengthen and grow their businesses. Banco Estado notes that the programme is designed to support women's financial empowerment and businesses growth.[88] In partnership with the Women's Ministry and organisations such as *Mujeres del Pacífico*, *Comunidad Mujer*, UN Women and *Mujeres Emprendedoras*, the programme offers a wide range of financial development, training and education opportunities.[89] The bank notes that 301,799 women were registered online in 2020, and 306,450 registrants were assisted in 2021.[90]

In alliance with UN Women, Banco Estado upholds the UN Women's Empowerment Principles (WEPs) by "promoting gender equality and women's empowerment through a variety of financial and non-financial services facilitating the economic and employment engagement of women".[91] Banco Estado supports the Win-Win equality initiative through its Ethical Principles for Gender-Sensitive Innovative Finance and Investment, an initiative that commits the bank to

> gender-sensitive innovative finance and investments that seek to attract private investment, strengthen the gender-sensitive investment ecosystem, and contribute to partnerships that help achieve Sustainable Development Goal No. 5. These principles seek to give women entrepreneurs access to capital and encourage investment in businesses that advance workplace gender equality and have a positive impact on the lives of girls and women.[92]

In support of initiatives headed by the Ministry for Women and Gender Equity, the Banco Estado website also provides information for victims and witnesses of gender violence in need of assistance.[93]

Data gathering includes statistics on the number of female customers and gender diversity among employees. The diversity and inclusion policy, which

88 Banco Estado, "Memoria Integrada 2020", Santiago, p. 167.
89 Ibid., p. 140.
90 Ibid.
91 Ibid., p. 30.
92 Ibid., p. 141.
93 Ibid., p. 30.

commits the bank to equality and non-discrimination, seeks to achieve gender balance by ensuring at least 40% representation of each gender across all positions.[94] At present, women account for 43% of the overall Banco Estado workforce and 63% the *Microempresas* subsidiary. Women in management, however, account for only 26% at Banco Estado and 32% across subsidiaries.[95] This is more or less the industry's average.[96] At board level, however, the state-owned enterprises in the services sector more than triple the participation of women compared to the private sector.[97] *Banco Estado Microempresas* is accredited under Chilean Standard NCh3262, "which commits companies to work towards a cultural change intended to narrow the gender gap".[98]

5.5 *Access to remedies*

Chilean law provides for civil, criminal, constitutional and administrative remedies for victims of corporate human rights violations.[99] In addition, some companies have internal grievance mechanisms. However, in practice, access to justice is often illusionary due to high litigation costs and the lack of pro bono legal representation, resources for the gathering of evidence and expert witnesses or reports. Also, studies reveal lengthy procedures and civil courts clogged by small claims seeking to enforce payment of debts.[100]

A specific remedy in the finance sector is tied to consumer law. Law 20.555, passed in 2012, amended consumer rights legislation to give the National Consumer Protection Service (SERNAC) jurisdiction over financial issues by creating *SERNAC Financiero*. This new legal framework grants consumers of financial products and services specific rights;[101] requires institutions to improve their dealings with customers, notably by providing streamlined information; and gives SERNAC new oversight tools and powers. The law created a SERNAC seal, certifying compliant financial services and contracts, and

94 Ibid., p. 194.

95 Ibid., p. 194.

96 For comparative figures, see Ministry of Finance/Chilemujeres/ILO, "Cuarto Reporte de Indicadores de Género en las Empresas en Chile 2022" (January 2023), available at www.chilemujeres.cl/wp-content/uploads/2023/03/4o-REPORTE-INDICADORES-DE-GENERO-EN-EMPRESAS-EN-CHILE.pdf (accessed 25 October 2023).

97 Ibid.

98 Banco Estado, "Memoria Integrada" (2021), p. 194.

99 Parra, Alejandra and Judith Schönsteiner (2022): "Chile", in: Cantú, Humberto (ed.), *Experiencias latinoamericanas sobre reparación en materia de empresas y derechos humanos* (Bogotá: Konrad Adenauer Stiftung), pp. 169–207.

100 See Lillo, Ricardo (2020): "la justicia civil en crisis. Estudio empírico en la ciudad de Santiago para aportar a una reforma judicial orientada hacia el acceso a la justicia", (formal), *Revista Chilena de Derecho*, Vol. 47, No. 1: pp. 127–165.

101 Valid for all financial products and services, including consumer loans, mortgages, credit cards and credit lines provided by financial institutions, businesses, insurance companies, compensation funds, savings and loan cooperatives and other providers of loan, insurance or financial services in general.

entitled customers to have a mediator settle disputes, complaints and claims, paid for by the financial institution.[102] Banco Estado is not participating in that initiative. The law was updated in 2021, through Law 21.398, which adds oversight functions for SERNAC regarding privacy and data protection. This law is fully applicable to Banco Estado.

Banco Estado has company-based grievance mechanisms for workers, clients and the general public. The bank has a separate channel for staff and another for individuals wishing to file complaints.[103] Confidentiality can be requested for complaints. These help Banco Estado "identify, manage and investigate queries and complaints involving ethical issues and deal with breaches of the Code of Ethics".[104] Banco Estado addresses complaints depending on significance and may take administrative sanctions ranging from salary cuts to dismissal. Additional channels available on the Banco Estado website enable staff and other parties to voice their concerns, including an "Ethics Committee mailbox and reporting channel for staff and the general public".[105] For reasons of time and resources, our study could not examine the efficacy of these mechanisms empirically. This would be necessary to assess whether the mechanism responds fully to Guiding Principle 31.

5.6 *Accessibility of financial services: Inclusion policies*

Pursuant to its charter, the banking and financial services Banco Estado provides are intended to further Chile's growth and development.[106] Banco Estado cites a range of its policies, programmes, operations and products as connected to financial inclusion and the reduction of gaps and inequalities. That said, the doctrine has shown that the Banco Estado strategy of financial inclusion and counter-cyclical credit delivery during global financial crises has also contributed to economic and financial stability and mitigated the impact of economic cycles.[107] We hold that these measures effectively combat Chile's structural socio-economic discrimination, a fact that sees a disproportionate 80–90% of the population impacted by both economic crises and the unwillingness of commercial banks to provide them with financial products.[108]

The bank recognises that it plays a social role "by leading financial inclusion efforts and supporting both small businesses and implementation of public

102 Baeza Soto, Javier (2014): *Impacto de la introducción de nuevos indicadores de gestión en el cumplimiento de las metas del Banco del Estado de Chile basados en la Ley 20.555 del SERNAC Financiero. Memoria para optar a título de Ingeniero Comercial* (Chillán: Facultad de Ciencias Empresariales, Universidad del Bío-Bío), pp. 5–7.

103 Banco Estado, "Memoria Integrada" (2021), p. 52.

104 Ibid., p. 52.

105 Ibid.

106 Art. 3, Decree-Law 2079: Charter of the State Bank of Chile.

107 Ochoa Castillo, Fernando, *Ob.Cit.*, p. 4.

108 This section is based on Francisco Sánchez's master's thesis, supervised by Judith Schönsteiner under ANID Proyecto Fondecyt No. 11150853, approved in 2020.

policy".[109] As its mission statement notes, "Banco Estado exists to make Chile more inclusive and equitable, a country with opportunities for everyone".[110] The bank also underlines the value of social inclusion: "At Banco Estado there is room for everyone, regardless of background. Our services are available to all, without exclusion and with equal dignity. That is our hallmark".[111] So noted the bank's 2014–2018 Strategic Plan, with its key tenets "to be financial inclusion leaders, work closely with government, and foster new relationships with and among staff."[112] This emphasis was confirmed in the 2018–2020 Strategic Plan, which reaffirmed that the Banco Estado's main pillars were "to strengthen financial inclusion 2.0 – more services and coverage – and consolidate the bank as a financial inclusion leader".[113]

The Smaller Enterprise Empathy Programme (EMT), an initiative that seems to have been discontinued in 2015,[114] sought to "offer quality financial and non-financial services designed to further business growth and development". Its goals included "prioritising financial services that give more companies access to financing", "creating specific new products for smaller companies across all sectors" and "optimising access to financial and non-financial services for micro- and small businesswomen through the *Crece Mujer Emprendedora*" programme.[115] Banco Estado's 2016 Annual Report explains that programme goals were agreed on with the Finance Ministry, based on capitalising this segment in 2014.[116] Progress achieved by 2016 included meeting 69% of the target for customers receiving financing and 111% of the target for commercial loans, plus 236,700 micro and small business customers receiving financing and total commercial loans of MMM$2,946.[117]

The bank notes that its *Banca Personas* division works to remove barriers to access through unrestricted banking products and services.[118] Banco Estado connects this portfolio to the sustainable development goal of eradicating poverty, highlighting the bank's standing as the industry's largest institution in terms of customer base and loan and transaction volume.[119] The Report on Financial Inclusion in Chile (SBIF, August 2016) notes that 98% of all Chilean adults hold at least one financial product, with Banco Estado serving fully 87% of this population. It also highlights that 35% of bank customers are served

109 Banco Estado, "Memoria Integrada" (2021), p. 26.
110 Ibid., p. 26.
111 Ibid., p. 27. Other values include commitment, accountability, excellence and collaboration.
112 Ibid., p. 29.
113 BancoEstado, available at https://corporativo.BancoEstado.cl/acerca-de-BancoEstado/plan-estrategico/lineamientos-estrategicos (accessed 25 October 2023).
114 Beginning in 2017, the annual reports no longer refer to the EMT.
115 Banco Estado, "Memoria Integrada" (2021), p. 29.
116 Ibid.
117 Ibid., p. 30. Programme target figures are not cited.
118 Ibid., p. 37.
119 Ibid.

exclusively by Banco Estado. The customer base in 2021 comprised 81% of the Chilean population.[120]

Of all personal banking products offered by the bank, the RUT account, a basic feature account based on a person's Chilean ID number that is issued at birth or when obtaining the first (temporary) residency, may well have the strongest connection to financial inclusion. This exclusive product is an on-demand account whose only prerequisite is to be an identity card holder.[121] The bank notes that RUT accounts are opened without complications. Account holders are issued a bank card that lets them deposit, transfer or withdraw funds and doubles as a debit card.[122] The bank considers this "universal product" emblematic of financial inclusion and claims that RUT accounts are now Chile's foremost form of payment.

Although service fees apply, Banco Estado data shows a close relationship between RUT accounts and access to the system by individuals or groups who would otherwise be excluded or struggle to obtain access, noting that 51% of customers are women;[123] 32% of clients of RUT accounts, in 2016, were residents of rural or remote areas;[124] in 2021, 54.1% of clients earned under \$400,000 CLP a month or had no income;[125] 8.6% of RUT account clients are migrants:[126] 1,200,000,[127] equivalent to 69% of the entire migrant population.[128]

Banco Estado also claims to contribute to financial inclusion through business loans, with its *Banco Estado Microempresas* subsidiary providing financial advice and financing opportunities to entrepreneurs traditionally excluded from the banking system or who lack the resources to grow their businesses. According to the bank, it has 879,214 clients who are micro-entrepreneurs, active in commerce, artisanal fishing, farming, passenger and cargo transport, professional and technical services, production, crafts and tourism.[129]

Through the elimination of conditions and requirements that the banking sector otherwise imposes on clients in order to access financial products, Banco Estado is carrying out a policy of financial inclusion that no public service or government actor is in charge of. This policy extends also to one specific human right: the right to housing, as the bank is offering mortgage contracts to financially vulnerable segments of the population. In effect, Banco Estado

120 Ibid. Disaggregated data to compare with 2016 is not available for 2021 or more recent years.
121 Yet not everyone holds an identity card: in particular, children, adolescents and migrants without residency permits.
122 Banco Estado, "Memoria Integrada" (2021), p. 41.
123 Banco Estado, "Memoria Integrada" (2022), p. 8.
124 Banco Estado, "Memoria" (2016), p. 41.
125 Banco Estado, "Memoria Integrada" (2022), p. 112.
126 Ibid., p. 112.
127 Banco Estado, "Memoria Integrada" (2021), p. 8.
128 Ibid., p. 41. Data for 2021 in Memoria Integrada (2021).
129 Banco Estado, "Memoria" (2022), p. 12.

reports having more mortgage customers than any other financial institution in Chile: 182,266 with state subsidies and 415,474 without.[130]

Caja Vecina, a network of banking correspondents operating through convenience stores, brings banking closer to people, especially in remote and poor areas.[131] It has nearly 36,000 locations across all districts.[132] Each location offers withdrawals, transfers, deposits, bill payment and mobile phone top-ups through extended hours compared to banks, without the need to travel to a branch (which, in some parts of the country, can take several hours).[133] In 2016, the *Banco Estado Contacto 24 Horas S.A.* subsidiary started offering customer service in Creole and Mapudungun in order to serve Haitian immigrants and Mapuche customers in their native languages.[134] This service is essential to accessing financial services, due to the geographical characteristics of the country and language obstacles regarding Spanish. Finally, Banco Estado executes, in the name of the state and pursuant to decisions of the family courts, on-demand savings accounts for the deposit of court-ordered alimony payments.[135]

A review of the data gathered on Banco Estado operations and programmes reveals a systematic approach to equality and non-discrimination in financial access by means of mostly positive or preventive measures. We were unable to ascertain the number of people who remain excluded from the financial system or whether prioritisation is connected to higher discrimination risk criteria. Only a human rights impact assessment could provide such data and enable Banco Estado to adopt inclusionary measures for the rest of the population. Such an evaluation needs to take into account, in addition to the impact of the state-owned enterprise itself, other government action to assess whether, overall, state action fulfils the human rights obligations of the state.[136] Such a "systemic approach"[137] has not yet been used to evaluate the implementation of human rights standards regarding access to financial services by both government agencies and state-owned enterprises. It would have to address social rights in particular, such as the right to housing (incipiently analysed earlier), the right to health, the right to education and the right to social security, in which different government agencies, regulators, and state-owned and private enterprises participate. Overall, it is certainly noteworthy that a state-owned enterprise carries out a public policy of non-discrimination and implements several others.

130 Ibid., p. 102.
131 Ibid., p. 22.
132 Ibid., pp. 8 and 20.
133 Ibid., p. 51.
134 Ibid., pp. 22 and 53.
135 Ibid., p. 128. Alimony recipients must be able to live modestly in a manner befitting their social status. Children under 21 are entitled to a primary and secondary education and to training in a profession or trade. Civil Code, art. 323.
136 Schönsteiner 2022.
137 Ibid., p. 10ff.

6 Conclusions

While the state-owned Banco Estado operates under the same laws as any other commercial bank in Chile and the executive does not seem to be involved in day-to-day decision-making, the state has an important control over appointments and removal of board members and CEOs. Several provisions of administrative law regarding accountability and transparency apply beyond what is required from privately owned banks. Thus, the bank responds to a double transparency scheme, both under the Financial Market Commission for private entities and under the Transparency Council for public entities. The bank is not obliged, however, to provide for citizen participation, contrary to public bodies. This means it needs to establish specific participation mechanisms under Pillar II of the UN Guiding Principles.

While the bank has not carried out a human rights due diligence process, it committed to do so in 2023, and it has adopted human rights policies, as well as different complaint mechanisms. It also carries out environmental due diligence. The bank has an explicit gender policy and an empowerment initiative for small enterprises run by women. Since 2023, Banco Estado reports under General Rule 461 of the Financial Market Commission; it is odd, however, that precisely for the human rights–related information, the Banco Estado report does not cross-reference the relevant sections of Rule 461, while it does so for all ESG indicators.

The main positive human rights impact, however, stems from its main purpose, financial inclusion, which calls the bank to provide financial services to inhabitants of Chilean territory who would otherwise not have access to them. The RUT account is the most prominent example; it is available to anyone who has a residency card (even temporary) and does not require fixed or regular income. Another salient example is mortgages for social housing, accessible to persons who do not have sufficient security to be accepted by privately owned commercial banks. In that sense, the bank carries out a public policy of financial inclusion, as stipulated in its purpose.

The picture is incomplete for human rights criteria in Banco Estado's finance (investments and assets). It is not clear from the information available whether green finance instruments offered by the bank are human rights compatible. The bank does not claim they are. Considering that only very few Chilean enterprises have a human rights policy and hardly any have carried out a proper human rights due diligence process, Banco Estado probably should presume that investee companies are likely to have a negative human rights impact and could generate responsibility for any bank, unless the bank itself extends its environmental due diligence procedures to human rights as required in the UN Guiding Principles and the OECD Due Diligence Guidance. This conclusion suggests itself even more as non-compliance with labour and environmental regulation remains deficient in Chile, oversight is still weak in certain sectors and regarding certain rights,[138] and the regulation itself shows considerable gaps regarding international human rights law.[139] These are issues Banco Estado cannot remedy (they depend on the government and Congress), and therefore, a corporate due diligence mechanism would allow them to identify human rights risks and impacts caused by investee companies even if they are not found in breach of the law.

Most probably, according to the argument that one of us proposed regarding inter-American standards,[140] the Inter-American Commission or Court would find state responsibility if the bank did not respect human rights, due to its public function and board-appointment mechanism. Most importantly, according to the UN Guiding Principles, the Working Group's interpretation and the OECD guidances for finance institutions, the absence of a human rights due diligence process would entail responsibility for human rights violations that occur in the companies it provides loans to. Regarding environmental issues, such due diligence procedures exist, and it would depend on the specific case whether they are correctly implemented and ensure that the bank (and through it, the state) cannot become responsible for remedying through compensation, for example, violations of the right to live in a healthy environment that occur in the companies Banco Estado provides loans to.

138 See for example, Toledo, César and Javiera Aravena (2022): "Ineficacia de las normas laborales", in: Schönsteiner, Judith (ed.), *Informe Anual sobre Derechos Humanos en Chile* (Santiago: Ediciones UDP), pp. 117–210.

139 Schönsteiner, Judith et al. (2016): "Estudio de Línea Base sobre Empresas y Derechos Humanos en Chile", commissioned by Danish Institute on Human Rights, available at https://derechoshumanos.udp.cl/cms/wp-content/uploads/2020/12/SchC3B6nsteiner_Estudio20Linea20Base20Chile2027.5.2016.pdf (accessed 25 October 2023).

140 Schönsteiner, Judith (2022): "Inter-American Elements for a Systemic Approach to State-Owned Enterprises", *Human Rights Obligations, Business and Human Rights Journal*, pp. 1–21.

6 State-owned enterprises and human rights in Finland

Mikko Rajavuori and Juho Saloranta

1 Introduction

State-owned enterprises (SOEs) are distinctive to the political economy of Finland. Historically, SOEs have played a significant role in the Finnish nation-building over the 20th century, but the state retains a large company portfolio through which it influences key sectors and industries to this day. While social policy has traditionally formed an important rationale for state ownership in Finland, human rights have never been at the core of either ownership policy or company operations. For the past decade, however, human rights, often with reference to the UN Guiding Principles on Business and Human Rights (UNGPs), have been progressively included to the legal and policy context in which Finnish state ownership operates. Similarly, Finnish SOEs increasingly confront different types of human rights claims, particularly in their global operations.

This chapter discusses Finnish SOEs and state ownership from a human rights perspective. The chapter is organized as follows. Section 2 introduces the landscape of state ownership and SOEs in the Finnish political economy. Section 3 focuses on the most significant law and policy instruments that structure the operating conditions of SOEs and discusses the integration of human rights into state ownership policy. Section 4 analyzes selected SOEs' human rights governance instruments and performance. Section 5 concludes.

2 State-owned enterprises in Finland: Past and present

2.1 State ownership in Finland: A brief history

State ownership has been a distinctive feature of the Finnish political economy throughout the 20th and 21st centuries.[1] Understanding this institutional backdrop helps in situating Finnish SOEs in the domestic law and policy frameworks, which also greatly affect their links with human rights issues and performance.

1 For a concise historical treatise, see Kuisma, Markku (2016): *Valtion yhtiöt: Nousu ja tuho* (Helsinki: Siltala).

DOI: 10.4324/9781003291428-6

After declaring independence from Russia in 1917, the Finnish government quickly decided to overcome underdeveloped capital markets and jump-start domestic industries with heavy state-led investment and equity ownership. Up until the Second World War, the most significant state-led sectors were forestry and mining, but later, the state also assumed strong entrepreneurial functions in energy and chemicals industries.[2]

Organizationally, state ownership was arranged in various ways. For example, the first major SOE, forestry company Enso Gutzeit (later Stora Enso), was acquired from Norwegian private investors through a stock purchase, whereas in many other cases, state ventures were initially set up as administrative agencies with heavy oversight by the parliament. Many public functions were also organized through state enterprises ('*valtion liikelaitos*'), which are administrative organs that follow business principles but are not incorporated. Over time, however, a joint-stock company became the most important organizational form for arranging state ownership.[3] It can thus be safely said that for the majority of the 20th century, Finland was, akin to other Nordic countries, essentially pursuing a developmental model that relied heavily on state-owned and state-operated ventures.[4]

Towards the end of the 20th century, both the operating conditions for SOEs and the prior developmental paradigms changed drastically. One important change was internationalization, as several SOEs started to establish subsidiaries abroad. Further structural changes were driven by liberalization and European economic integration, which affected the rationales and the constitution of the SOE sector. While the state retained a large company portfolio, the principle of competitive neutrality between public and private undertakings quickly emerged as the touchstone for ownership policy. The process took many forms, including partial privatizations of wholly or majority-owned SOEs, transforming administrative line organizations into state enterprises and subsequently corporatizing them.[5] Usually, this meant reducing direct influence that sectoral ministries exercised over SOE operations and institutionalizing law and policy frameworks that carefully elaborated the respective powers and competences of SOE boards or management and the state shareholder. Additionally, the use of supervisory boards, usually filled with political appointees, became an exception rather than the norm.[6]

2 See Puumalainen, Asko (1976): *Valtion teollinen yritystoiminta tuotantorakenteen täydentäjänä* (Helsinki: Helsingin yliopisto).

3 See Ahonen, Pertti (1987): *Valtion liiketoiminta, hallinnon reoriat ja finanssihallinto* (Turku: Åbo Akademis förlag).

4 See, e.g., Fellman, Susanna et al. (eds) (2008): *Creating Nordic Capitalism: The Development of a Competitive Periphery* (Houndmills: Palgrave Macmillan).

5 See, e.g., OECD (2003): Regulatory Reform in Finland: Marketisation of Government Services – State-Owned Enterprises, available at www.oecd.org/finland/32684881.pdf.

6 Nevalainen, Pasi, and Ville Yliaska (2021): "From State-Owned Smokestacks to Post-Industrial Dreams: The Finnish Government in Business, 1970–2010", *Business History*, Vol. 63: p. 1327.

In sum, the joint-stock company emerged as the default organizational form of state ownership over the 20th century. The number of other organizational forms, such as administrative agencies or state enterprises, was deliberately reduced, and the remaining entities run along commercial principles. At the same time, however, the absolute number of SOEs grew due to corporatization. The central administrative functions through which the state exercised control over the economy also shrank, leading to a transformation in the logic of state-company relationships. Most importantly, the state increasingly confined itself to a shareholder role, whereby the government usually set only the overarching goals for the company organs and management to deliver as they saw fit. Put simply, Finland's developmental model, which initially centered on the *entrepreneurial state*, has evolved into that of a *shareholder state*.[7]

2.2 *Present composition and size of the SOE sector*

The state retains a significant company portfolio to this day. Based on 2020 data, the Finnish state is a shareholder in 69 companies, which are valued at approximately 47 billion euros and have over 313 000 employees.[8] The companies are divided into three distinct groups based on their ownership rationale and further into two categories based on the size of the equity stake. These ownership rationales cover the state's 1) financial interest (e.g., telecommunications manufacturer Nokia and financial firm Sampo), 2) strategic interest (e.g., national airline Finnair and energy company Fortum) and 3) special assignments (e.g., public procurement company Hansel and national lottery company Veikkaus). Most of the companies are wholly or majority owned by the state, but, in the case of publicly traded companies (a total of 16 as of 2021), the state's ownership stake is usually below a non-controlling threshold.[9] Moreover, publicly listed companies are usually owned through state holding companies, and they cannot be classified as SOEs in the traditional sense, even though, in some cases, the companies have been majority state owned and operated in the past.

The state's portfolio covers a wide range of industries. The largest individual sector is energy, which constitutes roughly two thirds of the entire portfolio. Other major sectors are industry and finance, which make up roughly 10% of the total portfolio each. Smaller yet significant sectors are information technology and communications, transport and logistics and infrastructure.[10] The

7 Rajavuori, Mikko (2018): "Governing the Good State Shareholder: The Case of the OECD Guidelines on Corporate Governance of State-Owned Enterprises", *European Business Law Review*, Vol. 29: p. 103.

8 Hallituksen vuosikertomus 2020, Liite 4 Valtion yhtiöomistus (*Valtioneuvoston julkaisuja 2021:35*).

9 Valtioneuvoston kanslia (2021): Valtion omistuksen arvo ja avainluvut, available at https://vnk.fi/omistajaohjaus/omistuksen-arvo.

10 Valtioneuvoston kanslia (2021): Yhtiöt, available at https://vnk.fi/omistajaohjaus/yhtiot.

vast majority of portfolio valuations in these sectors consist of a few publicly listed companies such as energy (Fortum), chemicals (Neste), industrial goods and services (Outokumpu, Konecranes) and telecommunications (Elisa). By contrast, the valuation of most closely held portfolio companies is low, and the portfolio companies exist principally to deliver specific functions such as ferry traffic (Suomen Lauttaliikenne). Some special assignment companies, such as grid operator Fingrid, are by necessity fairly large, as are certain financial companies, including holding company Solidium and export credit agency Finnvera.

The majority of SOEs and other state-owned companies operate domestically. This is so particularly in the case of companies operating in basic infrastructure (Gasgrid), transport (VR) and fields adjacent to providing public functions such as defense (Leijona Catering). However, many companies also maintain an active international presence, publicly traded companies especially (Metso Outotec and Stora Enso) operate globally. This also applies to several non-listed companies in which the state is either a sole or a majority shareholder (icebreaker company Arctia and industrial development lender Finnfund). The most significant internationally operating majority-owned companies are energy company Fortum, chemicals company Neste and defense manufacturer Patria, all of which are publicly listed.

In sum, state ownership remains a significant feature of the Finnish political economy. While the dominant entrepreneurial state paradigm that fueled much of Finland's economic development over the 20th century has mostly ceded, SOEs and minority state ownership of private companies are critical actors in many sectors. Even though most SOEs operate domestically, there are several major companies with global reach.

3 State ownership and human rights in Finland: Law and policy instruments

The following section introduces, first, the key regulatory and policy instruments that shape the operating conditions of SOEs. The section then situates human rights in the overarching legal structure of state ownership. Finally, the section discusses the gradual mainstreaming of human rights concerns in Finnish state ownership policy.

3.1 Law and policy of state ownership

In Finland, state ownership is governed by a complex, multi-tiered legal framework spanning from corporate to constitutional law and from EU to soft law. State ownership is also a target of active policymaking, and the threshold between law and policy is often porous.

Due to the prominence of the joint-stock company as the dominant organizational form of contemporary state ownership, SOEs are principally governed by the Limited Liability Companies Act (osakeyhtiölaki, 624/2006,

'Companies Act'), which covers both listed and non-listed companies. The Companies Act defines the purposes, function and basic organizational structure of the company. While many default rules can be modified in the company's articles of association, the Companies Act contains several binding provisions on issues such as shareholder and creditor protection. From the perspective of the state ownership, the most important provisions in the Companies Act relate to the separate legal personality of the company, its default purpose to generate profits for the shareholders and the equal treatment of shareholders. Together, these rules assign shareholders and company organs different sets of powers and competences, thus effectively isolating the shareholder from company management and limiting the ability of even majority shareholders to dictate company operations beyond the formal venues for exercising control, such as the general meeting. In addition to the Companies Act, publicly traded state-owned companies are subject to further regulation, most importantly in the Securities Markets Act (arvopaperimarkkinalaki, 746/2012). Similarly, these companies are subject to the guidelines issued by the Financial Supervisory Authority, the Helsinki Stock Exchange and, in most cases, the national corporate governance code.

Several closely held special assignment companies also perform public functions. When delivering these functions, company operations are also bound by public law, principally the Administrative Procedure Act (hallintolaki, 434/2003), the Language Act (kielilaki, 423/2003) and the Act on the Openness of Government Activities (julkisuuslaki, 621/1999). In most cases, the functions are based in specific legislation, but companies can also be conceptualized as entities of indirect public administration.[11] Regardless of the classification, public law constraints only cover the specific public function and not the operation of the company as a whole. Thus, SOEs are not subject to public law regulation simply due to their ownership structure.

The operation of state shareholding is also regulated. The Constitution of Finland (Suomen perustuslaki, 731/1999) already stipulates that 'the competence and procedure in the use of shareholder authority in companies effectively controlled by the State are laid down by an Act', as are the 'provisions on the necessity for the consent of the Parliament for the acquisition or relinquishment of effective control by the State in a company'. The principal instrument that governs state ownership policy and steering is the State Shareholdings and Ownership Steering Act (Laki valtion yhtiöomistuksesta ja omistajaohjauksesta, 1368/2007, 'State Ownership Act'), and it applies to the decision-making involving state shareholdings in both state majority- and minority-owned companies. The State Ownership Act defines the powers of the government and the parliament when acquiring or relinquishing control in state-owned companies, and it further specifies the division of powers between the ministries responsible for exercising the state's ownership interest.

11 Mäenpää, Olli (2017): *Yleinen hallinto-oikeus* (Helsinki: Alma Talent), pp. 221–224.

According to the government bill, the state also adheres to international best practices in its operation as a shareholder.[12] The most prominent of the best practice codes are the OECD Guidelines on Corporate Governance of State-owned Enterprises,[13] but the government department responsible for state ownership steering also claims to follow general corporate governance codes, principally the G20/OECD Principles of Corporate Governance.[14]

While the conditions for exercising state ownership are exhaustively regulated, existing regulation tends to focus on the structural and institutional arrangements. Thus, the State Ownership Act principally identifies the actors involved in governing the use of state assets. In this scheme, the parliament is responsible for setting concrete ownership thresholds, whereas the government, either through the prime minister's office or different ministries, has the ability to exercise the state's shareholder rights within the limits set by the Companies Act and other relevant sectoral regulation. This regulatory framework is, however, limited to the broad institutional setting of state ownership, the formal exercise of shareholder power and reporting duties.[15] Thus, the relevant legislation does not constrain the substantive elements of ownership policy beyond requiring the state's assets 'to be used productively' in the State Budget Act (laki valtion talousarviosta, 423/1988).

The lack of substantive regulation on exercising state ownership is partly compensated for by state ownership policy. For the past decades, the Finnish government has periodically issued a document known as the Resolution on the State Ownership Policy (Valtion omistajapolitiikkaa koskeva periaatepäätös, 'Resolution'), the latest of which was published in 2020. This political document lays out the rationales, key principles and practical arrangements, such as the guidelines for director renumeration, of state ownership policy for the subsequent four-year period. The document is not binding as such but is used to outline the vision of the government for SOEs and state ownership and is thus viewed as an important signal for the public, portfolio companies and the market in general when it comes to the future behavior of the state shareholder. The document also forms a template for the ministries responsible for exercising the state's ownership interests in their portfolio companies to align, communicate and measure the performance of SOEs.

Despite the settled the framework governing its institutions and practices, the legal aspects of state shareholding have been under active debate over the past decade. In particular, there have been two major cases in which the

12 HE 233/2016 vp, s. 3.

13 OECD (2015): Guidelines on Corporate Governance of State-Owned Enterprises, available at www.oecd.org/daf/ca/OECD-Guidelines-Corporate-Governance-SOEs-2015.pdf.

14 Valtioneuvoston kanslia (2021): Omistajapolitiikka ja -ohjaus, available at https://vnk.fi/omistajaohjaus/omistajapolitiikka.

15 See Kankaanpää, Jari, Lasse Oulasvirta and Jani Wacker (2014): "Steering and Monitoring Model of State-Owned Enterprises", *International Journal of Public Administration*, Vol. 37: p. 409.

state has been accused of jeopardizing the pre-arranged competence structure between the shareholder and the company to further objectives the companies themselves have resisted. The wide margin of appreciation assigned to those exercising the state's ownership interests has thus been tested – and ultimately upheld – in judicial review.

The most detailed examination of the 'undue interference' has been conducted by the Chancellor of Justice. In the *Arctia Shipping* case, the ministry officials responsible for exercising ownership compelled the wholly state-owned icebreaker company to withdraw the complaint on a reported crime regarding a Greenpeace demonstration on its vessel.[16] The chancellor concluded the ministry's actions to be, from the perspective of public law and especially the legal framework sustaining state ownership, lawful, especially when considering the importance of ensuring constructive stakeholder communication with environmental groups. The corporate social responsibility (CSR) dimensions of the then-current ownership policy resolution were extensively used in the analysis. The *Finavia* case involved a broadly similar setting, wherein the shareholder ministry covertly negotiated a settlement agreement with an accountant firm with whom the company had an ongoing legal dispute.[17] In the decision, the vice chancellor considered the ministry to have unduly interfered with the operative management of the company, but due to wide substantive competence allotted to the state shareholder in the State Ownership Act, no public law violation was identified. Even though the state officials were exonerated, both cases suggest that the state shareholder has clear tendencies to step beyond its official competences regarding certain sensitive company operations.

As a whole, the law and policy instruments that structure the operation of SOEs and the exercise of the state's ownership interests put forward a framework in which the regulatory and ownership functions of the state are separated and the state shareholder insulated from operational management of SOEs. While the state shareholder commands great – and often decisive – influence over portfolio companies, this influence is channeled through multiple mediating devices and thresholds that include the institutional set-up of the state ownership between the parliament and the government and the varying competences of the shareholder and the firm. From the perspective of Finnish law, SOEs are thus seen as ordinary companies operating under the same regulatory conditions as other private operators.

3.2 *Human rights in the legal framework of state ownership*

The regulatory framework in which Finnish SOEs operate has not been designed with the protection of human rights in mind. Instead, its rationale

16 Valtioneuvoston oikeuskanslerin päätös OKV/1601/1/2013 (11.2.2014).
17 Valtioneuvoston apulaisoikeuskanslerin päätös OKV/934/1/2016 (10.05.2017).

has been to improve the utilization of the state's equity ownership by controlling the influence the state can exert over the company. Regardless, this legal conceptualization also defines the roles and responsibilities of Finnish SOEs in relation to human rights, including the possibility of finding SOEs or the state accountable for potential human rights violations.

As is the norm around the world, the Constitution of Finland places the obligation to 'guarantee the observance of basic rights and liberties and human rights' firmly on the public authorities. Additionally, the Constitution requires that the law, including the Constitution's Bill of Rights, shall 'be strictly observed' in 'all public activity'. While there is an active doctrinal debate on the horizontal application of basic and fundamental rights, as well as on what constitutes 'public activity', in the SOE context, the starting point of the analysis is that Finnish SOEs are strictly private law entities. There are a few exceptions to this rule in the case of companies performing limited public functions or forming entities of indirect public administration, such as Finnvera processing export credit applications, but in general, SOEs do not fall under comprehensive public law obligations. This includes the domestic basic rights provisions, which are structurally and operationally aligned with, and inspired by, the European Convention of Human Rights (ECHR). Put simply, Finnish legislation does not contain any independent human rights obligation, whether established in legislation or construed though horizontal application fundamental rights, that SOEs would have to fulfill due to their ownership structure. Naturally, some state-owned companies, such as large publicly listed companies, fall under the domestic Accounting Act (kirjanpitolaki, 1336/1998) and the EU Non-Financial Reporting Directive, which currently require the reporting of the company's human rights due diligence practices, but these instruments do not distinguish between SOEs and private companies.

Similarly, there is no distinct obligation in place for the state to operate as a shareholder bound by human rights. Despite the Constitutional provisions requiring public authorities to guarantee basic and human rights, the scope and content of this obligation has not been interpreted to establish independent obligation to operationalize human rights in the state's ownership function (as discussed in the section 3.3; however, human rights mainstreaming has recently occurred on the policy level). The practical operationalization of such an obligation would likely be hard and depend heavily on the scope and intensity of state ownership, given that the state's equity stakes range from minority (most publicly listed companies) to sole ownership (most companies performing special assignments).

In addition to the domestic legal framework, the international and European human rights treaty can also be seen to affect the human rights conceptualization of SOEs and the state shareholder. The requirements of the international human rights treaties and relevant case law are always consulted during law making and judicial review. Due to a dearth of substantive SOE obligations in international human rights treaties, however, their practical significance for the state shareholder is limited.[18] That said, international human rights case law provides external standards against which the domestic legal framework and SOE operations can be judged. Quite likely, the first international SOE-related human rights case involved Yleisradio, the Finnish public broadcasting company, in 1979. In that case, the UN Human Rights Committee approached the claimed violation of freedom of expression from the perspective of negative obligations, claiming the starting premise to be that 'the State party is responsible for actions of the Finnish Broadcasting Company (FBC), in which the State holds a dominant stake (90 per cent) and which is placed under specific government control'.[19] Accordingly, the committee considered both the ownership stake and the specific government control through legislation to allow attribution of company operations to the state. More recently, the relevant international standards for appraising the relationship between the state owner and SOEs in a human rights context have been developed in the case law of European Court of Human Rights (ECtHR).[20] Due to the institutional set-up of the Finnish state ownership legislation and practice, which generally protects the independence of the company management, attributing ECHR violations stemming from company conduct to the state is unlikely to succeed.[21] However, the cases examined by the Finnish chancellor of justice indicate that the state owner-SOE relationship may, at least in theory, contain operational interference that could influence the analysis in international or regional human rights treaty bodies.

3.3 *Human rights in state ownership policy*

Historically, human rights have been absent from state ownership policy. To be sure, social policy was a key driver of state ownership rationales, particularly in the early 20th century. As an example, one rationale for acquiring Enso Gutzeit, initially a Norwegian-owned forestry company (now Stora Enso), was land reform and balancing out the rights and duties of small farmers against large companies that held large quantities of arable land and forest. This policy, however, was not motivated by any notion of basic rights, which, as a legal system, were also

18 See Rajavuori, Mikko (2015): "How Should States Own? Heinisch v. Germany and the Emergence of Human Rights-Sensitive State Ownership Function", *European Journal of International Law*, Vol. 26: p. 727.

19 Leo Hertzberg et al. v. Finland, Communication No. 61/1979, UN Doc. CCPR/C/OP/1 (1985), at 9.1.

20 In the UN context, the only recent reference to Finnish SOEs was in the concluding observations of the CEDAW committee in 2008, where Finland was encouraged to increase the number of women in the 'board directors in State-owned or partly State-owned companies'; see CEDAW/C/FIN/CO/6 (CEDAW 2008). There have been many further opportunities for the UN treaty bodies to discuss Finnish SOEs' human rights impacts; see, e.g., Concluding observations on the seventh periodic report of Finland [E/C.12/FIN/CO/7] 2021.

21 See e.g. Schönsteiner, Judith (2019): "Attribution of State Responsibility for Actions or Omissions of State-Owned Enterprises in Human Rights Matters", *University of Pennsylvania Journal of International Law*, Vol. 40: p. 895.

underdeveloped in Finland until the mid-1990s. Similarly, labor policy, including labor rights, formed a key dimension of state ownership policy over the 20th century but, again, this was framed mostly as a question of collective bargaining. Towards the end of the 20th century, however, rights-sensitive issues such as gender equality regarding SOE hiring and board membership were increasingly included in the policy discussions. The first clear reference to human rights in ownership policy took place in 2011, when they were mentioned in a reporting template to be used by state-owned companies and the shareholder.[22]

The most important contemporary instruments linking state ownership and human rights are the Resolutions on the State Ownership Policy. These documents outline the key objectives, arrangements, expectations and performance metrics that the state shareholder pursues and uses in relation to its portfolio companies. The resolutions also signal to the market how the state is going to own companies in the coming years. Environmental, social and governance (ESG) matters, which are nowadays considered to include human rights performance, have been progressively integrated in the state ownership policy over the 2010s and early 2020s. Table 6.1 reviews the references to ESG issues in the resolutions issued over a period from 1999–2020. As the table conveys, ESG factors have become more prominent over each ownership policy iteration. Whereas environmental performance and good personnel policy where the only issues mentioned in the 1999 resolution, the most recent 2020 resolution includes diverse and clearly defined ESG targets, such as ambitions climate change mitigation goals and the expectation to conduct human rights due diligence across the company's value chain.

As a whole, the growing interest in ESG in the resolutions mirrors the progression and mainstreaming of corporate environmental and social responsibility in Finland over the past decades.[23] Accordingly, environmental concerns were the first to appear on the state owner's agenda, albeit in a diffuse way and without clear environmental performance metrics. Normatively, these objectives were tied to meeting the requirements set in legislation, international treaties and the legitimate expectations of various stakeholders. The same applied to the treatment of SOE personnel, but until the 2011 Resolution, no attention was paid to further stakeholder groups. One of the distinctive policy entry points has been SOEs' tax responsibility, which can be seen to bridge ESG discussion with the broader notions on the financial role of SOEs. Similarly, there is a clear move from framing ESG issues as function of the companies' competitive advantage to viewing environmental and social responsibility as self-standing objectives. The state has been proactive in assigning CSR and

22 Valtion omistajapolitiikkaa koskeva valtionneuvoston periaatepäätös, Liite 3 (2011), available at http://valtionomistus.fi/suomi/files/2012/01/VNn_periaatepaeaetoes_03112011.pdf.

23 See e.g. Mikkilä, Mirja, Virgilio Panapanaan and Lassi Linnanen (2015): "Corporate Social Responsibility in Finland: From Local Movements to Global Responsibility", in: Idowu, Samuel, René Schmidpeter and Matthias Fifka (eds), *Corporate Social Responsibility in Europe* (Cham: Springer).

Table 6.1 Evolution of state ownership policy

	Environment	*Social*	*Governance*	*Other*
1999	Isolated references to environmental issues and sustainable development	References to employment policy and collective bargaining (in the domestic context)	Good governance with a view of more competitiveness	SOEs have to be profitable over the long term
2004	Company operations need to be environmentally responsible, based on the requirements set in legislation and international treaties as well as stakeholders' legitimate expectations	Employees' position has to be considered	-	The state as an owner is ready to facilitate arrangements that aim at harmonizing economic and environmental factors in a way that increases the company's competitiveness
2007	Environmental responsibility is of particular importance Responsible operations are based on legislation, international treaties and respecting stakeholders' legitimate expectations	Respecting employees' rights is of particular importance	The basis for long-term shareholder value development is open and consistent ownership policy, appointing responsible and professional board members and considering other stakeholders' views	The state owner's most important tools are implementing independent ownership strategy and developing corporate governance
2011	Companies' environmental policies are expected to aim at exemplary and responsible behavior, based on requirements set in legislation and international treaties	State expects companies to pay attention to the transparency of their supply chains As a part of good employment policy, the state appreciates processes that can be used to eliminate and mitigate discrimination against minority groups	Companies wholly or majority owned by the state are required to report on responsibility issues with precise and comparable metrics	Even though SOEs operate along business principles and in a competitive setting, they are required to consider the legitimate expectations on responsibility and sustainability due to the state ownership interest

(Continued)

Table 6.1 (Continued)

	Environment	*Social*	*Governance*	*Other*
2016	Companies need to consider the environmental and social implications of their operations in addition to economic implications	Companies need to consider human rights, as set in UNGPs, in their operations and supply chains Stakeholders need to have a reliable way to inform company management of potential human rights violations	The state owner considers it a positive when companies utilize internationally recognized corporate social responsibility principles and guidelines, such as OECD MNE guidelines, UN Global Compact, ISO 26000 standard and UNGPs Companies need to understand the material CSR risks in their own operations and in their supply chains and integrate them into their risk management practices	Companies need to report on their tax footprint Aggressive tax planning is not allowed
2020	Companies need to recognize the impacts of their operations on climate, environment and biodiversity and set ambitious targets when compared to their peers State-owned companies are expected to take into account Finland's policy goals on carbon neutrality by 2035 and the aims of the Paris agreement to limit global warming to 1.5 degrees	Companies need to transparently take into account human rights and UNGPs in their own operations and supply chains and operationalize their due diligence duty Companies need to establish whistleblowing mechanisms for stakeholders to inform management of human and worker rights violations	Companies need to operate responsibly and report on their operations' impact on climate and other corporate responsibility issues To guarantee sustainability, long-term value creation and competitiveness, companies need to consider the impacts of climate change on their business operations Companies need to follow internationally recognized corporate social responsibility principles and guidelines such as OECD MNE Guidelines, Science Based Targets Initiative, Task Force on Climate-Related Financial Disclosures and ISO 26000	The state owner requires companies to report on their tax footprint Aggressive tax planning is not allowed

sustainability risks as material and subject to regular appraisal and reporting, particularly since 2016. Overall, however, explicit CSR terminology and different CSR instruments were included in the ownership policy fairly late. The first iteration of ownership policy that fully integrated CSR considerations was the 2016 Resolution, which stated the expectation to the portfolio companies to utilize internationally recognized corporate social responsibility guidelines and principles such as the OECD Guidelines for multinational enterprises, the UN Global Compact, the ISO 26000 Standard and the UNGPs. The 2020 Resolution increased the ambition of social performance and, further, imposed a requirement on portfolio companies to regularly report on CSR in the general meetings.

Over the past decade, the resolutions have also gradually mainstreamed human rights. In the 2011 Resolution, emphasis was put on the transparency of SOEs' supply chains. While this iteration of ownership policy refrained from using explicit human rights language (outside the annexed reporting template), starting with the 2016 Resolution, CSR policies and human were linked by embedding company operations in the framework of the UNGPs. Thus, portfolio companies were expected to integrate the duty to respect human rights into their operations and across their supply chains. Additionally, companies were expected to set up reliable mechanisms through which stakeholders could communicate potential human rights abuses to the company leadership. In terms of organizational boundaries, the ownership policies have covered both the company and its supply chain from 2011 onwards. Substantively, there is little guidance on what companies' human rights policies and institutions ought to do or look like. Ascertaining the availability of whistleblowing mechanisms is one of the few concrete human rights–related requirements, but other substantive issues seem to be outsourced to the UNGPs. The 2020 Resolution increased the expected human rights ambition, requiring portfolio companies to take human rights into account when fulfilling their due diligence obligation. Even though human rights were thus clearly integrated into the state ownership policy, the social dimensions of corporate responsibility were still communicated less ambitiously than environmental performance requirements. Most importantly, the 2020 Resolution necessitated portfolio companies to set emission reduction targets that were ambitious compared to those of their peers. No such comparative appraisal was required for companies' human rights impacts and performance.

From this, it is clear that human rights, and particularly the UNGPs framework, were been integrated into the Finnish SOE operations at least on the policy level over the course of the 2010s. Human rights due diligence and reporting have emerged as important dimensions of the broader CSR and sustainability discussion and policy, thus greatly adding to the diversity of ESG-related ownership policy, which was originally firmly rooted in environmental performance. Even though the materiality of human rights impacts, especially in the context of transnational supply chains, are increasingly highlighted in ownership policy, environmental issues, primally emission reduction targets and carbon risks, continue to surpass the emphasis on dedicated human rights policies, which may be well founded due to the prevalence of energy in the state's portfolio.

SOEs were also briefly mentioned in the national action plan (NAP) for the implementation of the UNGPs. In the NAP, the Finnish Ministry of Economic Affairs and Employment asserted that 'the state uses a separate accountability mechanism for dealing with human rights violations committed by State-owned companies'.[24] No public information on this mechanism is available, and it most likely relates to the shareholder communication between the state and the portfolio companies.

4 Human rights governance by state-owned enterprises

Currently, Finland has 69 SOEs or other companies in which the state has equity participation. This section reviews the human rights governance practices in a sample of six companies.

4.1 Remarks on method

In this section, we review the human rights governance instruments of practice in six state-owned companies: Stora Enso, Finnair, Fortum, Neste, Finnvera and Solidium. The companies have been selected due to 1) their global presence, either through sales, operations or finance; 2) their varied roles in the Finnish state ownership policy; and 3) their prominence in the Finnish policy debates on human rights. In the analysis, we rely largely on the companies' own materials, such as recent sustainability reports and human rights guidelines. In practice, we review the company disclosures against five variables that include factors such as the existence of a human rights and due diligence policy, the scope of risk assessment and access to remedy. In addition, we identify key human rights policy debates on each company, which we use to exemplify their most likely human rights impacts.

The results of the comparative analysis are presented in Table 6.2. As a whole, the evolution of the business and human rights agenda is clearly visible in practices of Finnish SOEs. There are, however, marked differences between publicly listed companies that operate in global markets and the closely held special assignment companies. We discuss a few key patterns that emerge from company data later in the chapter.

As a preliminary note, the human rights governance practices and performance of Finnish companies have not been systematically analyzed, with the exception of a recent government-funded research project.[25] This study

24 National Action Plan for the Implementation of the UN Guiding Principles on Business and Human Rights (2014), available at www.tem.fi/files/41214/TEMjul_46_2014_web_EN_21102014.pdf.

25 Tran-Nguyen, Elina et al. (2021): "Status of Human Rights Performance of Finnish Companies", *Publications of the Ministry of Economic Affairs and Employment*, p. 17, available at

Table 6.2 Human rights governance by select Finnish SOEs

Company	*Stora Enso*	*Finnair*	*Fortum*	*Neste*	*Finnvera*	*Solidium*
Industry	Pulp and paper	Airline	Energy	Chemicals	Export credit	Finance
Stake	10.7% (via Solidium)	55.9%	50.76%	35.9%	100%	100%
Ownership rationale	Finance interest	Strategic interest	Strategic interest	Strategic interest	Special purpose	Special purpose
Human rights policy	Independent human rights policy, integrated with supplier code of conduct 'Stora Enso respects all human rights established in the International Bill of Human Rights, and we are committed to implementing the UNGPs.'	Human rights management integrated in the code of conduct and the supplier code of conduct 'Finnair respects the UN Universal Declaration on Human Rights and the core conventions of the ILO. Finnair has signed the UN GC.'	Fortum respects the International Bill of Human Rights and recognizes in its operations the UNGPs, the OECD Guidelines, the UN GC, the ICC Anti-bribery and anti-corruption guidelines and the Bettercoal initiative's code on responsible coal mining	Human rights principles cover fair employment, health & safety, equality, rights of children & young workers, forced labour, fair treatment and social & economic development Business partners expected to respect and remediate human rights	Committed to the UNGPs and export credit guarantee and export credit operations by the World Bank Group's Environmental, Health, and Safety Guidelines (EHS Guidelines), the IFC Environmental and Social Performance Standards, and the OECD Recommendation on Common Approaches and the OECD Recommendation on Bribery and Officially Supported Export Credits	None

(*Continued*)

Table 6.2 (Continued)

Company	*Stora Enso*	*Finnair*	*Fortum*	*Neste*	*Finnvera*	*Solidium*
Due diligence policy	Human rights due diligence, which covers environmental and social impact assessments, community consultations, appropriate grievance and remediation mechanisms and accountability through transparent reporting Supplier code of conduct extends human rights due diligence to suppliers	Finnair aims to prevent any violations of human rights and the use of forced or child labour, both within its own operations and its supply chain and continuously develops practices ensuring that negative sustainability impacts can be mitigated	The UNGP is being followed in Fortum's own operations and in supply chain management Fortum's subsidiary Uniper performs a worldwide assessment, whose findings result in the implementation of modified due diligence requirements and mitigation measures	Regular supplier sustainability policy development and due diligence Neste's primary means of actions are based on engagement and cooperation with suppliers to remediate	Risk-based impact assessment seeking to identify for the environment, people and communities Enhanced due diligence in case of vulnerable groups or environmentally sensitive areas	None
Risk assessment	Integrated and detailed risk management procedures that also factor in human rights Highest priority human rights relevant to the forest products sector identified and subjected to due diligence	Emphasis on preventing modern slavery and trafficking SEDEX system to improve risk management, the evaluation of social impacts and traceability in the supply chain	Fortum's supplier qualification process and supplier audits cover the most important human rights aspects related to purchases Human rights impacts of the coal supply chain are addressed in the Bettercoal assessments	Neste has undertaken several initiatives to identify and understand how risks may be present in operations and supply chains Systematic controls for counterparty screening and monitoring of all potential business partners and suppliers	Environmental and social impact risk analysis as part of financing-related decision-making	Supply chain risks and corruption identified as key risks

(*Continued*)

Table 6.2 (Continued)

Company	*Stora Enso*	*Finnair*	*Fortum*	*Neste*	*Finnvera*	*Solidium*
	Priority areas: health and safety, fair employment conditions, forced labour, freedom of association, non-discrimination and non-harassment, land and natural resource rights acquisition and management, grievance mechanisms, children's rights (relevant to the forest sector)					
Access to remedy	Grievance mechanisms a priority area, including formal grievance mechanism open to all stakeholders; some grievance channels available in local languages	Internal whistleblower mechanism Finnair has a process and guidelines for continuous improvement in supply chain responsibility and for handling non-compliances	Internal and external reporting channels that cover suspected misconduct relating to the environment, labour practices or human rights violations	Externally operated misconduct reporting system available to all Neste's internal and external stakeholders Neste's investigation group is responsible for evaluating, investigating and following up reported cases	External consultant visits and reporting to Finnvera during the entire repayment period Corrective actions in case of noncompliance with environmental and social terms and conditions of the loan agreement	None

(*Continued*)

Table 6.2 (Continued)

Company	*Stora Enso*	*Finnair*	*Fortum*	*Neste*	*Finnvera*	*Solidium*
	In 2020, a total of 86 reports received through Stora Enso's various grievance channels were identified as potential non-compliance cases		In 2020, four on-site supplier audits were conducted The majority of the non-compliances identified in the audits were related to overtime, pay and occupational safety			
Key public debates	Exporting chemical pulp to Xinjiang Uygur autonomous region, linked to forced labour, production since stopped (2021) Suppliers using child labor in Pakistan led to organizational restructuring (2014) Land leasing practices in China, a complaint made to the UN Human Rights Council (2013)	Finnair's climate targets do not meet the requirements of climate science (2020) Finnair prohibits employees from supporting Hong Kong protests (2019)	Fortum's subsidiary Uniper seeks an aggressive ITA ruling to receive compensation for the closure of a coal-fired power plant in the Netherlands (2021)	Deforestation and human rights violations in the palm oil supply chain (2020)	Specific instance against Finnvera for its complicity in anticipated breach of the OECD Guidelines regarding the Botnia SA pulp mill project in Fray Bentos, Uruguay (2006)	Portfolio company Outokumpu linked to human rights violations and pollution in Brazil (2021) Human rights performance of portfolio companies considered meagre (2016)

analyzed approximately 80 public and private companies using Corporate Human Rights Benchmark (CHRB) methodologies. The results suggest that Finnish companies have committed themselves, on a general level, to respecting human rights, but the 'systematic integration of human rights responsibility and its monitoring as part of their core activities is still largely at an early stage'.[26] Approximately 10% of the investigated companies had no human rights policy commitments in place. Credible access and commitment to remedy were poor across the board, with some commitment to remedy found in only one in ten companies. Finally, Finnish companies were found to publish relatively little information related to their human rights governance or performance. As a whole, however, the human rights performance of Finnish companies was viewed approximately on the same level as the results of CHRB's global assessments. Due to the prominence of SOEs in the Finnish corporate sector, the effects of state ownership on human rights performance were also analyzed in some detail.[27] The results, first, suggest that state-owned companies as a group score lower than the sample as a whole. The majority state-owned companies fare better but still score only slightly above the average in the sample. Thus, the report concludes that SOEs are clearly not forerunners in implementing corporate human rights policies.[28]

4.2 *Human rights policy*

Five out of six investigated companies publicly commit to independent human rights policies. Two companies (Stora Enso, Finnair) explicitly state that their aim is to either prevent or remedy any violations of human rights and the use of forced or child labour, whereas Fortum and Finnvera opt for less committed language, such as following or respecting human rights. The primary reference frames for these commitments are most commonly the UNGPs, the Universal Declaration of Human Rights, select human rights conventions and the OECD Guidelines for Multinational Enterprises. Incidentally, the only company with no human rights policy is Solidium, the state holding company that exercises the state's equity interest in several public companies. Three companies explicitly extend their human rights policy to cover both company operations and those of third parties in their supply chains.

4.3 *Due diligence policy*

Four publicly listed companies claim to have human rights due diligence mechanisms in place. The policy of Stora Enso is explicitly aligned with the UNGPs,

https://julkaisut.valtioneuvosto.fi/bitstream/handle/10024/162936/TEM_2021_17.pdf?sequence=1&isAllowed=y.

26 Ibid., 75.

27 None of the companies analyzed in this section feature in the CHRB.

28 Elina Tran-Nguyen et al., pp. 73–74.

but the other three describe very similar procedures through which they assess and mitigate adverse human rights impacts. (Neste refers to their process as 'sustainability due diligence'.) The two closely held financial companies, Finnvera and Solidium, do not appear to have a self-standing due diligence policy. The former, however, does refer to the UNGPs and the OECDs on Common Approaches for Officially Supported Export Credits and Environmental and Social Due Diligence, whereas the latter merely mentions structural risk embedded in portfolio companies' foreign operations.

4.4 *Risk assessment and procedures*

Two of the publicly traded companies (Stora Enso, Finnair) spell out in detail their concrete risk assessment tools and metrics. Similarly, Neste describes its internally developed risk management tools in some detail and also highlights its partnership with BSR, a large sustainability consultancy. Closely held export credit agency Finnvera indicates that it has in place environmental and social risk assessment procedures, but these are not described in detail besides listing the number of investigated cases. State holding company Solidium has no publicly disclosed mechanisms in place. Thematically, anti-corruption is more prevalent than any other human rights-related issue.

Most companies integrate transparency (either financial, operational or supply chain transparency) into their sustainability policies. The most developed policies are used by Stora Enso, Fortum and Neste, who source globally, often hazardous materials (e.g. Neste's vegetable oils, waste and residue fats and crude oils). Finnvera and Solidium confine their transparency policies to open stakeholder communication reporting.

4.5 *Access to remedy*

Five of the six companies (excluding Solidium) operate a whistleblowing or a grievance reporting mechanism. Stora Enso and Neste appear to have the most developed mechanisms in place, with Stora Enso claiming that 'access to grievance mechanisms is one of . . . highest priority'. In most cases, whistleblowing or grievance mechanisms are outsourced to independent operators. Stora Enso and Fortum appear to have these mechanisms available also in local languages. Fortum and Neste also use external reporting mechanisms.

The most detailed assessment and follow-up procedures are used by Stora Enso and Neste, likely due to their presence in challenging regions such as Latin America and Central Asia. These include detailed environmental and social impact assessments, inclusion of supplier codes of conduct in supply contracts and regular stakeholder communication. Fortum claims to audit suppliers and require a plan for corrective actions Finnair outlines less ambitious human rights policies. Finnvera and Solidium do not appear to have credible human rights follow-up procedures in place.

No company voluntarily assumes any potential of liability for human rights violations.

4.6 Policy debates

Each company in our selection has faced human rights claims over the past decades. The human rights or wider sustainability issues have emerged either in the companies' global supply chains (Stora Enso, Neste) or in the operations of subsidiaries and portfolio companies (Fortum, Solidium). The most important exceptions to this are the treatment of in-flight personnel by Finnair in the case of Hong Kong democracy protests and the chemical pulp exports to Xinjiang region in China by Stora Enso.

There is limited information available on these and other SOEs' human rights issues impacts. Much of public information is based on NGO reporting, with Finnwatch being the most prominent actor both in and outside Finland.[29] In many cases, the companies have responded swiftly, with many of them building up dedicated human rights capacities after alleged violations.

The response of Stora Enso to a series of alleged human rights violations around 2013–2014 is a case in point. Pre-2013, Stora Enso was accused of corruption, unsustainable use of land and illegal land sales in Brazil,[30] as well as land disputes and environmental problems in China. The Finnwatch report on Stora Enso's operations in India regarding a factory (Stora Enso Inpac) suggested that the company, given its substantial state ownership, had not paid enough attention to introducing best practice compliance standards that were at least equivalent to those of key competitors. This stood in stark contrast with Stora Enso's own statements, which emphasized compliance with the key quality and environmental certificates, such as ISO 9001 and ISO 14001. Similarly, Stora Enso had indicated that it conducted human rights due diligence as a part of its human rights policy and also regarding its suppliers. Based on worker interviews, Finnwatch and Swedwatch claimed to have found out that the factory had inadequate work safety conditions (against the ILO standards), fixed-term contracts that breached Stora Enso's instructions: supplier's workers had minimal salaries and excessive working hours, and there were several gender inequality issues. After the Finnwatch report, Stora Enso improved the conditions regarding work safety, workers' social issues and women's rights and created a process for compensation. The factory was shut down due to decreased demand after a few years, and Stora Enso decided to provide its workers with monetary compensation and re-education.[31]

29 For reporting, see available at https://finnwatch.org/en/publications.

30 Finnwatch (2013): Stora Enso ja ihmisoikeudet. Työelämän oikeuksien toteutuminen Stora Enso Inpac Intiassa, available at https://finnwatch.org/images/stora_enso_intiassa_web.pdf.

31 Finnwatch (2016): Stora Enso tarjosi korvauksia ja koulutusta Intiassa irtisanotuille työntekijöille, available at https://finnwatch.org/fi/uutiset/363-stora-enso-tarjosi-korvauksia-ja-koulutusta-intiassa-irtisanotuille-tyoentekijoeille.

Besides NGO and company reporting, there is no extensive coverage of the alleged violations, which prevents further analysis. To our knowledge, Finnish SOEs' human rights impacts have not appeared before domestic or international courts, including the National Contact Points under the OECD Guidelines for multinational enterprises.

5 Conclusion

In this chapter, we have analyzed the legal framework that governs the operating conditions of the state shareholder and SOEs with reference to human rights practices. We have three key observations.

First, despite (or perhaps because of) the continuing relevance of state ownership in the Finnish political economy, the human rights performance of SOEs is not registered in the substantive domestic regulation. Instead, human rights issues are essentially delegated to individual shareholder relationships between the state owner and the investee company.

Second, the principal political instrument that defines the state's ownership interests and rationales, the Resolutions on the State Ownership Policy, has progressively integrated human rights concerns, mostly with reference to the UNGPs, as a part of the larger ESG mainstreaming. In the most recent policy iteration, however, climate change mitigation seems to have surpassed human rights risk analysis as the core policy rationale.

Third, the rift between publicly listed and closely held SOEs in mainstreaming human rights is wide. While the former group is naturally more responsive to market pressure and overall ESG trends, the weak state of independent human rights policies and reporting data in some of the largest financial SOEs – especially the state holding company Solidium – raises questions as to the effectiveness of ownership policy–based human rights integration in Finland. To put it bluntly, the key vehicle through which Finland manages its larger investment portfolio is mostly detached not only from business and human rights debates but also from the general human rights function of the state.

In sum, the emergence of the active business and human rights movement over the past decade has slowly made inroads into both the state ownership policy and SOE operations. At the moment, however, there are only very limited substantive legal grounds to either challenge the content of ownership policies (e.g., based on too modest human rights integration) or compel SOEs to obverse human rights, particularly in transnational contexts. It remains to be seen if future regulatory instruments, such as the domestic human rights due diligence law currently being drafted, adopt more stringent requirements on the human rights performance of SOEs.

7 Human rights responsibilities of state-owned companies in Germany

Development cooperation and sustainability financing as case studies

Markus Krajewski and Tina Brosi[1]

1 Introduction

The special responsibility of state-owned enterprises (SOE) and their impact on human rights has not been an important topic in the political and academic discourse on business and human rights in Germany. Similarly, the responsibility to respect human rights did not feature prominently in the otherwise lively debate on public enterprises and their legal, political and economic functions. In fact, there is hardly any academic scholarship in law and management studies which addresses SOEs and human rights.[2] Likewise, the political discussions on business and human rights did not address SOE in any particular way. Although Germany's National Action Plan (NAP) on Business and Human Rights of 2016 briefly addresses public enterprises, it does not contain any substantive special proposals or commitments in this regard.

The present chapter aims to fill the gap in research and public discourse by developing a framework in which the pertinent questions about SOE and business and human rights can be discussed and by assessing the human rights responsibilities of two particular SOEs. The chapter commences with an overview of SOEs in Germany, briefly addressing types of SOEs, questions of governance and the relevant sectors of SOEs (2). It will then assess different policy and legal instruments in the field of business and human rights, including Germany's National Action Plan on Business and Human Rights, the German Supply Chain Due Diligence Law (*Lieferkettensorgfaltspflichtengesetz*) and the EU's Draft Directive on Corporate Sustainability Due Diligence and discuss how they treat and regulate SOEs in Germany (3). The chapter then moves to analyse specific human rights risks of SOEs, addressing human rights both in

1 Parts of this research were presented at a seminar on international financing and human rights organized by the Centro de Derechos Humanos of Universidad Diego Portales and the Centre for Human Rights Erlangen-Nürnberg in Santiago de Chile on 4 April 2023. The authors would like to thank the organisers of the seminar and commentators for valuable input.

2 If at all, the topic is discussed as part of corporate social responsibility (CSR): Mann, Thomas and Franziska Schnuch (2019): "Corporate Social Responsibility öffentlicher Unternehmen", *DÖV*, Vol. 11: pp. 417–425.

DOI: 10.4324/9781003291428-7

Germany and abroad from the perspective of extraterritorial obligations (4). Based on these general observations and assessments, the chapter addresses two federal SOEs pursuing financial and technical development assistance, the *Gesellschaft für Internationale Zusammenarbeit* (GIZ) (5), Germany's agency for international cooperation, and the state-owned bank *Kreditanstalt für Wiederaufbau* (KfW) (6). The two entities were selected because their potential extraterritorial human rights impact is likely to be larger than the impact of other German SOEs, which exist mostly at the local and regional levels and are typically engaged in the provision of public services. While these SOEs may have an impact on human rights as well – in particular in the context of their supply chains – the cases of the KfW and the GIZ are of special interest as they have already been subject of complaints by rights holders in specific instances, and the treatment of these complaints sheds additional light on the fulfilment of the human rights responsibilities of the SOEs. The chapter concludes with a summary of its main findings and proposals for further research (7).

2 State-owned enterprises: Typology, legal forms and governance

2.1 Types and sectors of SOEs

A typology of state-owned enterprises (SOEs) in Germany needs to take Germany's multilevel system of governance and its principles of a social market economy into account. SOEs exist in Germany at the federal, state and local levels. As most SOEs are active in the field of public services which are usually provided, organised and financed by local government authorities, most SOEs can be found at the local level. SOEs at the local level are typically owned by larger cities, counties (*Landkreise*) or cooperations of smaller municipalities. The guarantee of local self-government (*kommunale Selbstverwaltung*) enshrined in Article 28 section 2 of the German Constitution (the *Grundgesetz* or Basic Law) allows municipalities to follow their public purpose on the local level by offering local services to the public.[3]

SOEs in Germany exist as either (purely) public enterprises or as so-called mixed-economic enterprises.[4] Public enterprises are characterised by a 100% holding of the Federation, a Land, a city/town or other public entity. These enterprises are directly bound by the constitutional fundamental rights as their activities are attributable to the state.[5] This also applies to mixed-economic enterprises which have a majority holding of a public entity because their activities are also attributed to the state under constitutional law and bound by the constitutional fundamental rights. If a public entity owns less than 50% of a

3 Ruthig and Storr, Öffentliches Wirtschaftsrecht (5th edition, 2020, para. 688).

4 Krajewski, Schuster, Sonder (2019): "Rechtliche Grundlagen der öffentlichen Wirtschaft", in: Mühlenkamp, Schulz-Nieswandt and Theuvsen Krajewski (eds), *Öffentliche Wirtschaft: Handbuch für Wissenschaft und Praxis* (Baden-Baden: Nomos), p. 233.

5 Ruthig and Storr, Öffentliches Wirtschaftsrecht (5th edition, 2020, para. 691).

company, the company is not attributable to the state.[6] As a consequence, the company would not be bound by fundamental rights. Instead, it may claim basic rights against state entities.

In a decision concerning Fraport Aktiengesellschaft – the private law company managing the international airport of Frankfurt – the Federal Constitutional Court ruled that Fraport had to respect the freedom of assembly of protesters against the deportation of rejected asylum seekers on airport premises, because the State of Hesse, the City of Frankfurt am Main and the Federal Republic of Germany together owned approximately 70% of the shares of Fraport.[7] The Constitutional Court stated:

> Like public enterprises that are in the sole ownership of the state and are organised in the forms of private law, enterprises owned both by private shareholders and the state over which the state has a controlling influence are directly bound by the fundamental rights.[8]

SOEs exist in a variety of different sectors of the economy. On the federal level, they include railways (Deutsche Bahn AG) and infrastructure as well as the financial sector such as the KfW and development cooperation *inter alia* by the GIZ.[9] At the state level, the most important sectors are transport infrastructure (ports, airports), state banks and, in some cases, also housing companies. As mentioned, most SOEs can be found at the local level where they cover a broad range of different sectors including *inter alia* local public transportation, energy, water distribution and waste management, as well as health, social and housing services.[10]

2.2 *Legal forms*

SOEs can be organised and constituted under public and private law. Due to the neutrality of economic policy, the German Constitution prefers neither public law nor private law organisational forms in order to economically fulfil public purposes.[11]

SOEs organised under public law take different organisational forms. SOEs without a separate legal identity (*Regiebetrieb*) depend legally, organisationally, personally and financially on the public entity. Legally, they are not separate enterprises but part of the public administration. In a similar manner

6 Ruthig and Storr, Öffentliches Wirtschaftsrecht (5th edition, 2020, para. 692).
7 Federal Constitutional Court, Judgment of the First Senate of 22 February 2011, 1 BvR 699/06, para 2.
8 Federal Constitutional Court, Judgment of the First Senate of 22 February 2011, 1 BvR 699/06, para 46.
9 See sections 5 and 6.
10 Krajewski et al. 2019, p. 240.
11 Fisahn and Viotto (2008): "Privatisierung und Public-Private-Partnership", *KritV*, Vol. 91, No. 3: pp. 265, 266.

so-called *Eigenbetriebe* have a separate organisation and a separate budget, but they are still legally part of the administration.[12] SOEs can also be formed in the legal form of an institution of public law (*Anstalt des öffentlichen Rechts*) (AöR). They constitute separate legal entities and therefore have personnel and financial resources which are separate from the public administration. If several local entities cooperate in order to fulfil a common task, they can form a purpose-specific joint administrative entity (*Zweckverband*).[13] All companies organised under public law are directly managed by the respective public entity (Federation, Land or the competent local entity). The respective entity is also liable for all debts of the SOE.

State-owned enterprises using the organisational form of private law usually choose between the limited liability company (*Gesellschaft mit beschränkter Haftung*) (GmbH) or joint stock company (*Aktiengesellschaft*) (AG).[14] The establishment of private law SOEs is only permissible if public law forms are not effective enough. They must perform the respective tasks better and more cost-effectively than in other organisational forms.[15] Additionally, the public entity (Federation, Land, municipality) must have an adequate influence in the supervisory body in order to secure the public interest.[16] Despite these legal restrictions, limited liability companies and stock companies are very popular private law organisational forms for SOEs in Germany because they give the entities more managerial and commercial freedom and allow them to operate without direct influence of the public administration.

A limited liability company (GmbH) requires at least one shareholder (*Gesellschafter*) and a minimum share capital of 25.000€.[17] The shareholders are only liable for the size of their shareholding in the company, and it is the company that is liable to creditors with its assets. A joint stock company (AG) is a public limited company with the possibility of being publicly listed on the stock exchange.[18] However, most SOEs which are organised as stock companies are not listed on the stock exchange because the public entity holds all or a majority of the shares. The minimum share capital is 50000€, and the minimum number of shareholders is one.[19] Again, only the company's assets are liable to the creditors of the company for its obligations.[20]

12 Ruthig and Storr, Öffentliches Wirtschaftsrecht (5th edition, 2020, para. 714).

13 Krajewski et al. 2019, p. 245.

14 Krajewski et al. 2019, p. 249.

15 Public Corporate Governance Code of the Federation, Preamble.

16 § 65 I Federal Budget Code (*Bundeshaushaltsordnung*). See also the respective regulations at the Länder level, Art. 65 Bayerische Haushaltsordnung; § 65 I Landeshaushaltsordnung für Baden-Württemberg; § 65 I Landeshaushaltsordnung Nordrhein-Westfalen.

17 Act on Limited Liability Companies, Section 1, Section 5 para. 1, available at www.gesetze-im-internet.de/englisch_gmbhg/ (accessed 10 January 2024).

18 Stock Corporation Act, Section 1 para. 1, available at www.gesetze-im-internet.de/englisch_aktg/ (accessed 10 January 2024).

19 Stock Corporation Act, Section, 2 Section 7.

20 Stock Corporation Act, Section 1 para. 1.

2.3 Governance

While the governance of SOEs established under public law follows the principles of the respective public entities and is governed by public administrative law, the governance of SOEs constituted as private law companies follows the respective rules for the GmbH and the AG. The statutory organs of a GmbH are the shareholders and the managing director (*Geschäftsführer*).[21] The GmbH may also have a supervisory board (*Aufsichtsrat*); if it has more than 500 employees, a supervisory board must be established. The statutory organs of the *Aktiengesesellschaft* are the management board (*Vorstand*), the supervisory board (*Aufsichtsrat*) and the general meeting (*Hauptversammlung*) of the shareholders.[22]

SOEs organised as private law companies are also subject to the requirements of corporate financial and non-financial reporting, which are based on the EU's Directive on Non-Financial Reporting[23] and laid down in the German Commercial Code (*Handelsgesetzbuch*). Accordingly, all companies with more than 250 employees must include information *inter alia* on how the company respected human rights in its business activities.[24] For these purposes, the company may rely on international standards, such as the UN Guiding Principles, the OECD Guidelines for Multinational Enterprises or the ILO Tripartite Declaration of Principles concerning Multinational Enterprises and Social Policy.[25] These obligations also cover SOEs if they are constituted as GmbH or as AG.

In order to involve employees in the decision-making processes, German labour and corporate law provides for special institutions and procedures of co-determination. Companies with five and more employees are obligated to allow the establishment of a works council (*Betriebsrat*) if the employees opt for such a body.[26] In larger companies, the employees also elect one third or half of the members of the supervisory board, depending on the size of the company.[27]

In addition to the applicable statutory requirements, SOEs are also subject to special regulatory instruments. Publicly listed companies are expected to follow the German Corporate Governance Code. Furthermore, the federal

21 Act on Limited Liability Companies, Sections 6 and 45.

22 Stock Corporation Act, Sections 76 et seq.

23 Directive 2014/95/EU of 22 October 2014 as amended.

24 Commercial Code, Section 289c, para 2 No. 5, available at www.gesetze-im-internet.de/englisch_hgb/ (accessed 10 January 2024).

25 Commercial Code, Section 289d. See also Krajewski, Markus (2018): "Legitimationsfragen internationaler Rahmenwerke für die CSR-Berichterstattung: Inhalt, Regelgeber und Durchsetzungsmechanismen", *ZGR*, Vol. 47.

26 Works Constitution Act, Section 1, available at www.gesetze-im-internet.de/englisch_betrvg/ (accessed 10 January 2024).

27 See Institut für den öffentlichen Sektor, Der Aufsichtsrat in öffentlichen Unternehmen, available at https://publicgovernance.de/html/de/Aufsichtsrat-in-oeffentlichen-Unternehmen.htm (accessed 10 January 2024).

government adopted the Public Corporate Governance Code of the Federation (PCGC) as part of the Principles of Good Corporate Governance and Active Management of Federal Holdings.[28] The PCGC is applicable to companies in which the Federation has a majority holding which are not publicly listed.[29] It complements existing corporate law by recommending standards of good and responsible corporate governance.[30] Annually, the management and supervisory body submit a corporate governance report stating their compliance with the PCGC or explaining and justifying their deviations from the recommendations.[31]

Similar instruments exist at the Länder and local level: Twelve of the sixteen Länder and 43 municipalities have their own public corporate governance codes recommending standards for good corporate governance to the respective SOEs.[32]

3 The relevance of the topic of business and human rights for SOEs in Germany

3.1 The National Action Plan (NAP)

As mentioned at the outset, the German National Action Plan on Business and Human Rights of 2016 (NAP) does not treat the topic of SOEs extensively. The NAP acknowledges that if a business enterprise is under state control or if its actions may otherwise be attributed to the state, such an enterprise bears special responsibility under the UN Guiding Principles to respect human rights.[33] The NAP claims that the general standard of protection given to human rights by public enterprises is already very high since these entities – at least of the state holding a controlling stake – are directly bound by the enshrined constitutional fundamental rights. Nevertheless, the federal

28 Bundesministerium der Finanzen, Grundsätze guter Unternehmens- und aktiver Beteiligungsführung im Bereich des Bundes, p. 9f, available at www.bundesfinanzministerium.de/Content/DE/Downloads/Broschueren_Bestellservice/grundsaetze-beteiligungsfuehrung.pdf?__blob=publicationFile&v=7 (accessed 10 January 2024).

29 Beteiligungsbericht des Bundes (2022), p. 19, available at www.bundesfinanzministerium.de/Content/DE/Downloads/Broschueren_Bestellservice/beteiligungsbericht-des-bundes-2022.pdf?__blob=publicationFile&v=4 (accessed 10 January 2024).

30 Public Corporate Governance Model Code, Preamble, available at https://pcg-musterkodex.de/wp-content/uploads/2022/03/German-Public-Corporate-Governance-Modelcode_Version_2022-03-14-1.pdf (accessed 10 January 2024).

31 Public Corporate Governance Model Code, 7.1.

32 See Institut für den öffentlichen Sektor, Kodizes der Länder, available at https://publicgovernance.de/html/de/2382.htm (accessed 10 January 2024) and Ibid., Kodizes der Kommunen, available at https://publicgovernance.de/html/de/2393.htm (accessed 10 January 2024).

33 The Federal Government (2016–2020): National Action Plan Implementation of the UN Guiding Principles on Business and Human Rights, p. 18, available at https://globalnaps.org/wp-content/uploads/2018/04/germany-national-action-plan-business-and-human-rights.pdf (accessed 10 January 2024).

government committed to two concrete measures: First, the government aimed to expand the training courses of the federal holding management bodies to include sustainability matters and so focus its attention on responsibility for human rights in the enterprises in which the Federation holds a direct majority share. Second, the government was keen to increase the percentage of enterprises in which it holds a majority share that apply the German Sustainability Code, including its obligation to report on human rights.[34] In 2022 the code was applied to a total of eleven SOEs owned solely by the Federation (including the GIZ) and six further SOEs including the KfW.[35]

The NAP therefore only contained two rather limited measures with regards to public enterprises. Furthermore, it only applied to enterprises owned or dominated by the Federation. The NAP did not refer to public enterprises at the Länder or local level even though the majority of these enterprises exist at these levels. It is unclear to what extent business and human rights and SOEs are topics recognised at the Länder and local level. There is no centralised information available regarding the extent to which these companies follow the UN Guiding Principles or engage in human rights due diligence beyond their statutory requirements. Cursory information suggests the topic is not treated as a high priority. For example, the reports of the two largest Länder, Bavaria and North Rhine-Westphalia, about public asset management of 2022 do not mention the term "human rights" as an element of corporate responsibility.[36]

3.2 *Statutory human rights due diligence obligations*

To the extent SOEs are subject to relevant legislation in the areas of business and human rights, their statutory obligations require them to engage with the subject. As mentioned earlier, this concerns non-financial reporting requirements. Moreover, the German Supply Chain Due Diligence Act of 2021 (*Lieferkettensorgfaltspflichtengesetz*), which came into force on 1 January 2023 for companies with more than 3,000 employees, is also applicable to some SOEs as the act applies to enterprises regardless of their form.[37] Hence, SOEs are subject to the act in the same way as other companies. The number of SOEs

34 German NAP, p 18f.

35 Beteiligungsbericht des Bundes (2022), p. 33, available at www.bundesfinanzministerium.de/Content/DE/Downloads/Broschueren_Bestellservice/beteiligungsbericht-des-bundes-2022.html (accessed 10 January 2024).

36 Beteiligungsbericht des Freistaats Bayern (2022), available at www.stmfh.bayern.de/beteiligungen/beteiligungsbericht/ (accessed 10 January 2024) and Beteiligungsbericht Nordrhein-Westfalen (2022), available at www.finanzverwaltung.nrw.de/system/files/media/document/file/231212_Beteiligungsbericht%202022%20final.pdf (accessed 10 January 2024).

37 Act on Corporate Due Diligence Obligations for the Prevention of Human Rights Violations in Supply Chains (Supply Chain Due Diligence Act), Section 1, available at www.csr-in-deutschland.de/SharedDocs/Downloads/EN/act-corporate-due-diligence-obligations-supply-chains.pdf?__blob=publicationFile#linkicon (accessed 10 January 2024).

subject to the Supply Chain Law rose on 1 January 2024 when the act became applicable to companies with more than 1,000 employees. While many SOEs established at the local level may still be too small to fall into the scope, a number of larger energy supply companies or transportation companies are now subject to the Supply Chain Due Diligence Act.[38]

The Supply Chain Due Diligence Act requires companies to engage in human rights and environmental risk assessment and risk management as well as to adopt preventive and remedial measures as necessary.[39] Companies are also required to establish a complaint mechanism and to report on their activities.[40] The relevant due diligence obligations extend to the company's own activities and the activities of its direct suppliers. They may encompass indirect suppliers if the company has substantiated knowledge about human rights and environmental risks in its supply chains.[41]

The Draft EU Directive on Corporate Sustainability Due Diligence (EU CSDDD)[42] would also cover SOEs. As an EU Directive, it would only become directly applicable for companies after its implementation in domestic law. However, it is already clear that the EU CSDDD would not exempt SOEs from its scope of application. In fact, it might even increase the number of companies subject to human rights and environmental due diligence standards as it applies to companies with more than 500 employees. After the implementation of this new threshold into domestic German law, many SOEs even at the local level could be subject to the due diligence obligations.

4 Human rights risks of SOEs in Germany

One of the reasons business and human rights have not played a significant role for SOEs in Germany could be that it is generally assumed that these companies are subject to a high level of human rights, environmental and labour rights standards and therefore have a very low risk of negatively impacting human rights. In particular, since SOEs are directly bound to the basic rights of the Constitution[43] and therefore also subject to strict scrutiny and judicial oversight by the competent courts, actual violations of human rights within the direct sphere of SOEs may indeed be limited. For example, the regulation of labour and employment matters and the protection of employees may be quite high due to the relative proximity of these employment relationships to the status of public servants in the administration. In addition, SOEs are often

38 See for example, the local energy supplier N-ERGIE, which operates in the city of Nuremberg and surrounding municipalities with 2,500 employees.

39 Supply Chain Due Diligence Law, Sections 4 to 7.

40 Supply Chain Due Diligence Law, Sections 8 and 10.

41 Supply Chain Due Diligence Law, Section 9 paragraph 2.

42 European Commission Proposal for a Directive of the European Parliament and the Council on Corporate Sustainability Due Diligence and amending Directive (EU) 2019/1937, COM/2022/71 final, 23 February 2022.

43 See section 2 a.

also seen as "role models" in public discourse[44] and may therefore be specifically keen on maintaining their reputations in these fields.

However, with regards to human rights and environmental risks in the supply chain, SOEs may be linked to similar if not the same risks as other companies as well.[45] To the extent that SOEs rely on global supply chains for their economic activities, they may be associated with pertinent risks concerning human rights violations or environmental damages. However, it should be noted that most SOEs supply (public) services in Germany and are therefore not engaged in the production of goods which require the importation of other products or raw materials. Nevertheless, two areas in which SOEs may be directly linked to negative human rights impacts through their supply chain can be identified.

As mentioned earlier, a number of SOEs at the local level produce and supply energy. The production of energy may depend on the importation of hard coal, gas and oil, the production of which is often linked to human rights violations in the mining industry or environmental damages associated with petroleum production.[46] SOEs engaged in the production of solar or wind energy rely on the import of technical equipment such as solar panels, which may have been produced in the context of forced labour.[47]

Another important area of human rights risks of SOEs in Germany is the potential activities of these entities abroad. This raises the question of extraterritorial effects of human rights due diligence and of the impact of extraterritorial obligations (ETOs) on SOEs in Germany.[48] It should be recalled that the Maastricht Principles on Extraterritorial Obligations of States in the Area of Economic, Social and Cultural Rights establish a state's obligations to respect, protect and fulfil human rights *inter alia* in

> situations in which the State, acting separately or jointly, whether through its executive, legislative or judicial branches, is in a position to exercise decisive influence or to take measures to realize economic, social and cultural rights extraterritorially, in accordance with international law.[49]

44 Grundsätze guter Unternehmens- und aktiver Beteiligungsführung im Bereich des Bundes, p. 6.

45 German Institute for Human Rights, "Development of the Human Rights Situation in Germany July 2020–June 2021", p. 6.

46 See with regards to the importation of hard coal, Deutscher Bundestag, Wissenschaftliche Dienste, 'Lieferkettensorgfaltspflicht der deutschen Steinkohleimporteure, Sachstand", 'WD 5-3000-017/23, 23.03.2023.

47 See with regards to the importation of solar panels from China, "Solarmodule aus China: Tolerieren wir Zwangsarbeit von Uiguren?" (2023), available at www.energie-experten.org/news/solarmodule-aus-china-tolerieren-wir-zwangsarbeit-von-uiguren (accessed 10 January 2024).

48 On ETOs in general, see Gibney, Mark, Gamze Erdem Türkelli, Markus Krajewski and Wouter Vandenhole (eds) (2021): *The Routledge Handbook on Extraterritorial Human Rights Obligations* (Milton Park: Routledge).

49 Maastricht Principles on Extraterritorial Obligations of States in the Area of Economic, Social and Cultural Rights (2011), available at www.fidh.org/IMG/pdf/maastricht-eto-principles-uk_web.pdf (accessed 10 January 2024).

While most SOEs at the local and regional level do not operate or maintain subsidiaries and cooperate projects outside Germany, some federal SOEs do. For example, Deutsche Bahn, the German state-owned railway company, operates in a number of different countries through subsidiaries and joint ventures, including in freight trains in Uruguay,[50] regional rapid trains in India[51] and consultancy services in Kazakhstan.[52]

ETOs are of particular relevance in the case of the Gesellschaft für Internationale Zusammenarbeit GmbH (GIZ), Germany's agency for international cooperation, aimed at sustainable development and the technical counterpart of the government's foreign development policies, and the state-owned financial institution Kreditanstalt für Wiederaufbau (KfW), which provides financial support for development projects outside Germany.[53] Both GIZ and KfW have headquarters and branch offices in Germany, but many of their operational activities lie outside Germany, in particular in the so-called Global South. Both entities are also involved in projects with significant human rights impacts abroad. Indeed, development cooperation has been rightly characterised as an extraterritorial activity which engages human rights duties and responsibilities of different agencies and states.[54]

5 SOE in the field of development cooperation: *Gesellschaft für Internationale Zusammenarbeit* (GIZ)

The *Gesellschaft für Internationale Zusammenarbeit* (German Society for International Cooperation) (GIZ) provides services in the field of international cooperation and international education concerning economic development, the environment, energy, employment promotion, peace and security.[55] While GIZ cooperates with European Union institutions, the United Nations, private actors and governments, its main partner is the German Federal

50 DB E.C.O. Group (2022): "A New Era for Rail Freight Transportation in Uruguay", available at https://db-eco.com/en/a-new-era-for-rail-freight-transportation-in-uruguay/ (accessed 10 January 2024).

51 DB E.C.O. Group (2022): "Multi-Million-Euro Contract to Operate a New Regional Rapid Transit System in India between Delhi and Meerut", available at https://db-eco.com/en/multi-million-euro-contract-for-new-rrts-in-india/ (accessed 10 January 2024).

52 DB E.C.O. Group (2023): "Kazakh Railways Awards Further Consulting Work to DB E.C.O. Group", available at https://db-eco.com/en/kazakh-railways-awards-further-consulting-work-to-db-e-c-o-group/ (accessed 10 January 2024).

53 On ETOs in the field of development cooperation. see Chenwi, Lilian (2021): "Human Rights-Based Approaches to Development Assistance and Policies", in: Gibney, Mark, Gamze Erdem Türkelli, Markus Krajewski and Wouter Vandenhole (eds), *The Routledge Handbook on Extraterritorial Human Rights Obligations* (Abingdon-on-Thames: Routledge), pp. 213–225.

54 Chenwi, Lilian (2021): "Human Rights-Based Approaches to Development Assistance and Policies", in: Gibney, Mark, Gamze Erdem Türkelli, Markus Krajewski and Wouter Vandenhole (eds), *The Routledge Handbook on Extraterritorial Human Rights Obligations* (Abingdon-on-Thames: Routledge), p. 223.

55 GIZ, "GIZ Profile: Sustainable Development for a Liveable Future", available at www.giz.de/en/aboutgiz/profile.html (accessed 10 January 2024).

Ministry for Economic Cooperation and Development. As part of the German government, the ministry has the responsibility of ensuring that GIZ as its implementing agency complies with human rights requirements. In general, GIZ supports the development policy of the German government[56] by implementing the Sustainable Development Goals as part of the UN 2030 Agenda in, with and by Germany in bilateral and international cooperation.[57]

5.1 Legal status and governance

GIZ is a limited liability company (GmbH) and therefore has shareholders and a management board as statutory organs. Due to its size, it also has a supervisory body.[58] The Federation is the sole shareholder of GIZ and is represented by the Federal Ministry for Economic Cooperation and Development (BMZ) and the Federal Ministry of Finance (BMF).[59]

The management board consists of three members.[60] The supervisory body includes ten shareholder representatives and ten employee representatives. The shareholder representatives consist of four members of the German federal government, five representatives of the German Parliament and one representative of the Bavarian State Chancellery.[61] Since 2011, GIZ has also had a board of trustees and a private sector advisory board, which serve as advisory bodies. While the supervisory board consists of representatives of government and parliament and even though the Federation is the only shareholder, politicians and government officials usually do not interfere directly with the daily management of GIZ or with its various projects and programmes.

Pillar II of the UNGP, the corporate responsibility to respect human rights, applies to GIZ as a private commercial company (GmbH) as stipulated in UNGP 14. The federal government also committed GIZ to the voluntary due diligence and reporting standards of the German NAP.[62] Finally, GIZ has also been subject to the Supply Chain Due Diligence Act since 1 January 2023 due to its character as a commercial entity and its size (approximately 25,000 employees).

56 GIZ, "Identity", available at www.giz.de/en/aboutgiz/identity.html (accessed 10 January 2024).
57 GIZ, "GIZ and the 2030 Agenda", available at https://reporting.giz.de/2016/our-strategic-direction/our-strategy-and-our-business-model-focus-on-the-future/giz-and-the-2030-agenda/ (accessed 10 January 2024).
58 GIZ, "Organisation", available at www.giz.de/en/aboutgiz/organisation.html (accessed 10 January 2024).
59 GIZ, "Shareholder", available at www.giz.de/en/aboutgiz/shareholder.html (accessed 10 January 2024).
60 GIZ, "Management Board", available at www.giz.de/en/aboutgiz/management_board.html (accessed 10 January 2024).
61 GIZ, "Supervisory Board", available at www.giz.de/en/aboutgiz/supervisory_board.html (accessed 10 January 2024).
62 Beteiligungsbericht des Bundes (2022), p. 36.

5.2 *Corporate responsibility and human rights due diligence*

While the overall strategy of GIZ orients itself towards the 2030 Agenda for Sustainable Development,[63] respect for human rights features prominently on GIZ's corporate agenda. In fact, GIZ claims that "human rights constitute the frame of reference for everything we do".[64]

In 2023, GIZ adopted its Human Rights Strategy Policy Statement, which builds on earlier human rights statements. According to the 2023 statement, GIZ is committed to upholding the Universal Declaration of Human Rights, the core UN human rights instruments, the ILO Core Labour Standards and the European Convention on Human Rights, as well as to the UN Global Compact, the UN Guiding Principles on Business and Human Rights and the OECD Guidelines for Multinational Enterprises.[65] The statement not only contains the general commitment but also describes GIZ's risk management system and identified risks as well as preventive and remedial measures. The statement also mentions the designated human rights officer of GIZ and was authored by the management board. It is safe to conclude that the statement complies with UNGP 15 (b) as well Section 6 paragraph 2 of the German Supply Chain Due Diligence Act.

For its risk management system, GIZ uses a four-step approach involving systematically addressing risks at each project level. The four steps consist of identifying and describing all risks and potential adverse impacts, scoring and analysing the risks to assess the importance of the risks based on the probability of occurrence and the potential damage, developing appropriate risk control measures by the relevant manager and submitting a risk report to the next management level.[66] GIZ states that the risk management system covers GIZ's own business area as well as its suppliers.[67] However, GIZ does not specify whether the risk management system applies only to its direct suppliers or also its indirect suppliers. For its direct suppliers, GIZ relies on a code of conduct for contractual relations, establishing sustainability standards for its own procurement.[68]

In its human rights policy statement, GIZ also remains very general with respect to the identified risks as it only states the following: "Protection of

63 GIZ, "2030 Agenda for Sustainable Development", available at www.giz.de/en/aboutgiz/40669.html (accessed 10 January 2024).

64 GIZ, "GIZ Human Rights Policy", available at www.giz.de/de/downloads/giz2021-en-human-rights-policy.pdf (accessed 10 January 2024).

65 GIZ (2023): "GIZ Human Rights Strategy Policy Statement", available at www.giz.de/de/downloads/giz2023-en-human-rights-strategy-policy-statement.pdf (accessed 10 January 2024).

66 Ibid.

67 GIZ (2023): "GIZ Human Rights Strategy Policy Statement", available at www.giz.de/de/downloads/giz2023-en-human-rights-strategy-policy-statement.pdf (accessed 10 January 2024).

68 GIZ (2023): "Integrated Company Report 2022: Understand, Embrace, Transform", p. 43, available at reporting.giz.de/2022 (accessed 10 January 2024).

vulnerable groups; fair working conditions; occupational safety; freedom from discrimination; no economic or social exploitation of children; prevention of forced or compulsory labour; and protection against sexual assault at the workplace."[69]

Since 2014 GIZ has compiled financial and non-financial information in its integrated company report. With this voluntary reporting format, GIZ claims to take a holistic view of its activities and organisation and to illustrate how responsibility for sustainability is strategically anchored and implemented at GIZ.[70] In addition, GIZ also publishes an annual statement of accounts, which provides details of GIZ's assets, financial position and income; a public corporate governance report in line with the German Government's Public Corporate Governance Code (PCGC);[71] a non-financial declaration as set out in Section 289 et seq. of the German Commercial Code;[72] a report on GIZ's climate and environmental indicators; an EMAS Environmental Statement, which reports on GIZ's corporate environmental management; and, biannually, a stakeholder dialogue results report showing how GIZ's stakeholders rate its sustainability.[73] While these reporting activities seem extensive, it is not clear to what extent they fully comply with Section 10 paragraph 2 of the German Supply Chain Due Diligence Act which requires the report to

> state in a comprehensible manner, (1) whether the enterprise has identified any human rights and environment-related risks or violations of a human rights-related or environment-related obligation, and if so, which ones, (2) what the enterprise has done to fulfil its due diligence obligations . . .; this also includes . . . the measures taken by the enterprise as a result of complaints (3) how the enterprise assesses the impact and effectiveness of the measures and (4) what conclusions it draws from the assessment for future measures.[74]

5.3 *Complaint mechanism*

According to UNGP Principle 22 and Section 8 of the German Supply Chain Due Diligence Act, businesses shall ensure that an appropriate internal complaints procedure is in place. In order to fulfil this requirement, GIZ relies on its whistleblower system, which allows complaints and information on

69 GIZ (2023): "GIZ Human Rights Strategy Policy Statement", available at www.giz.de/de/downloads/giz2023-en-human-rights-strategy-policy-statement.pdf (accessed 10 January 2024).

70 GIZ (2023): "Integrated Company Report 2022: Understand, Embrace, Transform", p. iii, available at reporting.giz.de/2022 (accessed 10 January 2024).

71 On the PCGC, see 2 c.

72 On these requirements, see 2 c.

73 GIZ (2023): "Integrated Company Report 2022: Understand, Embrace, Transform", p. iii, available at reporting.giz.de/2022 (accessed 10 January 2024).

74 Supply Chain Due Diligence Law, Section 10 paragraph 2.

violations of human rights and environmental law in addition to the more "typical" topics of whistleblowing: e.g., sexual misconduct and sexual exploitation, corruption and bribery, misappropriation, fraud and embezzlement as, well as conflicts of interest.[75] For these complaints, GIZ maintains a special whistleblower portal for confidential reporting of information.[76] Complaints can be submitted anonymously, and GIZ attempts to ensure that there won't be negative consequences for any whistleblower. Complaints concerning GIZ's human rights actions can also be sent to the Compliance and Integrity Advisory Services by email and to an external ombudsman as a point of contact outside GIZ. The ombudsman has the duty of confidentiality towards the complainants as he is an independent lawyer.[77]

It should be noted that the whistleblower portal is only available in English, French, Spanish and German, so it requires knowledge of these languages to submit a report. It is questionable whether this meets the requirements of an easily accessible complaint mechanism according to Section 8 paragraph 3 of the German Supply Chain Due Diligence Act and UNGP 31 b) as these require mechanisms to overcome lack of language skills, reading and writing difficulties and other challenges of persons in vulnerable situations.[78]

GIZ published a flow chart entitled Compliance and Integrity Case Management Process, which details how complaints are handled.[79] The information provided is very general and does not contain detailed and specific time frames. It only states that "[a]fter three months at the most, the whistleblower is informed about the measures taken".[80] It is questionable if this meets the requirements of "specific rules of procedure in text form" as required by Section 8 paragraph 2 of the German Supply Chain Due Diligence Act. Accordingly, the specific rules should at least describe what procedural steps are envisaged, what routes the procedure can take, who is responsible, how the responsible persons can be addressed, what form is envisaged for notifications and the time frame for the individual procedural steps.[81]

Finally, GIZ provides little information on actual complaints and measures taken. The relevant websites and reports do not contain any easily accessible

75 GIZ, "Whistle Blowing", available at www.giz.de/en/aboutgiz/39089.html (accessed 10 January 2024).

76 GIZ, "Confidential Reporting of Information", available at www.bkms-system.com/bkwebanon/report/clientInfo?cin=26zig7&c=-1&language=eng (accessed 10 January 2024).

77 GIZ, "Whistle Blowing", available at www.giz.de/en/aboutgiz/39089.html (accessed 10 January 2024).

78 Kocher, Eva (2023): "LkSG § 8 Beschwerdeverfahren", in: Kaltenborn, Markus, Markus Krajewski, Giesela Rühl and Miriam Saage-Maaß (eds), *Lieferkettensorgfaltspflichtenrecht* (München: C.H. Beck), p. 592.

79 GIZ, "GIZ Compliance and Integrity Case Management Process", available at www.giz.de/en/downloads_els/fallbearbeitungsprozess-aussendarstellung-en.pdf (accessed 10 January 2024).

80 Ibid.

81 Kocher 2023, p. 586.

information on remedial actions and measures taken based on complaints received. A "case register" contains the information that "as of 22 September 2023, no complaints have been filed with GIZ".[82] However, this seems to contradict the Integrated Company Report of 2018, in which GIZ mentions it received one case related to a complaint in Côte d'Ivoire in 2018, which was addressed in 2019.[83] However, no outcome report was published. This contradicts the UNGP Principle 21 b), which asks for information that is sufficient to evaluate the adequacy of enterprise's response to the particular human rights impact involved.

6 SOE in the field of sustainability financing: *Kreditanstalt für Wiederaufbau* (KfW)

The *Kreditanstalt für Wiederaufbau* (KfW) (Credit Agency for Reconstruction) was founded in 1948 as an institution to financially support German reconstruction after World War II.[84] Today, it is a state-owned financial institution to support development projects abroad and social-ecological projects in Germany under the motto of "responsible banking" and with a mandate to promote global development.[85] KfW acts on behalf of the Federal Republic of Germany and the federal states and aligns its financing and promotional services with the UN Agenda 2030 and the Sustainable Development Goals (SDGs).[86] Hence, KfW performs public functions.[87]

6.1 Legal status and governance

The KfW is a public law entity (*Anstalt des öffentlichen Rechts*)[88] and does not operate under commercial or corporate law per se.[89] As *Anstalt des öffentlichen Rechts* is a KfW, it is not an entity of the state but has a separate legal personality. However, it is bound by basic freedoms of the constitution like state agencies.[90] The legal basis is the Law Concerning KfW, which was enacted

82 GIZ, "Case Register", available at www.giz.de/en/workingwithgiz/132063.html (accessed 20 January 2024).

83 GIZ, "Integrated Company Report 2018", available at https://reporting.giz.de/2018/corporate-sustainability/focus-theme-human-rights/human-rights-a-yardstick-for-our-processes/index.html (accessed 10 January 2024).

84 On the KfW's history see KfW, "History of KfW", available at www.kfw.de/About-KfW/F%C3%B6rderauftrag-und-Geschichte/Geschichte-der-KfW/ (accessed 10 January 2024).

85 KfW, "KfW – Responsible Banking', available at www.kfw.de/About-KfW/ (accessed 10 January 2024).

86 Ibid.

87 German Institute for Human Rights (2020): "KfW's Human Rights Obligations in Conversation Work – The Example of La Salonga National Park", Berlin, p. 6.

88 See 2 b.

89 KfW, "Law Concerning Kreditanstalt für Wiederaufbau", Article 1 Section 1, available at www.kfw.de/PDF/Download-Center/Law-Concerning-KfW/KfW-Gesetz-DE-EN.pdf (accessed 10 January 2024).

90 On the differences between public and private law institutions, see 2 a.

in 1948 and amended multiple times since then. The Federation participates with 3 billion euros and the Länder with 750 million euros;[91] thus KfW is owned 80% by the Federation and 20% by the Länder.

The KfW Group consists of the KfW Development Bank and three subsidiaries organised as private law companies and thus subject to private corporate and commercial law: the IPEX Bank (organised as a GmbH), which finances projects for German and European companies in the global markets; the KfW DEG (organised as a GmbH), which finances and advises German and local companies active in developing and emerging countries; and the KfW Capital (organised as a GmbH and Co. KG), which supplies venture and growth capital for innovative technology companies in Germany.[92] As private law companies, these entities are also subject to the reporting requirements of the Commercial Code.[93]

KfW's governance structure follows the model of private banks. It has an executive board with the functions of a board of directors and a board of supervisory directors with similar functions as a supervisory board.[94] The executive board conducts the business and manages KfW on a daily basis. It is appointed by the board of supervisory directors. The board of supervisory directors consists of seven Federal ministers, seven Länder ministers and seven members of Federal Parliament, as well as representatives of financial institutions, industry associations and trade unions.

Based on its legal status, ownership and governance structure, it can be argued that KfW is subject to Pillars I and II of the UNGP. While KfW is not a state organ within the meaning of Article 4 Draft Articles on State Responsibility,[95] because of its separate legal personality or another entity exercising governmental authority within the meaning of Article 5 Draft Article on State Responsibility as KfW does not exercise governmental authority, its activities are nevertheless attributable to the state as a person wholly controlled by the state under Article 8 Draft Articles on State Responsibility. While its management may be independent from state organs, the executive board depends on the board of supervisory directors, and KfW is wholly owned by the state. Hence, state human rights obligations (Pillar I) apply directly to KfW.[96]

91 KfW, "Law Concerning Kreditanstalt für Wiederaufbau", Article 1 Section 2, available at www.kfw.de/PDF/Download-Center/Law-Concerning-KfW/KfW-Gesetz-DE-EN.pdf (accessed 10 January 2024).

92 KfW, "Promotional Mandate and History", available at www.kfw.de/About-KfW/F%C3%B6rderauftrag-und-Geschichte/ (accessed 10 January 2024).

93 See 3 c.

94 KfW, "Law Concerning Kreditanstalt für Wiederaufbau", Article 6 and 7, available at www.kfw.de/PDF/Download-Center/Law-Concerning-KfW/KfW-Gesetz-DE-EN.pdf (accessed 10 January 2024).

95 International Law Commission (2001): "Draft Articles on Responsibility of States for Internationally Wrongful Acts, with commentaries", available at https://legal.un.org/ilc/texts/instruments/english/commentaries/9_6_2001.pdf (accessed 10 January 2024).

96 German Institute for Human Rights 2020, p. 6, available at Position_Paper_KfWs_Human_Rights_Obligations_in_Conservation_Work.pdf (accessed 10 January 2024).

However, due to its commercial activities, KfW is also subject to UNGP Pillar II. KfW conducts financial activities and is therefore a business entity in this regard. The corporate duty to respect human rights applies to all business entities regardless of ownership and structure (UNGP 14). It should also be noted that UNGP IV requires additional steps to protect against human rights abuses by business enterprises that are owned or controlled by the state. This applies *inter alia* to development finance institutions organised as SOEs.[97] Furthermore, the UN Working Group on the issue of human rights and transnational corporations and other business enterprises views human rights violations of SOEs as violations of the state's duty to respect by performing public functions or having delegating authority.[98] While KfW does not have delegated authority, it performs public functions as mentioned earlier. On this basis, human rights due diligence of SOE's carrying out public functions despite their incorporation under private law should be based on states' human rights obligations and responsibilities of businesses.[99] KfW itself is also "aware of its role model function as a state-owned financial institution".[100]

KfW is also subject to the German Supply Chain Due Diligence Act. The law applies to "companies" without specifying legal forms. Hence, public law entities engaged in commercial activities are also covered by the Supply Chain Due Diligence Act.[101] With approximately 7,700 employees, KfW has been subject to the Act since 1 January 2023.

6.2 Corporate responsibility and human rights due diligence

In 2023, KfW published its latest policy statement on human rights and on its human rights strategy.[102] The statement was approved by KfW's executive board on 4 April 2023 and replaces the first declaration on respect for human rights in its business operations from 2008. When referring to "human rights", KfW considers the Universal Declaration of Human Rights; all core human rights instruments developed within the framework of the United Nations, including the Covenants on Civil and Political Rights and on Economic, Social and Cultural Rights; and the UN Guiding Principles on Business and Human Rights. KfW also mentions the European Convention on Human

97 UN Guiding Principles on Business and Human Rights (2011), p. 7.

98 UN/HRC/32/45, 2016, para. 30–35; German Institute for Human Rights 2020, p. 7.

99 German Institute for Human Rights 2020, p. 7.

100 KfW (2023): "KfW 2022 Sustainability Report – Data According to GRI, HGB and TCFD", available at www.kfw.de/PDF/Download-Center/Konzernthemen/Nachhaltigkeit/englisch/Sustainability-Report-2022.pdf (accessed 10 January 2024).

101 Mittwoch, Anne-Christin and Fernanda Bremenkamp (2023): "LkSG § 1 Anwendungsbereich", in: Kaltenborn, Markus, Markus Krajewski, Giesela Rühl and Miriam Saage-Maaß (eds), *Lieferkettensorgfaltspflichtenrecht* (München: C.H.Beck), p. 77.

102 KfW, "Policy Statement of KfW and Its Subsidiaries' on Human Rights and on Its Human Rights Strategy", (April), available at www.kfw.de/nachhaltigkeit/Dokumente/Sonstiges/KfW-Group%27s-Human-Rights-Policy-Statement.pdf (accessed 10 January 2024).

Rights, the core labour standards of the International Labour Organisation and the OECD Guidelines for Multinational Enterprises.[103]

According to its human rights policy statement, KfW "protects and respects international human rights within its sphere of influence and employs appropriate procedures to exclude its participation in human rights violations". Furthermore, "KfW is also committed to actively supporting the implementation of international human rights".[104] The statement summarises the main elements of KfW's risk management system concerning its own banking operations, with regards to its procurement and – most importantly – concerning its banking business: i.e., the financial services for its clients. In its 2019 sustainability report KfW openly stated in this regard: "The biggest risk of possible human rights violations lies within our core business. It is essential to identify human rights risks resulting from financing measures at an early stage so that we can counteract them accordingly".[105] Unfortunately, the same openness is missing in KfW's current human rights statement. Instead, the 2023 document only refers in general terms to "vulnerable and disadvantaged groups such as women, indigenous communities, children and people with disabilities".[106]

In light of the general nature of the steps of the risk management system and the identified risks mentioned in the statement, it is unclear if the statement in its current form fulfils the requirement of Section 6 paragraph 2 of the German Supply Chain Due Diligence Act.

6.3 Complaint mechanism

KfW offers bank-wide complaint mechanisms in order to submit a complaint if one is negatively affected by activities of the KfW Group.[107] Complaints can be addressed by telephone, in writing or online by using a complaint form.[108] In addition to KfW itself, IPEX-Bank, KfW Development Bank, DEG and KfW Capital have separate complaint mechanisms. It should be noted that the online complaint form is only available in English,[109] which does not fulfil international and domestic requirements of accessibility.[110]

103 Ibid., p. 2.

104 Ibid.

105 KfW, "Protecting and Preserving Human Rights", available at www.kfw.de/microsites/Microsite/nachhaltigkeitsbericht.kfw.de/archiv-2019/en/discourse/human-rights-due-diligence.html (accessed 10 January 2024).

106 KfW, "Policy Statement of KfW and Its Subsidiaries' on Human Rights and on Its Human Rights Strategy", (April), p. 5, available at www.kfw.de/nachhaltigkeit/Dokumente/Sonstiges/KfW-Group%27s-Human-Rights-Policy-Statement.pdf (accessed 10 January 2024).

107 Ibid., p. 6.

108 Ibid.

109 KfW, "Online Complaint Form", available at www.kfw-entwicklungsbank.de/International-financing/KfW-Development-Bank/Formulare/FZ-Beschwerdeformular/ (accessed 10 January 2024).

110 See 5 c.

In the case of the online complaint form, complainants can be individuals, companies, organisations or other parties affected by KfW projects or programmes supported by the KfW Group.[111] Within 14 business days, the complainant receives a confirmation, and the complaints office coordinates the complaint.[112] The complainant will be informed if additional information is required and receive the results of the complaint in writing.[113] KfW also publishes complaints reports with information about the complaints since 2018.[114] While KfW's webpage on complaints contains basic information on the complaints procedure, this information does not fully satisfy the requirement of Section 8 paragraph 2 of the Supply Chain Due Diligence Act (publicly available rules of procedure in text form).

The KfW Group also offers an external ombudsperson as a contact for all employees and third parties in order to inform themselves about possible compliance claims. The contact is anonymous, and contractual regulations guarantee the secrecy of the identity of the whistleblower. The ombudsperson as well as the Compliance Whistleblowing System addresses suspected criminal activities.[115]

In recent years, complaints submitted to and handled by KfW concerned a number of different projects, including a road construction project in Mombasa (Kenya) relating to the resettlement of people and insufficient compensation,[116] a school construction in Palestine allegedly without the consent of the landowner[117] and a water treatment plant in India, where the complainants claim a lack of civil participation, pollution, odour nuisance and the destruction of argan trees.[118] IPEX-Bank received one complaint in 2021 about the Coastal Gaslink project in Canada. The complaint mainly concerned the lack of free, prior and informed consent of those affected and the impact of natural gas on the climate.[119] A special and noteworthy case was the involvement of GIZ in the La Salonga National Park project in DR Congo and the alleged human rights abuses by park guards, which will be analysed in the next section.

111 KfW, "Complaints", available at www.kfw-entwicklungsbank.de/International-financing/KfW-Development-Bank/Service/Complaints/ (accessed 10 January 2024).

112 Ibid.

113 Ibid.

114 Ibid.

115 Ibid.

116 KfW, "Sustainability Report 2020", p. 93, available at www.kfw.de/PDF/Download-Center/Konzernthemen/Nachhaltigkeit/englisch/Sustainability-Report-2020.pdf (accessed 20 January 2024).

117 KfW, "2021 Complaints Report", p. 10, available at www.kfw-entwicklungsbank.de/PDF/Beschwerdebericht/2021_Beschwerdebericht_EN.pdf (accessed 10 January 2024).

118 Ibid.

119 Sustainability Report (2021), p. 89.

6.4 *Case study: The La Salonga National Park Project*

The La Salonga National Park in DR Congo was managed by Institut Congolais pour la Conservation de la Nature (ICCN), with consultancy services provided by the World Wildlife Fund (WWF).[120] ICCN was responsible for the hiring, equipping and discipline of park staff, (e.g., the ecoguards and rangers). KfW and other international financing institutions provided financial support to the project with the aim of nature conservation as part of sustainable development. In 2016, international NGOs including Rainforest UK reported allegations that park rangers and ecoguards committed serious human rights violations, such as physical abuse resulting in injuries, rape and murder. It was also claimed that the staff did not receive adequate training, and the incentive system encouraged them to arrest poachers. Furthermore, the lack of participation of the local communities in the establishment, management and benefit sharing of this and other parks was also criticised.

In light of these allegations, KfW commissioned Monkey Forest Consulting (MFC), a consulting company specialising in security and community participation issues, to assess the security, environmental and social management systems at La Salonga in 2019. KfW also requested the German Institute for Human Rights to advise it and MFC on the inclusion and evaluation of human rights aspects in this assessment. The German Institute for Human Rights did not participate in the field investigations undertaken by MFC and did not verify the allegations against Congolese ecoguards in La Salonga.[121]

However, the German Institute for Human Rights analysed how KfW should discharge its own human rights obligations and responsibilities and made recommendations in this regard. The institute recalled that KfW remains the human rights duty bearer even if some activities to implement human rights obligations can be outsourced. Hence, KfW cannot discharge its obligations by relying on its contracting partners.[122]

The German Institute for Human Rights recommended that KfW should exercise human rights due diligence regarding partner capacity. In particular, it should assess the capacity of partners and contractors to implement the activities in line with human rights due diligence requirements. In cases of management weaknesses of local partners, financial cooperation should be complemented by technical cooperation, especially in the areas of good governance, including judiciary and security sector reform. The pre-engagement assessment of partners' will and capacity to reform should also include conditions which would result in the suspension of the cooperation. Any de-investment or withdrawal

120 For a summary of the facts, see German Institute for Human Rights 2020, p. 4, available at www.institut-fuer-menschenrechte.de/fileadmin/Redaktion/Publikationen/Stellungnahmen/Position_Paper_KfWs_Human_Rights_Obligations_in_Conservation_Work.pdf (accessed 15 January 2024).

121 German Institute for Human Rights 2020, p. 4.

122 Ibid., p. 10.

from the project, however, should also be subject to special human rights due diligence considerations.[123]

The German Institute for Human Rights also recommended that KfW should increase transparency about project assessments and project progress.[124] This is not only essential for complaint procedures as well as for stakeholder dialogue but would also support public dialogue and further accountability. Furthermore, KfW should increase transparency with respect to how it dealt with the results of investigations into the alleged human rights allegations.[125] In addition, KfW should establish a complaint mechanism in line with UNGP 31. Finally, KfW should be guided by the findings of forums for exchange among researchers and practitioners and research aimed at expanding the knowledge base. In this regard, the German Institute for Human Rights pointed to "community-based forest management, including security management, engaging local nature conservation institutions and effective and accessible grievance mechanisms in difficult-to-access areas as well as the protection of human rights defenders and whistle blowers, especially in fragile contexts".[126]

The case study and the assessment of KfW's activities by the German Institute for Human Rights show that it is not enough for an institution to simply commit itself to respect human rights and to engage in projects which are generally perceived as sustainable. Instead, procedures need to be in place and implemented which allow scrutiny before new projects begin and during the operation of a project. The La Salonga case also highlights the importance of an accessible and effective complaint mechanism not to only to ensure access to remedies by rights holders, but also to provide information and learning opportunities for the respective entities to react to alleged human rights abuses and to improve the general human rights record of a project. It is not clear if the current KfW complaint mechanism as described in the previous section takes the recommendations of the German Institute for Human Rights sufficiently into account.

The La Salonga case and KfW's involvement also indicate that SOEs are faced with similar if not the same human rights challenges as commercial actors. KfW did not cause or contribute actively to human rights abuses in the La Salonga case. Rather, the allegations concerned an actor involved in a project financed by KfW. In the language of the German Supply Chain Due Diligence Law, ICCN could be seen as an "indirect supplier" as KfW did not have a direct contractual relationship with ICCN. In such cases, it is important to assess the leverage one business entity may have over the other, which is primarily determined by the financial input of KfW in the project. As these questions are also relevant for commercial actors, KfW and other SOEs may also learn from the experiences of these actors.

123 Ibid., p. 11.
124 Ibid., p. 12.
125 German Institute for Human Rights 2020, p. 12.
126 Ibid., pp. 12–13.

It should be noted that it is unclear if the allegations of human rights abuses in the La Salonga National Park were ever the subject of a proper enquiry or judicial proceedings. It is therefore difficult to assess if and how rights holders whose rights were violated received compensation or whether other forms of remediation were applied. Considering the fact that KfW is a SOE directly bound by domestic constitutional law and international human rights law, the lack of knowledge about access to justice and remedies remains deplorable.

7 Conclusion

State-owned enterprises in Germany are typically not engaged in the production of goods, extraction of minerals or petroleum or other high-risk activities with significant negative impacts on human rights. In fact, most activities of SOEs in Germany concern the delivery of public services in Germany and are therefore subject to environmental, labour, social and other laws aimed at protecting human rights. Nevertheless, SOEs may rely on imported goods and services which could be connected with human rights abuses in global supply chains and production networks.

In this regard, it is important to recall that SOEs are directly bound to fundamental rights as protected by the constitution. In light of the important role and special responsibilities of SOEs with regards to human rights, it is unfortunate that the public discourse on business and human rights in Germany does not pay a lot of attention to SOEs in this regard. The National Action Plan on Business and Human Rights only focused on federal SOEs. There is, hence, a gap with regards to SOEs at the Länder and local level, even though this is where most of the SOEs exist and operate.

Human rights responsibilities of SOEs are specifically relevant if these entities engage in activities outside Germany. This chapter took a closer look at GIZ and KfW as two SOEs which operate in the field of development cooperation and financing. The chapter showed that both entities and their public owners (i.e., the federation and partly the Länder) are aware of the human rights responsibilities of GIZ and KfW and aim to ensure that their activities not only avoid negative impacts on human rights ("do no harm") but also positively contribute to the realisation of human rights ("do good").[127] Both GIZ and KfW have adopted respective human rights declarations and claim to exercise due diligence with regards to their activities in Germany and their projects abroad.

However, the assessment of the complaint mechanisms of both entities and of the La Salonga case study showed that SOEs may be faced with challenges similar to those of private law companies. A preliminary conclusion suggests that both GIZ and KfW need to improve their strategies and policies concerning access to remedies and to complaint mechanisms. Furthermore, there

127 See also Report of the Special Rapporteur on the Right to Development, "Role of business in realizing the right to development" A/78/160 para 77.

seems to a be a lack of transparency with regards to the relevant procedures and their outcomes.

This also leads to the need for further empirical research concerning the human rights obligations and responsibilities of SOEs in Germany. In particular, it would be important to assess the follow-ups of the cases which reached the complaint mechanisms of GIZ and KfW. It might also be interesting to analyse the performance of both entities under the German Supply Chain Due Diligence Act and the future EU Directive on Corporate Sustainability Due Diligence. Finally, the exact mode and scope of attribution of the activities of SOEs, in particular of GIZ and KfW, to the German state need to be studied further to determine whether and how these entities have direct obligations under domestic constitutional and international human rights law.

8 A review of the regulatory framework relating to human rights and environmental concerns for state-owned enterprises in France

Mihaela Maria Barnes[1]

1 Introduction

State-owned enterprises (SOEs) have a long history in France,[2] with King Henry IV having created the first French East India Company in 1604 as a Crown entity. In 1664, Jean-Baptiste Colbert (minister to King Louis XIV) created the second French East India Company as a joint-stock company with a hybrid legal status (partly private, partly owned by the Crown), whose purpose was to compete with the English and Dutch trading companies that were already operating in the East Indies. While the second French East India Company was liquidated in 1794, during the upheaval of the French Revolution, the novel ideas that flowed from this period of radical political and societal change ultimately set the foundations for socialism as an accepted political, social and economic system; in this process, the state was reimagined as a producer, buyer and seller.[3]

Although the importance of state corporate ownership gradually increased in France from the late 18th century, its popularity ebbed and flowed, and it was linked with the ideology of the main political party(ies) in charge of the government at a given point in time. For example, in French contemporary economic history, there have been three major cycles of nationalisations: in 1936–37, 1945–46 and 1982, and by the time of the last cycle of nationalisations took place, few industries remained completely independent of state

1 The author would like to thank Professor Judith Schönsteiner and Professor Markus Krajewski for their helpful comments and suggestions. Thank you also to all the other participants in the author workshop organised by the Centre for Human Rights Erlangen-Nürnberg and the Human Rights Centre at the University of Diego Portales, Chile, on 20–21 September 2021.

2 Bottini, Fabien (2020): "Legal Aspects of Public Enterprises: Remarks Based on a Comparative Study of French, European and American Legislation", in: Bernier, Luc, Massimo Florio and Philippe Bance (eds), *The Routledge Handbook of State-Owned Enterprises* (Abingdon-on-Thames: Routledge), pp. 256–266.

3 Chadeau, Emmanuel (2000): "The Rise and Decline of State-Owned Industry in Twentieth-Century France", in: Toninelli, Pier Angelo (ed.), *The Rise and Fall of State-Owned Enterprise in the Western World* (Cambridge: Cambridge University Press), pp. 191–197.

DOI: 10.4324/9781003291428-8

ownership.[4] In the second half of the 1980s, however, SOEs started to fall out of favour, and a strong move towards privatisation and deregulation ensued, which, to a certain extent, continues to this day. Nevertheless, state corporate ownership continues to remain significant in France,[5] and its importance is likely to increase in the aftermath of the COVID-19 pandemic.[6] There are currently 12 listed entities in which the French state maintains a shareholding: Aeroports de Paris (50.63%), Airbus Group (11.03%), Air France-KLM (14.29%), CNP Assurances (holds 1.11%; controls 66%), Dexia (5.73%), Électricité de France ('EDF', the 'Company') (83.68%), ENGIE (24.10 %), Orange (a direct 13.39% stake and a 9.60% stake through Bpifrance), Renault (15.1%), Safran (14 % of shares and 21.9% of voting rights) and Thales (25.76%).[7] There are also some large companies in which the state maintains ownership and which are unlisted, such as SNCF (rail), RATP (public transport), CDC (*Caisse des dépots et consignations*) and La Banque Postale (bank).[8] Overall, the French government maintains a stake (either majority or minority) in some 81 firms, in various sectors.[9] The state's share portfolio is administered by the L'Agence des participations de l'État, which operates under the authority of the Minister of the Economy.[10]

With this brief background in mind, the purpose of this chapter is to review the current regulatory framework for SOEs in France as applicable to human rights and environmental sustainability matters and to examine – through two case studies – how this regulatory framework is implemented in practice. Thus, to clarify, given space constraints, the present contribution is not an exhaustive review of the whole regulatory framework for French SOEs.[11] Instead, as discussed in the next section, the focus is solely on the provisions of Law 2017–399 of 27 March 2017 (Duty of Vigilance Law),[12] although it should

4 Ibid., pp. 185–191.

5 European Commission and Directorate-General for Economic and Financial Affairs (2016): *State-Owned Enterprises in the EU: Lessons Learnt and Ways Forward in a Post-Crisis Context* (Brussels: Publications Office), pp. 1, 5, 7, 12, 30.

6 "The COVID-19 Crisis and State Ownership in the Economy: Issues and Policy Considerations" (2020) OECD Policy Responses to Coronavirus (COVID-19), available at www.oecd-ilibrary.org/economics/the-covid-19-crisis-and-state-ownership-in-the-economy-issues-and-policy-considerations_ce417c46-en (accessed 17 November 2021).

7 "France and Monaco" (*United States Department of State*), available at www.state.gov/reports/2018-investment-climate-statements/france-and-monaco/ (accessed 17 November 2021).

8 Ibid.

9 Ibid.

10 "Agence des participations de l'État", available at www.economie.gouv.fr/agence-participations-etat/notre-mission-statement (accessed 17 November 2021).

11 For a more comprehensive overall review of the regulatory framework for SOEs in France, see Fabien Bottini's book chapter cited earlier.

12 Law No. 2017–399 (27 March 2017) on the Duty of Care of Parent Companies and Ordering Companies, available at www.legifrance.gouv.fr/loda/id/JORFTEXT000034290626/ (accessed 12 June 2023).

be borne in mind that there may be other legal provisions that are concomitantly applicable to SOEs in this area, such as certain provisions of the French Criminal Code[13] and other rules and regulations applicable to listed entities.

Nevertheless, before proceeding with the core analysis, several broad remarks are in order about certain aspects of the regulatory environment for SOEs in France. First, in line with classical liberal thought, the regulatory framework distinguishes between non-trade activities (non–profit making or sovereign activities such as regulation, policing or the provision of essential services to the most vulnerable members of the society) and trade activities (profit making).[14] This distinction is often blurred and has been susceptible to change over time. For example, there was a period in France when road and railway construction was deemed to be a sovereign activity as it enabled control over a territory, a situation that changed over time.[15] Second, SOEs are, in essence, hybrids, enjoying a hybrid legal status and the regulatory framework for SOEs is constructed at the intersection of two conflicting purposes, both of general interest: the achievement of social, economic and societal goals and free market competition.[16] Given that the overall aim of the various regulatory frameworks for SOEs is largely to ensure competitive neutrality between the public and the private sectors, in cases in which certain competitive advantages bestowed on SOEs alter this balance, certain measures have been designed to apply exclusively to SOEs in order to restore the level playing field with the private sector.[17] Thus, as Bottini remarks, '[I]n practical terms, the goal assigned by most states to a public enterprise has an impact on its legal regime. . . . [T]hey will be personalised to enable the entity to fulfill its purpose as efficiently as possible' and '[T]his is why some public enterprises are not subject to general rules', whilst, at the same time, they are being subjected to specific obligations.[18] Third, the definition of entities that can be considered SOEs does not appear to be static and is often dependent on the legal regime in question (public law or private law), some entities having separate

13 French Criminal Code (31 December 2005) Article L.121–2. Addresses the criminal liability of legal entities, available at www.legifrance.gouv.fr/codes/article_lc/LEGIARTI000006417204/ (accessed 17 November 2021).

14 Chadeau (n 2) 192; Bottini (n 1) 257; OECD (2015): *OECD Guidelines on Corporate Governance of State-Owned Enterprises, 2015 Edition* (Paris: OECD Publishing). The OECD defines a trade activity as one in which goods and services are offered 'on a given market and which could, at least in principle, be carried on by a private operator to make profits'.

15 Bottini (n 1) 258.

16 Ibid., 259.

17 Willemyns, Ines (2016): "Disciplines on State-Owned Enterprises in International Economic Law: Are We Moving in the Right Direction?" *Journal of International Economic Law*, Vol. 19: p. 657; Chaisse, Julien (2016): "Untangling the Triangle: Issues for State-Controlled Entities in Trade, Investment, and Competition Law", in: Chaisse, Julien and Lin Tsai-Yu (eds), *International Economic Law and Governance Essays in Honour of Mitsuo Matsushita* (Oxford: Oxford University Press), pp. 233–258.

18 Bottini (n 1) 262.

legal personalities and some lacking them.[19] Currently, in French domestic law, an SOE will be regarded as public in nature if it is an entity in which the state has the majority of the share capital, holds the majority of votes in deliberative bodies, or exercises, directly or indirectly, significant management and decision-making power.[20]

2 Duty of Vigilance Law

The process of drafting and adopting the Duty of Vigilance Law was 'highly contested',[21] but at the time of its adoption in 2017, it was the 'first comprehensive and legally binding'[22] human rights due diligence instrument worldwide that imposed obligations on parent companies to identify and prevent adverse human rights and environmental impacts, which are a consequence either of their own activities, the activities of entities that they control or those resulting from certain commercial relationships involving subcontractors or suppliers.[23] The Duty of Vigilance Law applies to companies that: 1) are registered in France (French subsidiaries of foreign groups are also included), 2) are under a prescribed corporate form and (c) have a certain number of employees (≥ 5,000 employees at the end of two consecutive financial years if the company's head office is located on French territory or ≥ 10,000 employees if its head office is located on French territory or abroad). Recent research, however, shows that it is often difficult to identify the entities to which the Vigilance Law applies, largely due to the lack of available public data or certain other peculiarities found in corporations (such as the evolution of corporate entities and groups following mergers, acquisitions or restructuring.)[24]

19 Ibid.

20 Code des Juridictions Financières Article 133–1; Ordinance No. 2016–1360 of 13 October 2016 Article 9; Law No. 83–675 (26 July 1983) on Public Sector Democratization; Ordinance No. 2014–948 of 20 August 2014, on Governance and Capital Transactions of Publicly Owned Companies; Law of 11 February 1982, concerning the Competence of the Board of Directors of Public Companies; Law No. 82–155, 11 February 1982) on Nationalization; Ordinance No. 2015–899 of 23 July 2015. Article 11. All instruments are available at www.legifrance.gouv.fr (accessed 12 June 2023).

21 Almut Schilling-Vacaflor (2021): "Putting the French Duty of Vigilance Law in Context: Towards Corporate Accountability for Human Rights Violations in the Global South?", *Human Rights Review*, Vol. 22: pp. 109, 115–116.

22 Ibid., 111; Brabant, Stéphane and Elsa Savourey, "Loi Sur Le Devoir de Vigilance, Pour Une Approche Contextualisée' Revue Internationale de la Compliance et de l'Ethique des Affaires." English translation available with the Business and Human Rights Resource Centre, available at www.business-humanrights.org/en/latest-news/frances-law-on-the-corporate-duty-of-vigilance-a-practical-and-multidimensional-analysis-in-english/ (accessed 6 October 2021).

23 Cossart, Sandra, Jérôme Chaplier and Tiphaine Beau De Lomenie (2017): "The French Law on Duty of Care: A Historic Step Towards Making Globalization Work for All", *Business and Human Rights Journal*, Vol. 2: p. 317.

24 Savourey, Elsa and Stéphane Brabant (2021): "The French Law on the Duty of Vigilance: Theoretical and Practical Challenges Since Its Adoption", *Business and Human Rights Journal*, Vol. 6: pp. 141, 142–143. See also, in this context, the research done by the non-governmental

The entities[25] that are covered by the law must establish and implement a vigilance plan that identifies and prevents risks of serious violations of human rights and fundamental freedoms and the health and safety of persons and the environment resulting, directly or indirectly, from the operations of the company or the entities it controls, directly or indirectly, or the operations of subcontractors and suppliers with whom it maintains an established commercial relationship.[26] The vigilance plan must be publicly disclosed and drafted by collaborating with the relevant stakeholders. In the case of entities with multiple subsidiaries, it envisages a multiparty collaborative process involving all relevant subsidiaries at territorial level. An appropriate vigilance plan is drafted, preferably by engaging all the relevant 'stakeholders',[27] has five elements and includes: *a risk mapping* that identifies, analyses and ranks the relevant risks; *procedures to regularly assess* – in accordance with the risk mapping – the situation of subsidiaries, subcontractors or suppliers with whom the company maintains an established commercial relationship; *appropriate action* to mitigate the

organisations (NGOs) Sherpa, Terre Solidaire and the Business and Human Rights Centre: Duty of Vigilance Radar – List of Companies Subject to the Duty of Vigilance, available at https://vigilance-plan.org/ (accessed 6 October 2021). As identified by other authors, there are other interpretative difficulties with the Vigilance Law that continue to persist, chiefly among those being its ambit *rationae personae* and *rationae materiae*, the meaning of an 'established commercial relationship', etc. In this context, see Stéphane Brabant, Elsa Savourey and Charlotte Michon, 'The Vigilance Plan: Cornerstone of the Law of the Law on the Corporate Duty of Vigilance', originally published in the International Review of Compliance and Business Ethics [Revue Internationale de la Compliance et de l'Ethique des Affaires] in December 2017, with an English translation available with the Business and Human Rights Resource Centre, available at www.business-humanrights.org/en/latest-news/frances-law-on-the-corporate-duty-of-vigilance-a-practical-and-multidimensional-analysis-in-english/ (accessed 6 October 2021), where the authors rightly suggest that where there is potential for ambiguity, reference should be made to international standards such as the United Nations Guiding Principles on Business and Human Rights (UNGPs), which should be used as a benchmark.

25 Brabant, Stéphane and Elsa Savourey (2017): "Le Champ de La Loi. Les Sociétés Soumises Aux Obligations de Vigilance", *Revue Internationale de la Compliance et de l'Ethique des Affaires*. English translation available with the Business and Human Rights Resource Centre, available at www.business-humanrights.org/en/latest-news/frances-law-on-the-corporate-duty-of-vigilance-a-practical-and-multidimensional-analysis-in-english/ (accessed 6 October 2021).

26 Law No. 2017–399 (27 March 2017) on the Duty of Care of Parent Companies and Ordering Companies Article L. 225–102–4. – I.

27 For an analysis of the possible meaning of 'stakeholder' in the Vigilance Law, see Tiphaine Beau de Loménie and Sandra Cossart, 'Parties Prenantes et Devoir de Vigilance' [2017] Revue Internationale de la Compliance et de l'Ethique des Affaires. English translation available with the Business and Human Rights Resource Centre, available at www.business-humanrights.org/en/latest-news/frances-law-on-the-corporate-duty-of-vigilance-a-practical-and-multidimensional-analysis-in-english/ (accessed 6 October 2021), which clarifies that while France's Constitutional Court approved the presence of the word 'stakeholders' in the Vigilance Law, specifically because this process of engagement was not made mandatory, their implication in the creation of the vigilance plan is 'anything but trivial and remains the responsibility of the companies'.

risks or to prevent serious violations; an ***alert mechanism***, which is developed in partnership with the trade union organisation representatives, that collects the reporting of existing or actual risks; and ***a monitoring scheme*** for the purpose of following up on the measures implemented and assessing their efficiency.[28] Companies that need to publish or implement vigilance plans are given a three months formal notice to comply with the legal requirements; if they fail to do so, they may be subject to a court ordered injunction or penalties.[29] The Vigilance Law allows for the commencement of civil actions in tort so harmed individuals may make a claim for damages that results from a company's failure to comply with any legal requirements therein and where such compliance would have prevented the harm.[30] The Vigilance Law does not expressly mention SOEs in its text, so for its provisions to be applicable to a SOE, the conditions discussed here concerning registration, corporate form and number of employees would also have to be satisfied, meaning that the Vigilance Law does not offer blanket coverage to all SOEs, but only those of a certain size.

3 Case studies

For the purposes of the case studies, the general quality of the vigilance plans published and implemented by EDF and Air France-KLM will be assessed. The choice of corporations has largely been based on the size of a particular entity and the number of countries it operates in (an important factor to consider in the analysis of the relationship between parent company and subsidiaries), as well as diverse sectors of operation. The ultimate aim is to provide the reader with a snapshot view of how the Duty of Vigilance Law is implemented by certain SOEs that operate in different countries and in different economic sectors. Additionally, in the case of EDF, the change in status from a public undertaking to a limited liability company has also been a factor that has been taken into consideration, while in the case of Air France-KLM, its multi-sovereign ownership structure was factored in as an element when making this choice.

The case studies thus seek to answer the following questions: 1) Is the plan published in a stand-alone, formalized and accessible manner? 2) Does the plan clearly cover the parent company and its subsidiaries? Does it present the consolidation method that allows precise identification of the subsidiaries? 3) Does the plan demonstrate the integration of subcontractors and suppliers of the parent company and controlled companies within the scope of vigilance? Does it allow them to be identified precisely? 4) Does the plan clearly cover the risks of serious violations of human rights, the environment and health and safety? Does it identify the benchmarks of the company? 5) Does the plan

28 Law No. 2017–399 (27 March 2017) on the Duty of Care of Parent Companies and Ordering Companies Article L. 225–102–4. – I.

29 Ibid., Article L 225–102–4. I.

30 Ibid., Article L. 225–102–5.

identify the stakeholders of the company? Does it present the methodology of their consultation, as well as the results of the latter? 6) Does the plan outline the initiatives in which the company is involved? If applicable, does it indicate the company's level of involvement in them as well as the objectives pursued? 7) Is the vigilance plan updated on a regular basis? Is there a whistleblowing system in place? Are there any operational grievance mechanisms in place?[31]

3.1 Électricité de France (EDF)

EDF is a French multinational electric utility company whose main business is electricity generation, building transmission and distribution networks, providing energy to customers and engaging in energy trading.[32] The company is majority owned by the French state (83.68%), with the remaining share capital being split between institutional retail investors (14.94%) and EDF employees (1.36%).[33] The company is headquartered in France, but it has partners and affiliates throughout Europe (in France, the United Kingdom, Italy, Belgium, Greece, the Netherlands, Germany, Portugal, Switzerland and Poland), the Americas (the United States, Brazil, Canada, Chile and Mexico), the Middle East (Turkey, Israel and the United Arab Emirates), Africa (South Africa and Egypt) and Asia (China, Laos, Vietnam and India).[34] It generated approximately €69 billion in sales in 2020, employs 165,200 people throughout the world, has a research and development budget of approximately €685 million and claims that approximately 90% of its electricity production is free of CO_2.[35] The company's raison d'être was recently changed to read: 'to build a net zero energy future with electricity and innovative solutions and services, to help us save the planet and drive well-being and economic development', a statement that is now part of its Articles of Association.[36]

The company has a long and complex history, having been created in 1946 by law[37] as a public undertaking (Public and Industrial Commercial

31 Some of the questions asked in this methodology have been proposed by the non-governmental organisations Sherpa, Terre Solidaire and the Business and Human Rights Centre, and this methodology has been consistently used in the assessment of the vigilance plans of several hundred companies that report under the Vigilance Law. For further information see "Duty of Vigilance Radar – List of Companies Subject to the Duty of Vigilance", available at https://vigilance-plan.org/ (accessed 15 November 2021).

32 "EDF at a Glance" (*EDF France*), available at www.edf.fr/en/the-edf-group/edf-at-a-glance (accessed 4 November 2021).

33 "EDF 2020 Facts and Figures", p. 53, available at www.edf.fr/en/the-edf-group/dedicated-sections/investors-shareholders/financial-and-extra-financial-performance/edf-group-s-facts-and-figures (accessed 4 November 2021).

34 "EDF at a Glance" (n 31), p. 59.

35 "EDF 2020 Facts and Figures" (n 32), p. 59.

36 "EDF Universal Registration Document 2020", p. 198, available at https://labrador.cld.bz/EDF-2020-Universal-Registration-Document/198/ (accessed 9 November 2021).

37 Law No. 46–628 (8 April 1946), available at www.legifrance.gouv.fr/loda/id/JORFTEXT000000868448/ (accessed 4 November 2021).

Establishment or EPIC)[38] after the nationalisation of approximately 1,700 smaller energy producers and transporters, and it enjoyed a monopoly in electricity generation until 1999, when it was mandated by the EU[39] to open up 20% of its business to competition.[40] After the 1946 nationalisation, one of the first tasks of EDF was the unification and standardisation of the power distribution network, with the second being to meet the rapid growth of the electricity market and consumption through dam building.[41] In 2004, EDF was converted from an EPIC to a limited liability company (Société Anonyme), governed by a board of directors, with the chairman and chief executive officer appointed by the French Council of Ministers following a proposal from the board of directors.[42] Unless expressly specified in the Commercial Code, the Energy Code, Order No. 2014–948[43] or its articles of association, the company is governed by the laws applicable to commercial companies. The 2004 law also stipulates that the French state must hold at least 70% of the capital and the voting rights.[44] While this change in legal status has allowed the company to broaden its commercial offer beyond solely supplying electricity,[45] and it signed a public service contract for an unlimited period of time with the French State, which establishes the terms and conditions for carrying out its public service missions (including the development of a balanced supply of electricity from various sources, including renewables),[46] being an

38 Public Industrial and Commercial Establishments (établissement public à caractère industriel et commercial, also found in literature under the abbreviation EPIC) are a special type of public undertaking, which, according to Article 34 of the French Constitution, can only be created by Parliament through a special law.

39 Directive 96/92/EC of the European Parliament and of the Council of 19 December 1996 (the 'Electricity Directive').

40 "Legal Status" (*EDF France*, 23 March 2015), available at www.edf.fr/en/the-edf-group/dedicated-sections/investors-shareholders/legal-status (accessed 19 September 2021); "EDF 2020 Facts and Figures" (n 32), p. 8; Law No. 2006-1537 (7 December 2006); Law No. 2004-803 (9 August 2004), available at www.legifrance.gouv.fr/loda/id/JORFTEXT000000868448/ (accessed 8 November 2021).

41 "History" (*EDF France*, 5 May 2015), available at www.edf.fr/en/the-edf-group/edf-at-a-glance/history (accessed 4 November 2021).

42 Law No. 2004-803 (9 August 2004). See also the Company's Articles of Association as approved by Decree 2004–1224 (17 November 2004) and Law No. 2004-803 (9 August 2004). For a summary on relevant provisions see Universal Registration Document 2020, available at https://edf.publispeak.com/2020-universal-registration-document/article/510/ (accessed 8 November 2021).

43 Ordinance No. 2014-948 (20 August 2014) on the Governance and Capital Transactions of Companies with State Holdings; Decree No. 2014-949 (20 August 2014).

44 Law No. 2004-803 (9 August 2004) l Article 24.

45 "Legal Status" (n 39).

46 Ibid. Among others, the Public Service Contract deals with the rules of financial compensation for service commitments. The public service mission is stipulated in Article L. 121 to L. 124–5 of the French Energy Code, which states that the public electricity service must provide a balanced supply of electricity, develop and operate public electricity networks and supply electricity at regulated sales tariffs: available at www.legifrance.gouv.fr/codes/texte_lc/LEGITEXT000023983208/ (accessed 8 November 2021). At the same time, development

undertaking majority owned by the State, it still remains subject to special audit procedures.[47]

Given its size, the company is subject to the reporting requirements set out in the Duty of Vigilance Law and it joined the United Nations Global Compact as early as 2001. In 2013 it rolled out its first ethics charter ('Charter'), which is based on the company's core values (respect, solidarity and responsibility) covering the company's human rights obligations.[48] The company has a group ethics and compliance division (GECD), composed of around 50 ethics and compliance officers based at French and international entities, who report directly to the directors of the respective entities and have the means and power to implement and ensure compliance with the relevant programmes and policies.[49] The director of the GECD reports to the general secretary, who is a member of the Group Executive Committee (GEC), while the board of directors (BD), through the Corporate and Social Responsibility Committee, oversees the implementation of ethical and compliance considerations in

---

of a balanced supply of electricity must be compatible with the provisions of Decree No. 2020-457 (21 April 2020) on Greenhouse Gas Emission Targets and the Low Carbon Strategy available at www.legifrance.gouv.fr/jorf/id/JORFTEXT000041814459 (accessed 8 November 2021), while Decree No. 2020–456 (21 April 2020) sets out multi-year energy programmes for the years 2019–2023 and 2024–2028 available at www.legifrance.gouv.fr/jorf/id/JORFTEXT000041814432 (accessed 8 November 2021). Of further interest are Articles L. 121–5 which states that the supply of electricity at regulated tariffs must contribute to social cohesion and Article L. 115–3 of the French Social Action and Families Code, available at www.legifrance.gouv.fr/codes/section_lc/LEGITEXT000006074069/LEGISCTA000006157555/#LEGISCTA000006157555 (accessed 8 November 2021), which prohibits electricity suppliers from cutting off the electricity supplies to primary residences during winter, and Article L. 2224–31 of the French Local Authorities Code (available at www.legifrance.gouv.fr/codes/id/LEGITEXT000006070633/ (accessed 8 November 2021).

47 Decree No. 53-707 (9 August 1953) on State Evaluation of National Public Undertakings and Certain Organisations with an Econmic or Social Component; Decree No. 55–733 (26 May 1955) on State Economic and Financial Evaluation. In addition, EDF must undergo special audit procedures as required by the French General Accounting Office and the Parliament. Its activities as a buyer are governed by the French Public Procurement Code, available at www.legifrance.gouv.fr/codes/id/LEGITEXT000037701019/ (accessed 8 November 2021).

48 "EDF Ethics Charter" (*EDF France*, 3 May 2018), available at www.edf.fr/en/the-edf-group/our-commitments/ethics-compliance/ethics-compliance-policy/respect-for-the-group-s-values (accessed 8 November 2021). This document makes reference to the Universal Declaration of Human Rights (1948), the Convention on the Elimination of All Forms of Discrimination against Women (1979), the International Convention on the Rights of the Child (1989), the OECD Convention on Combating Bribery of Foreign Public Officials in International Business Transactions (1999), ILO Conventions guaranteeing the fundamental principles and rights of employment and fighting against discrimination, the OECD Guidelines for Multinational Enterprises (2011) and the UN Convention against Corruption (2005).

49 "EDF Group Ethics and Compliance Division" (*EDF France*, 26 April 2018), available at www.edf.fr/en/the-edf-group/taking-action-as-a-responsible-company/ethics-and-compliance-programme/the-edf-group-s-commitment-to-ethics-and-compliance (accessed 8 November 2021).

the company.[50] The GECD has set up a company-wide ethics and compliance programme[51] and a company-wide ethics and compliance policy, which in January 2020 included a body of internal rules aimed at ensuring compliance with national and international rules and regulations in 13 different areas: the prevention of corruption and influence peddling;[52] the prevention of conflicts of interest; anti-fraud measures; compliance with international sanctions programmes; prevention of harassment and discrimination; prevention of market abuse; prevention of the risk of money laundering and financing of terrorism; compliance with derivatives reporting regulations; preventing breaches of competition laws; personal data protection; export control regulations; and a duty of care plan, as required by the Vigilance Law.[53]

To comply with its obligations under the Vigilance Law, each year, the company draws up a vigilance plan and reports on the implementation of the previous year's plan, having so far published in its yearly annual report[54] four vigilance plans (which appear to be continuously updated and improved[55]) and reported on the implementation of three others.[56] Although the company presents its vigilance plan in a formalised manner as part of its annual report,

50 Ibid.

51 "EDF Group Ethics and Compliance Programme Implementation", available at www.edf.fr/en/the-edf-group/taking-action-as-a-responsible-company/ethics-and-compliance-programme/the-edf-group-s-commitment-to-ethics-and-compliance (accessed 8 November 2021).

52 See also in this context the requirement of Law No. 2016–1691 (9 December 2016) – Sapin II; "Preventing the Risk of Corruption" (*EDF France*, 4 May 2018), available at www.edf.fr/en/the-edf-group/our-commitments/ethics-compliance/ethics-compliance-policy/preventing-the-risk-of-corruption (accessed 9 November 2021). According to the Sapin II law, companies with more than 500 employees which operate in France and their directors are required to implement a special internal compliance programme to fight corruption and trading in influence. Broadly, the compliance programme is required to have a specific code of conduct which addresses anti-corruption rules and procedures; an internal whistleblowing process; a risk mapping to identify corruption risks based on the country of operation as well as the sector of operation; a due diligence process for clients, suppliers and intermediaries; accounting control procedures; training sessions for employees; a disciplinary system to sanction violations; and an internal control and audit process of the various measures and procedures that have been implemented.

53 "EDF Group Ethics and Compliance Policy 2020", available at www.edf.fr/en/the-edf-group/taking-action-as-a-responsible-company/ethics-and-compliance-programme/the-edf-group-s-commitment-to-ethics-and-compliance (accessed 8 November 2021); "EDF Group's Duty of Vigilance" (*EDF France*, 23 July 2021), available at www.edf.fr/en/the-edf-group/taking-action-as-a-responsible-company/duty-of-vigilance (accessed 19 September 2021).

54 Also known in some years as 'Reference Document' or 'Universal Registration Document'.

55 "EDF Universal Registration Document 2020" (n 35), pp. 202, 203.

56 "EDF 2017 Reference Document", pp. 155–157, available at www.edf.fr/en/the-edf-group/dedicated-sections/investors-shareholders/reference-documents (accessed 9 November 2021); "EDF 2018 Reference Document", pp. 215–217, available at www.edf.fr/en/the-edf-group/dedicated-sections/investors-shareholders/reference-documents (accessed 9 November 2021); "EDF 2019 Universal Registration Document", pp. 187–191, available at www.edf.fr/en/the-edf-group/dedicated-sections/investors-shareholders/reference-

rather than as a stand-alone document, the vigilance plan is easily accessible on the company's website and appears to be drawn within the framework of several international standards, such as the United Nations Guiding Principles on Business and Human Rights (UNGPs), the OECD Guidelines for Multinational Enterprises and the core conventions of the International Labour Organisation and the International Bill of Rights. The plan is currently available only in English and French, so a translation into all the languages in which the company currently operates would be welcome. The vigilance plan also appears to be tailored to respond to various on-the-ground conditions. For example, while most of the company's activities are based in OECD countries, in cases in which certain assets and projects are based in countries that are deemed 'higher-risk', special procedures are triggered which are applicable to the entire supply chain.[57] The vigilance plan covers the activities of the company, some of its subsidiaries[58] and those suppliers and contractors with which the company has established commercial relations 'to the extent their activities are related to those relations.'[59] EDF has not published a list of suppliers and subcontractors yet, which is an issue that should be given further attention.

The vigilance plan is prepared by taking into consideration the input of the Duty of Care Committee, the Group Duty of Care Compliance Officer, various corporate divisions[60] and trade union organisations and is based on the following documents: mandatory group policies which are binding on all controlled entities,[61] internal documents that have been made public,[62] external sources in the form of various international standards[63] and the Company's

documents (accessed 9 November 2021); "EDF Universal Registration Document 2020" (n 35), pp. 198–203.

57 "EDF Universal Registration Document 2020" (n 35), p. 198. It is unclear from the text of the Universal Registration Document how EDF determines country risk, so further information in this area would be welcome. Nevertheless, several references to 'OECD countries' and 'non-OECD countries' would appear to suggest that the threshold could be triggered by the presence or lack of OECD membership.

58 Although no exhaustive list of all EDF's subsidiaries has yet been published, some independently managed subsidiaries such as RTE and Enedis (the French power transmission and distribution system operators) appear to publish their own vigilance plans.

59 "EDF Universal Registration Document 2020" (n 35), p. 198.

60 Such as the Sustainable Development Division, Legal Division, Risks Division, Ethics and Compliance Division, Procurement Division, HR Division, International Division and all other EDF Business Divisions heading up projects in France or abroad.

61 Such as those relating to risk management and internal control, the governance of subsidiaries and holdings, project management, ethics and compliance, sustainable development, health and safety and procurement.

62 For example, the Company's Ethics Charter, the Code of Conduct for Ethics and Compliance, Sustainable Development Charter for Suppliers, Global Framework Agreement on Corporate Social Responsibility.

63 UN Global Compact, UNGPs, OECD Guidelines for Multinational Enterprises, World Business Council for Sustainable Development CEO Guide to Human Rights, the core conventions of the International Labour Organization, the Convention on the Elimination of All Forms of Discrimination against Women (1979), the International Convention on the Rights

reference framework.[64] While there is indeed reference to various international standards, the company does not expressly clarify whether the intention is to respect all the human rights that those standards address or only some of them. The same issue was encountered in relation to environmental, health and safety standards and to the company's membership in various sectoral and regional initiatives, such as those dealing with the responsible sourcing of minerals.[65] For example, the company could also clarify the extent to which Regulation (EU) 2017/821 of the European Parliament and of the Council of 17 May 2017, laying down supply chain due diligence obligations for EU importers of tin, tantalum and tungsten; their ores; and gold originating from conflict-affected and high-risk areas is applicable to its operations.

Country-specific risks and cultural peculiarities appear to be taken into consideration in three broad areas: risks of harm to communities, indigenous peoples and vulnerable groups; risks due to working conditions, including forced labour and child labour; and risks relating to the practices of security services providers.[66] Various internal stakeholders (the company's trade unions and two international trade union federations) have been engaged in the preparation of the vigilance plan, but there is a need for further clarification of whether other external stakeholders have been engaged in this process at all.[67] A more precise identification and consultation process with internal and external stakeholders could potentially avoid the repeat of a situation such as that present in Mexico, whereby representatives of the local community of Union Hidalgo and several non-governmental organisations have commenced legal proceedings in France under the Vigilance Law against EDF, claiming a violation of the right to free, prior and informed consent.[68] EDF has also decided to abandon a plan concerning a wind turbine project in China as the 'production capacity was not consistent with the number of families that would have to be displaced'.[69]

---

of the Child (1989), Global Reporting Initiative (GRI), Supplier Relations and Responsible Procurement Label (RF&AR).

64 "EDF 2019 Universal Registration Document" (n 55), p. 198.

65 For an in-dept analysis concerning the quality of the company's vigilance measures relating to the use of minerals necessary for the energy transition, see "EDF: Quality of Vigilance Measures in the Company's Value Chain Relating to the Use of Minerals Necessary for the Energy Transition", available at https://plan-vigilance.org/company/electricite-de-france-edf/ (accessed 11 November 2021).

66 "EDF 2019 Universal Registration Document" (n 55), p. 199.

67 For example, the identification of various internal and external stakeholders appears to be dealt with in other sections of the annual report, such as those involving corporate social responsibility or responsible development, rather than under the section dealing with the mandatory vigilance plan. See, in this context, "EDF 2019 Universal Registration Document" (n 55), pp. 130, 143, 178–179.

68 "Lawsuit Filed Against EDF for Alleged Failure to Respect French Duty of Vigilance Law Over Wind Project in Mexico" (*Business & Human Rights Resource Centre*, 13 October 2020), available at www.business-humanrights.org/pt/%C3%BAltimas-not%C3%ADcias/devoir-de-vigilance-edf-assign%C3%A9-en-justice-pour-ses-activit%C3%A9s-au-mexique/ (accessed 11 November 2021).

69 "EDF Universal Registration Document 2020" (n 35), p. 205.

The company claims that the risks covered under the vigilance plan meet the criteria for 'salient risks' according to the UNGPs, and the process for identifying and prioritising risks is carried out by 'each Group entity' and is based on two complementary approaches: a 'general risk mapping' (which includes the iteration of several risks relating to the duty of care standard required by the Vigilance Law, such as ethics and compliance risks, climate change risks, industrial safety risk, the management of large projects and their impact on human rights and the operational continuity of supply chains and contractual relationships) and an 'additional risk mapping' (which specifically focuses on the duty of care standard required under the Vigilance Law and addresses operations and projects 'in the field' as well as an interim summary in which each entity, on the basis of the 'field" risk assessment, identifies and assesses exposures to potential human rights violations).[70] Although the risk mapping process can be considered adequate, it is vague in several places, and additional details (e.g., the provision of a list of the main suppliers and subcontractors[71] and a more detailed presentation of the risk mapping and procedures for its regular updating) would improve the overall quality of the vigilance plan.

The company has in place a single whistleblowing system that covers reporting under the Sapin II Law and the Vigilance Law, as well as allegations of harassment and discrimination, with the GECD being the first point of contact in the system.[72] The company has reported that its whistleblowing system is managed via an independent platform that is not connected with its internet system but may be accessed anytime via its website, with the interface being available in several languages, allowing group employees, external staff or occasional employees and third parties to anonymously (in countries where this is allowed) report wrongdoing of which the EDF group or its staff are the culprits or victims.[73] After a complaint has been submitted, the next step in the process is an analysis of its admissibility, which is usually processed within 72 hours from receipt and involves an investigation whether the facts are 'well-founded or not'.[74] Once a ruling has been made on admissibility, the whistleblower is informed of the protective measures from which they benefit under the relevant laws.[75] After a particular complaint passes the admissibility stage, a case

70 "EDF 2019 Universal Registration Document" (n 55), p. 199.

71 "EDF Universal Registration Document 2020" (n 35), pp. 184–186. The sections deal with responsible procurement strategies and practices, its coal and uranium supply chain and responsible subcontracting.

72 Ibid., p. 202. Given that the subsidiaries Enedis and RTE operate in the regulated sector, they have their own whistleblowing in place in order to maintain their managerial independence.

73 Ibid.

74 Ibid.

75 Ibid. For example, such measures could be legal protections under the Sapin II Law, under the French Labour Code, etc. and vary according to the status of the person making the complaint (victim, witness, individual, corporation, etc.), their relationship to the company (employee, external service provider, third party, etc.) and the issue at stake (e.g. fraud, harassment, environmental damage).

manager is appointed to conduct further investigations and draws up a report, which will include an action plan. The implementation of the action plan is monitored by the ethics and compliance department.[76] Although the whistle-blowing system appears to be comprehensive, further detail would be welcome concerning the time frames for the processing of the admissible reports and the implementation of the action plans, as well as the appointment procedures for staff handling the complaints. Various systems have been created by the company for monitoring the implementation and effectiveness of the measures taken, such as the appointment of a companywide duty of care compliance officer, who liaises with various other departments[77] in the company for this purpose and is further supported by a network of duty of care" officers.

3.2 *The Air France-KLM Group*

Air France traces its roots back to 1933, when the private airlines existent at that time[78] were nationalised and amalgamated into a new entity called Air France (the 1933 Air France).[79] This entity was later incorporated by the Vichy Air Ministry into the Air Transport Administration, but by July 1945, a new entity had been created (the 1945 Air France), wherein the State became the sole shareholder and remained so until 1999, when Air France listed its shares on the Paris Stock Exchange.[80] Currently, the Air France-KLM Group (Air France-KLM, the Group) is a Franco-Dutch airline holding company incorporated under French law and is the result of a merger in 2004 between Air France and the Dutch state-owned carrier KLM. The Group holds particularly relevance for the purpose of this chapter, due to its multi-sovereign ownership, which currently stands at French state (14.29%); Dutch state (14%); China Eastern Airlines (8.8%).[81]

The Group is subject to the obligations imposed by the Vigilance Law[82] and has responded to these regulatory changes having so far published in its

76 Ibid. For example, such measures could be legal protections under the Sapin II Law, under the French Labour Code, etc. and vary according to the status of the person making the complaint (victim, witness, individual, corporation, etc.), their relationship to the company (employee, external service provider, third party, etc.) and the issue at stake (e.g. fraud, harassment, environmental damage).

77 Such as the Sustainable Development Department, the Legal Department, the Group Ethics and Compliance Department and any other departments and subsidiaries affected.

78 Air Union, Air Orient, Société Générale de Transport Aérien (SGTA), CIDNA and Aéropostale.

79 Chadeau (n 2), pp. 188–189.

80 "History" (*Air France KLM*, 26 November 2014), available at www.airfranceklm.com/en/group/history (accessed 29 October 2021).

81 "Air France-KLM 2020 Universal Registration Document" (2020), p. 124, available at www.airfranceklm.com/en/finance/publications (accessed 15 November 2021).

82 The Dutch Child Labour Due Diligence Law, which was due to come into effect in mid-2022, will also be applicable to the operations of the Group, available at https://zoek.officielebekendmakingen.nl/stb-2019-401.html (accessed 21 February 2022).

yearly annual report three vigilance plans which are updated and appear to be improved from year to year and reported on the implementation of two others.[83] In its annual reports, the Group deals with its reporting obligations under the Vigilance Law via a special section that sits under the broader theme of corporate social responsibility, rather than as a stand-alone document.[84] The annual reports are available in English and French, easily accessible on the Group's website and have been drawn up within the framework of several international standards such as the ten principles of the Global Compact (which it joined in 2003), the Universal Declaration of Human Rights, the OECD Guidelines for Multinational Enterprises, the core conventions of the International Labour Organisations and the Children's Rights and Business Principles,[85] as well as internal policy documents such as the Air France-KLM Principles which are aligned with the UNGPs,[86] with the Group having started to take specific actions in this area in 2003.[87]

It is not specified, however, whether the intention of the Group is to respect all the human rights that are included in those standards or only some, and further clarification in this area is desirable. No list of subsidiaries could be located yet, but the Group has stated that it 'delegates to its subsidiaries the responsibility of respecting and promoting the content of these commitments locally', whilst paying due regard to 'national provisions and legislation specific to each country'.[88] During its risk-mapping process, the Group has expressly

83 "Air France-KLM 2018 Registration Document" (2018), available at www.airfranceklm.com/en/publications/2018-registration-document (accessed 15 November 2021); "Air France – KLM 2019 Universal Registration Document", available at www.airfranceklm.com/en/system/files/universalregistrationdocument2019va.pdf (accessed 15 November 2021); "Air France-KLM 2020 Universal Registration Document" (n 80).

84 "Air France-KLM 2018 Registration Document" (n 81), pp. 147–196; "Air France-KLM 2019 Universal Registration Document" (n 81), pp. 155–215; "Air France-KLM 2020 Universal Registration Document" (n 80), pp. 161–230. The Group's corporate social responsibility chapter, which is a legal requirement under the French Code of Commerce (Article L. 225-102-1), is consistent from year to year and deals with topics such as creating long term value for all stakeholders (presentation of the business model, identification of the key priorities for building long-term relationships and the role of business responsibility); human resources (working conditions and employee engagement; resource adaptation and employee dialogue; development of human capital and talent management; diversity and equality; and health, safety and quality of life in the workplace); environmental impact (carbon emissions, noise and air quality, waste and the circular economy and biodiversity); customer trust (operational safety for stakeholders, confidentiality and data protection, accessibility of products and services); ethics and compliance (company reference texts, human rights, business ethics); and societal value (local development, sustainable procurement and reporting under the Vigilance Law).

85 "Air France-KLM 2020 Universal Registration Document" (n 80), p. 219.

86 "Air France-KLM Principles" (2020), available at https://sustainabilityreport2019.airfranceklm.com/air-france-klm-principles/ (accessed 15 November 2021). The 'Air France-KLM Principles' are an update of the Group's Social Rights and Ethics Charter.

87 "Air France-KLM", available at https://sustainabilityreport2020.airfranceklm.com/en/english-ethics/ (accessed 15 November 2021).

88 "Air France-KLM 2020 Universal Registration Document" (n 80), p. 228.

identified several areas which bear human rights risks, such as procurement, the environment, the health and safety of individuals, equal opportunity and diversity, achieving a better work/life balance and data protection procedures for its customers and employees, and it runs awareness-raising actions for its employees on human trafficking and other forms of human exploitation.[89]

While the Group employs people largely from France and the Netherlands,[90] it expressly undertakes to apply the labour legislation of the European Union and its member states and all national collective agreements and to respect the exercise of trade union rights in all relevant countries.[91] This risk mapping is presented as a stand-alone section in the corporate social responsibility chapter and also in the Vigilance Law section, in parts dealing specifically with human rights and fundamental liberties, health and safety, environment and the supply chain.[92] A specific human rights risk-mapping section would be welcome in the Vigilance Law section itself, rather than having to cross-reference to other chapters and sections. Alternatively, a detailed human rights risks section could be included in Chapter 3 of the annual report, which deals specifically with risk and risk management.

On the board of directors, the Group has a Sustainable Development and Compliance Committee that, twice yearly, reviews risks related to climate change and the remedial measures in place to address them.[93] Similarly to EDF, the Group also has obligations under anti-corruption laws and anti-competitive behaviour, having developed several internal policies in this area.[94]

The Group is heavily dependent on procurement, which represents around €13 billion per year.[95] Although the Group does not disclose a detailed supplier list, a responsible procurement policy is in place, and all suppliers are invited to sign the Group's Sustainable Development Charter.[96] The responsible procurement policy is composed of several steps. First is the initial supplier referencing process, and assuming suppliers pass this stage, they are then invited to sign the Sustainable Development Charter (which is based on the principles of the UN Global Compact) and a supplier code of conduct or to provide their own equivalent document, which may be approved following analysis; the tender documents, which lists the criteria enabling the evaluation of the environmental impact of the product or service; and, ultimately,

89 Ibid., p. 219.

90 Ibid., p. 182. See breakdown: Continental France: 50,403 people; The Netherlands: 31,609 people; Europe (other): 3,116 people; North & South America: 1,848 people; Caribbean/ Indian Ocean: 695 people; Asia/Pacific: 1,654 people and Africa/Middle East 1,061 people.

91 Ibid., p. 228.

92 Ibid., pp. 228–229.

93 Ibid., pp. 168, 189–195.

94 See the Anti-Bribery Manual and the Gift & Hospitality Policy both available at https://sustainabilityreport2020.airfranceklm.com/en/english-ethics/ (accessed 15 November 2021).

95 Representing largely fuel purchasing, aircraft maintenance and components, airport and navigation fees and airport handling.

96 Ibid., p. 219.

the supplier contracts, which include an ethical and environmental clause.[97] The Group uses country/sector risk-mapping processes, which are evaluated independently,[98] and it identifies its stakeholders as its employees, shareholders, customers, suppliers, authorities, local communities and other players in the civil society such as NGOs.[99] While the Group has whistleblowing procedures in place, these matters are not comprehensively dealt with in the section dealing with the Vigilance Law, so further detail in these areas would be welcome.[100] The Group states that it regularly evaluates the perception of its stakeholders, and it has a number of feedback channels in place enabling stakeholders (particularly employees, customers and local residents around airports) to communicate complaints, but it is not clear where these systems are, how they can be accessed or the indicative timelines for resolving operational level grievances.

4 Conclusion

State corporate ownership has a long history in France, and its relevance continues at present, with some of the largest French companies that operate in strategic sectors remaining state-owned. The regulatory framework distinguishes between non-trade activities and trade activities, but this distinction is fluid and has been susceptible to change over time, as has the definition of what constitutes a SOE. Overall, in France, SOEs often enjoy a hybrid legal status, and the regulatory framework for SOEs has been built at the intersection of two conflicting goals of general interest: the achievement of social, economic and societal goals and free market competition. For certain SOEs, the Duty of Vigilance Law is currently the most important tool for addressing human rights concerns. The Vigilance Law was, at the time of its enactment, the first comprehensive and legally binding human rights due diligence worldwide that imposed obligations on parent companies to identify and prevent adverse human rights and environmental impacts which are either a consequence of their own activities or the activities of entities that they control or result from certain commercial relationships involving subcontractors and suppliers. The Vigilance Law hardens corporate accountability norms and poses challenges to the limited liability and separation doctrines. However, challenges persist about how the requirements of this law are actually understood by corporations. For this purpose, the Vigilance Law requires that companies which fall within its sphere of application prepare a vigilance plan with the involvement of all relevant stakeholders. Such a plan must include a human rights risk-mapping assessment; the creation of relevant procedures to regularly assess the situation of subsidiaries, subcontractors or suppliers with

97 "Air France-KLM 2020 Universal Registration Document" (n 80), p. 226.

98 Ibid.

99 Ibid., p. 162.

100 Ibid., 229.

whom the company maintains an established commercial relationship; appropriate action to mitigate risks or to prevent serious violations; and the creation of alert mechanisms and monitoring schemes for the purpose of following up on the measures implemented.

The case studies analysed the quality of the vigilance plans published by EDF and Air France-KLM. On the one hand, the overall conclusion that can be drawn is that the requirements of the Vigilance Law appear to be understood differently by corporates, and currently, there does not appear to be a solid baseline from which to start an assessment of the quality of the vigilance plans. For example, gaps have been identified in both case studies in relation to the disclosure of the relevant subsidiaries, the disclosure of the suppliers list, the identification of relevant stakeholders, the procedures that are in place to continuously assess the situation of subsidiaries and suppliers and those relating to the alert mechanisms, operational-level grievance mechanisms and the monitoring schemes of the vigilance plan itself. The cross-references in the Vigilance Law section to other sections that deal with corporate social responsibility issues are also problematic, given that the Vigilance Law uses human rights language, rather than corporate social responsibility terminology. On the other hand, the Vigilance Law is still relatively new, and it has been a learning exercise for all involved. Evidence of this is the length of the vigilance plans examined in this chapter, which appear to be longer and more comprehensive from year to year, demonstrating that while it may be a while before a certain minimum qualitative baseline emerges, the course appears to have been set in the right direction. Government commitment to the implementation of the Vigilance Law, accompanied by strong monitoring and enforcement mechanisms could also iron out these initial 'teething' issues.

9 Chinese state-owned companies and investment in Latin America and Europe

Larry Catá Backer (白 轲)[1]

中央企业境外投资应当遵循以下原则：＊ ＊ ＊ （二）依法合规。遵守我国和投资所在国（地区）法律法规、商业规则和文化习俗，合规经营，有序发展 [The overseas investment of central enterprises shall follow the following principles: . . . (2) Compliance with laws and regulations. Abide by the laws and regulations, business rules and cultural customs of my country and the country (region) where the investment is located, operate in compliance with regulations, and develop in an orderly manner.][2]

对于境外特别重大投资项目，中央企业应建立投资决策前风险评估制度，委托独立第三方有资质咨询机构对投资所在国（地区）政治、经济、社会、文化、市场、法律、政策等风险做全面评估。[For particularly major overseas investment projects, central enterprises should establish a pre-investment risk assessment system and entrust an independent third-party qualified consulting agency to conduct a comprehensive assessment evaluation of the political, economic, social, cultural, market, legal, and policy risks of the country (region) where the investment is located.][3]

In all contexts, business enterprises should: (a) Comply with all applicable laws and respect internationally recognized human rights, wherever they operate; (b) Seek ways to honour the principles of internationally recognized human rights when faced with conflicting requirements; (c) Treat the risk of causing or contributing to gross human rights abuses as a legal compliance issue wherever they operate.[4]

SOEs should observe high standards of responsible business conduct, including with regards to the environment, employees, public health and safety, and human rights. Their actions should be guided by relevant international standards,

1 An earlier version was first presented at the Workshop–Book Project: "Human Rights and environmental sustainability in state-owned enterprises in Latin America and Europe" (21 September 2021), with great thanks to Markus Krajewski and Judith Schönsteiner for their organization and the vision around which this project was organized.

2 China State-Owned Assets Supervision and Administration Commission of the State Council (SASAC), Measures for the Supervision and Administration of Overseas Investment by Central Enterprises (18 January 2017) [国务院国有资产监督管理委员会 中央企业境外投资监督管理办法], art. 6(2) (hereafter, Measures for Supervision of Overseas Investment 2017).

3 Ibid., art. 25.

4 UN Office of the High Commissioner for Human Rights (2011): Guiding Principles for Business and Human Rights: Implementing the United Nations 'Protect, Respect, and Remedy' Framework (New York and Geneva: United Nations) (hereafter "UNGP").

DOI: 10.4324/9781003291428-9

including: the OECD Guidelines for Multinational Enterprises, which have been adopted by all OECD member countries.[5]

1 Introduction: Scope of inquiry: Chinese SOEs, human rights, and sustainability

The Chinese state-owned enterprise (CSOE) presents an anomaly in the operation of the well-ordered construction of a self-referencing and closed system of liberal democratic internationalism, especially as that system touches on business responsibilities under national and international human rights and environmental law and market-driven norms. That anomaly is perhaps quite clearly evident in the application of international framework systems.[6] The anomaly is sourced from the increasingly distinct and autonomous framework principles emerging as between liberal democratic and Marxist-Leninist systems, within which it is possible to develop conduct-based systems respectful of both human and environmental rights. Anomaly produces deviation in theory and practice. That deviation is commonly measured in the distance between that anomalous concept (Marxist-Leninist) and practice from the at-times rough consensus of what is thought of as the common (liberal democratic) standard. Marxist-Leninist *anomalia*, especially that which has developed in the 21st century and embodied in the CSOE, produces regulatory and operational friction in two distinct fields of governance at the heart of the UNGPs. The first is formal, identified with the UNGP's first pillar: State Duty to Respect Human Rights (and its balancing of the authority of national and international law and norms).[7] These are the terrains of public law. The second is identified with the UNGP's second pillar: Corporate Responsibility to Respect Human Rights (and its private law–based market- driven internationalism).[8] It exists as well in the distance between the OECD-SOE principles of distinguishing between public and economic objectives in advancing the ideal of more or less open borders as a function of level playing field principles.[9] And it is augmented by the OECD-MNE framework that generalizes OECD-SE principles.[10] That

5 Organization for Economic Cooperation and Development (2015): OECD Guidelines on Corporate Governance of State-Owned Enterprises (Paris: OECD), Annotations to Chapter V: Stakeholder relations and responsible business, p. 60 (hereafter OECD-SOE).

6 Perhaps principal among them in the discourse, the UNGPs, the OECD-SOE, and the Organization for Economic Cooperation and Development (2011): OECD Guidelines for Multinational Enterprises (Paris: OECD) (hereafter OECD-MNE).

7 UNGP, supra, Principles 1–10.

8 Ibid., Principles 11–24.

9 On one expression of the Chinese variation, Larry Catá Backer, 对各类市场主体一视同仁 ["Treat All Market Players Equally"]: Developing the Formal Legal Framework for Markets-Based Activities in China, Law at the End of the Day (23 October 2019); available at https://lcbackerblog.blogspot.com/2019/10/treat-all-market-players-equally.html (accessed 9 August 2023).

10 Canadian National Contact Point: Final Statement on the Request for Review regarding the Operations of China Gold International Resources Corp. Ltd., at the Copper Polymetallic

friction is especially augmented where the public and private spheres meet[11] – incarnated as the state-owned enterprise, the operational premises of which are also divided by ideological basis between the expectations of a liberal democratic sensibility and those of (Chinese) Marxist-Leninism.[12]

In the early decades of the 21st century, it was possible to finesse difference. During that period, the liberal democratic vision of SOE conduct, of human rights, of internationalism, and of environmental policy and sustainability could suppose itself unchallenged. And that self-reflexive stance was indeed much in evidence in the liberal democratic heartland during those first two decades of this century. The assumption, almost uncontested and accelerated after 1989, was that all states, irrespective of their governing ideologies, would be required, one way or another, to receive and conform to the ordering principles of liberal democratic internationalism and their manifestations in rights regimes.[13] In the context of Chinese economic interaction, it was most visible in the context of projecting liberal democratic human rights sensibilities into China through the private law governance regimes of foreign multinational enterprises operating in Chinese territory[14] and in the use of public law administrative and regulatory extraterritorialism through projects like the once well-discussed "Brussels Effect."[15]

But beneath the surface of this converging internationalism, the currents of opposition were becoming increasingly evident. One more benign strain was interpretive – it signaled adherence to the core documents and principles of internationalism, including those which centered human rights but insisted on interpretive flexibility.[16] The other presented a more fundamental

Mine at the Gyama Valley, Tibet Autonomous Region (April 8, 2015); available at www.international.gc.ca/trade-agreements-accords-commerciaux/ncp-pcn/statement-gyama-valley.aspx?lang=eng (accessed 9 August 2023).

11 See, e.g., Holland, Tom, "China's 'Go Out' Policy Means Trouble," *South China Morning Post* (26 April 2007) ("In recent years Chinese state-backed companies have bolstered their chances of winning lucrative resource contracts by pledging to invest generously in local infrastructure in countries where few other businesses would dare venture. . . . By extending no strings attached loans to African governments, Beijing has also been accused of undermining international efforts to promote sound governance." Ibid.).

12 Catá Backer, Larry (2017): "The Human Rights Obligations of State-Owned Enterprises (SOEs): Emerging Conceptual Structures and Principles in National and International Law and Policy", *Vanderbilt Journal of Transnational Law*, Vol. 50, No. 4: pp. 827–888.

13 Cf., Langlois, Anthony J. (2001): *The Politics of Justice and Human Rights: Southeast Asia and Universalist Theory* (Cambridge: Cambridge University Press).

14 See, e.g., Catá Backer, Larry (2007): "Economic Globalization and the Rise of Efficient Systems of Global Private Law Making: Wal-Mart as Global Legislator", *Connecticut Law Review*, Vol. 39, No. 4: pp. 1739–1784.

15 Bradford, Anu (2012): "The Brussels Effect", *Northwestern University Law Review*, Vol. 107, No. 1: pp. 1–67.

16 See, e.g., Final Declaration of the Regional Meeting for Asia of the World Conference on Human Rights, Report of the Regional Meeting for Asia of the World Conference on Human Rights, A/Conf.157/ASRM/8; A/Conf.157/PC/59 (29 March – 2 April 1993; Bangkok, Thailand) (hereafter, Bangkok Declaration 1993).

challenge and became inevitable when the People's Republic began operationalizing its post–Mao Zedong era socialist modernization objectives[17] through a Reform and Opening Up Policy,[18] its global manifestation as its "going out" strategy.[19] By 2022, the areas of normative conflict, already smoldering in their post-Soviet manifestation in 1993,[20] produced not just resistance but a more fully formed ideology of socialist human rights[21] as a more specific manifestation of a broader challenge to liberal democratic normative leadership over the narratives of internationalism.[22] At the same time, one saw manifested a

17 Hui, Kao (1991): "A Study of the CCP's Concept of 'Socialist Modernization'", *Issues and Studies*, Vol. 27, No. 7: p. 18.

18 Catá Backer, Larry (2016): "Central Planning Versus Markets Marxism: Their Differences and Consequences for the International Ordering of State, Law, Politics, and Economy", *Connecticut Journal of International Law*, Vol. 32, No. 1: pp. 1–47.

19 Nash, Paul, "China's 'Going Out' Strategy," *Diplomatic Courier* (10 May 2012).

20 Bangkok Declaration 1993, supra.

21 China, State Council of the People's Republic of China (2021), *The Communist Party of China and Human Rights – a 100 Year Quest* (Beijing, State Council Information Office). On its contemporary origins, see Przetacznik, Franciszek (1971): "The Socialist Concept of Protection of Human Rights", *Social Research*, Vol. 38, No. 2: pp. 337–361. For its implications under New Era Marxist-Leninism since 2022, see Catá Backer, Larry, The Rise of Socialist Human Rights–Larry Cata Backer Remarks: "Brief Reflections on the Building of a Theory and Practice of Community with a Shared Future for Mankind and Global Human Rights Governance "[建立具有人类共同未来的社区理论和实践以及全球人权治理的简要思考] (English and Chines Versions), Law at the End of the Day (28 September 2022). It is true that, in some fundamental respects, Soviet-era approaches to internationalism helped forge the foundational premises that contributed to contemporary Chinese human rights – especially its focus on social, economic, and cultural rights on the one hand and its attachment of rights systems to colonial self-determination on the other. See, Weitz, Eric D. (2019): *A World Divided: The Global Struggle for Human Rights in the Age of Nation-States* (Princeton, NJ: Princeton University Press). But as discussed *infra*, the Soviet-era focus on class struggle, proletarian revolution, and the fundamental position that human rights is an expression of the internal competence of states or otherwise bound up in dialectics of class struggle. See, e.g., Szawlowski, Richard (1979): "The International Protection of Human Rights: A Soviet and a Polish View", *The International and Comparative Law Quarterly*, Vol. 28, No. 4: pp. 775–781. That approach has given way to a distinct expression of the basic focus on economic, social, and cultural rights, now coupled with a focus on development and collective stability, along with collective sustainability-based objectives. These are realized not through the Communist International but within the operational structures of the Belt and Road Initiative.

22 习近平：共同构建人类命ff共同体 2021–01–01 [Xi Jinping: Jointly build a community with a shared future for mankind] ("China's plan is to build a community with a shared future for mankind and achieve win-win and shared benefits. . . . The key to building a community with a shared future for mankind lies in action. I believe that the international community should make efforts in terms of partnership, security structure, economic development, civilization exchanges, and ecological construction"); Yi, Wang, "Striding Forward Holding High the Banner of Building a Community with a Shared Future for Mankind," Ministry of Foreign Affairs of the People's Republic of China (1 January 2023); considered in Catá Backer, Larry, 外交部副部长谢锋：推动构建人类命ff共同体是应对世界之变、时代之变、历史之变的中国方案 [Vice Foreign Minister Xie Feng: Promoting the building of a community with a shared future for mankind is China's solution to changes in the world, times, and history], Law at the End of the Day (21 January 2023).

quite robust counter-thrust in the context of Chinese human rights policies and their operationalization in the Xinjiang Uyghur Administrative Region,[23] which itself generated a vigorous pushback.[24] The stakes are high. Control of the narratives of business, the analytics of risk, and the way that human rights and sustainability are embedded in these narratives and risk calculus can help shape the normative-practice environment within which global economic activity can be understood and managed.[25]

It is in this normative environment, one moving further and further from global normative human rights convergence, that one might more effectively consider the tensions and challenges in the human rights and environmental governance of CSOEs. These tensions are manifested within China and its political governance ideology and when CSOEs operate abroad in an ideological ecology the application of which may not be compatible with its own. The excerpts at the start of this chapter sketched out the borders of that terrain: the nature of CSOPEs as both economic and political actors, the different conceptions of the role of the state shareholder in Marxist-Leninist and liberal democratic regimes, the application of notions of sovereignty to hierarchies of law, the spaces for authoritative governance through public or private legal regimes and the now-open contests for the control of the narrative of the SOE when they are projected abroad. CSOEs might be required to obey the laws of the home and host states but not international law, except to the extent that it has been domesticated. The risk analysis expected of CSOEs before projection of operations abroad – political, economic, social, cultural, market, legal, and policy risks – embed international and foreign human rights and environmental norms, but the calculus does not foreground them. The CSOE may be guided by international and multilateral instruments in the calculus of risk and in the formulation of behavior expectations, but it is clear that those will be interpreted within the guiding ideology and political principles of the home state. Nonetheless, it is unlikely that at the level of pragmatics, the differences will be deeply felt in every case of CSOE operations. However, where international and multilateral instruments play a significant role in CSOE

23 Office of the UN High Commissioner for Human Rights, "OHCHR Assessment of Human Rights Concerns in the Xinjiang Uyghur Autonomous Region, People's Republic of China" (31 August 2022), available at www.ohchr.org/sites/default/files/documents/countries/2022-08-31/22-08-31-final-assesment.pdf (accessed 9 August 2023).

24 Permanent Mission of the People's Republic of China to the United Nations Office at Geneva and Other International Organizations in Switzerland, "Fight Against Terrorism and Extremism in Xinjiang: Truth and Facts," No. GJ/56/2022 (31 August 2022) (prepared by the Information Office of the People's Government of Xinjiang Uyghur Autonomous Region, August 2022).

25 This comes as no surprise. John Ruggie understood the importance of narrative in framing what became the UNGPs. See Ruggie, John G. (2013): *Just Business: Multinational Corporations and Human Rights* (New York: W.W. Norton & Co.), p. xxvi. For a perceptive recounting, see Slaughter, Joseph R. (2007): *Human Rights, Inc.: The World Novel, Narrative Form, and International Law* (New York: Fordham University Press).

investment risk calculus, investment protection and exit strategies[26] may serve as the templates rather the capstones of the liberal democratic human-rights architecture for business based on human rights–infused compliance-based prevent-mitigate-remedy principles.[27]

The chapter first situates the CSOE within the political ideology of its home state. The manifestation of Marxist-Leninist ideology now operationalized through the New Era principles, refined and announced at the Communist Party of China's (CPC) 20th Party Congress, shape the relationship of the state to CSOEs, the responsibilities, authorities, and expectations of each in important ways. The theory of CSOEs emerging in the Chinese Leninist New Era from the start of the leadership of Xi Jinping is then considered, situated within the political ideology and objectives of Chinese outbound investment organized through the Belt and Road Initiative (BRI) and its Asian Infrastructure Investment Bank (AIIB) financing mechanism. The object is to focus on China as a home state for outbound investment, with respect to which there appears to be little literature.[28] The chapter then moves from the structure of CSOEs to the human rights structures within which CSOEs are expected to operate. Again, this requires amalgamating political imperative under the leadership of the CPC, with those behaviors identified as human rights. In that context, the chapter considers the shape and consequences of the emerging framework of Chinese human rights internationalism. The chapter then considers applications drawn from CSOE-host state interaction, principally drawing from the experience in Latin America,[29] but also in and Europe. What emerges is closely aligned with the normative framework of CSOEs – the most pronounced effect tends to center on investment decisions closely aligned to state objectives; operationally, CSOEs tend to favor collective (development-oriented) value in assessing human rights effects.

26 This is particularly the case in the context of investment in Belt and Road states, where CSOE investment is framed by the bilateral investment treaties that define the framework of China host state economic relations. See, infra.

27 Consider Fasciglione, Marco (2020): "Implementing 'Responsible Business Conduct' Approaches Under the UN Guiding Principles on Business and Human Rights at the Time of COVID-19", *European Papers*, Vol. 5, No. 3: pp. 1435–1450.

28 "While the rise in Chinese investment in the region is mentioned frequently across the literature, our review did not yield a single work focused on China as a home state." Vizarreta, Cristina Blanco and Weronika Betta (2022): "Business and Human Rights in Latin America: A Systematic Review of Scholarship", *Business and Human Rights Journal*, Vol. 7: pp. 342–274, 361.

29 See Enrique Dussel Peters, Monitor of Chinese OFDI in Latin America and the Caribbean 2023 (15 April 2023) Red Académica de América Latina y el Caribe sobre China, available at www.redalc-china.org/monitor/images/pdfs/menuprincipal/DusselPeters_Monitor-OFDI_2023_Eng.pdf (accessed 9 August 2023). A listing of the 600 investments by Chinese enterprises in Latin America and the Caribbean through early 2023 may be available at www.redalc-china.org/monitor/images/pdfs/menuprincipal/DusselPeters_Monitor_OFDI_Database_2023.xlsx (accessed 9 August 2023).

2 The CSOE in its legal-normative context

The CSOE is a specific, though critically important, manifestation of the organization of governmental power for the achievement of state objectives in the context of economic activities and within markets. CSOEs represent an intermediate step in the core political objective of the state led by its Communist Party vanguard to establish a communist society in China. To that end, a Chinese socialist system was established "governed by a people's democratic dictatorship."[30] The Socialist system incorporates two key fundamental Leninist principles. The first is that "leadership by the Communist Party of China is the determining feature of socialism with Chinese characteristics."[31] The second is that both the CPC and state institutions "shall practice democratic centralism."[32] CSOEs, then, operate within the ordering of Chinese Marxist-Leninism as expressed through law and implemented under the leadership of the vanguard CPC.

Within that broad constraint of constitutionalized political-economy principles, including the fundamental principle of CPC leadership, Marxist principles are then constitutionally rationalized for operationalization within a state system moving towards communism. The grounding principle is the commitment of "socialist public ownership of the means of production."[33] The exercise of public ownership, direct or indirect, has been subject to considerable development since 1949,[34] but the means of *exercise* of ownership has not called into question the grounding principle of public ownership. In the current period of socialist development, and certainly since the reforms post–cultural revolution, there is a constitutionally protected space for a non-state economic sector over which the state exercises oversight and regulation in furtherance of the operation of "the socialist market economy."[35] In the development of the socialist market economy, the "state sector of the economy . . . shall be the leading force in the economy. The state shall ensure

30 Xianfa, art. 1 (1982 as amended) (China). See Zedong, Mao, "On the People's Democratic Dictatorship," Remarks in Commemoration of the 28th Anniversary of the Communist Party of China (30 June 1949); available at www.marxists.org/reference/archive/mao/selected-works/volume-4/mswv4_65.htm (accessed 9 August 2023).

31 Xianfa art. 1 (1982) (China).

32 Ibid., art. 3. See, V.I. Lenin 1965 (1906): "Freedom to Criticise and Unity of Action," in: Lenin (ed.), *Collected Works* (Moscow: Progress Publishers), Vol. 10: pp. 442–443, reproduced in available at www.marxists.org/archive/lenin/works/1906/may/20c.htm (accessed 9 August 2023).

33 Xianfa art 6 (1982) (China).

34 See, e.g., Backer, "Central Planning Versus Markets Marxism," supra.

35 Xianfa, supra, art. 11. See Sigley, Gary (2006): "Chinese Governmentalities: Government, Governance, and the Socialist Market Economy", *Economy & Society*, Vol. 35, No. 4: pp. 487–508; Huang, Philip C. C. (2012): "Profit-Making State Firms and China's Development Experience: 'State Capitalism' or 'Socialist Market Economy'?", *Modern China*, Vol. 38, No. 6: pp. 591–629.

the consolidation and development of the state sector of the economy."[36] Private entities may be managed through regulation, administrative application and compliance programs, and increasingly, the strategic use of "golden shares."[37] While the focus here is on CSOEs, it ought to be borne in mind that state control exists within a broad spectrum of measures of control.

Within this broad constitutionally mandatory set of principles, it is possible to develop the framework within which the contemporary concept of the CSOE can be developed. That framework might fit comfortably within the broad definition for SOEs in the OECD-SOE[38] but not necessarily within its core governance principles.[39] The normative foundation of that framework, as well as the legal structures within which CSOEs are constituted, have been formally expressed through the State-Owned Assets in Enterprises Law (SOAEL).[40] The primary distinction between CSOEs and other operations of states is marked by assets – the CSOE are constituted as vehicles for the management of state assets at the operational level. That is to be distinguished from state organs with a regulatory role and governmental administrative units charged with the development of public policy for purely non-financial objectives in the form of oversight, management, control, or use of the police-prosecutorial power. That regulatory or supervisory role is exercised elsewhere – in the case of CSOEs, by the State-Owned Assets Supervision and Administration Commission (SASAC),[41] an institution directly under the management of the State Council.[42] Thus, the regulatory context for CSOEs

36 Xianfa, supra, art 7. Special reference is made to the exploitation and protection of natural resources, supra art 9, and the protection of what is described as socialist public property, supra, art. 12.

37 See, Wei, Lingling (2023): "China's New Way to Control Its Biggest Companies: Golden Shares" *The Wall Street Journal* (8 March), available at www.wsj.com/articles/xi-jinpings-subtle-strategy-to-control-chinas-biggest-companies-ad001a63 (accessed 9 August 2023).

38 OECD-SOE, supra, p. 14 ("defining an SOE).

39 Cf., Holz, Carsten A. (2018): "The Unfinished Business of State-owned Enterprise Reform in the People's Republic of China" (2 December), available at https://ssrn.com/abstract=3392986 (accessed 9 August 2023), p. 5.

40 Law of the People's Republic of China on State-Owned Assets in Enterprises [中华人民共和国企业国有资产法] (Adopted at the 5th meeting of the Standing Committee of the Eleventh National People's Congress on 28 October 2008) (hereafter SOAEL).

41 SOAEL, supra, art. 6 ("in adherence to the principles of separating government administration from enterprise management, separating the functions of public affairs administration from the functions of the State-owned assets contributor, and non-intervention in the lawful and independent business operations of enterprises."); see also Ibid., arts. 12–15.

42 SASAC was created in its current form in 2003 through the consolidation of various other industry-specific ministries. It is responsible for managing SOEs, including appointing top executives and approving any mergers or sales of stock or assets, as well as drafting laws related to SOEs. Its principal role is as a high-level coordinating and supervisory agency and the state organ charged with ensuring that the financial objectives of the CSOE is undertaken in conformity with the political objectives of the CPC and, when projected abroad, with the social/cultural/security objectives of BRI (SCC). See, Wang, Junmin, Doug Guthrie and Zhixing Xiao (2011): "The Rise of SASAC: Asset Management, Ownership Concentration, and Firm

consists of both its internal institutional regulation (SOAEL) and the supervisory regulatory framework exercised by the state through SASC. A distinction is made in the regulations between central SOEs – those under the direct supervision of national regulatory-supervisory organs[43] – and all others. After reorganization, by 2022, Chinese authorities counted 97 central CSOEs.[44] All other CSOEs are supervised by inferior state organs (provincial level and the like). Lower-tiered administrative structures are influenced by national level policy action.

CSOEs, then, are vessels for the realization of socialist modernization[45] under the direction of the state and subject to the overall leadership of the CPC.[46] One focuses on independence, state aids, and economic objectives in the construction of SOEs in the context of OECD-SOE and OECD-MNE principles and in the presumptions if the UNGP. The organization of the CSOE vessel, in contrast, focuses on systems of control and discretion. These organizational systems are built in ways that ensure that the state and its political vanguard are invariably present. A decade ago, Lin and Milhaupt usefully described these then emerging organizational systems as grounded in principles of networked hierarchy and institutional bridging.[47] That vessel, however,

Performance in China's Capital Markets", *Management and Organization Review*, Vol. 8, No. 2: pp. 253–281.

43 中央企业境外投资监督管理办法，国务院国有资产监督管理委员会令 第35号(11 August 2021) [Measures for the Supervision and Administration of Overseas Investment by Central Enterprises. Order of State Owned Assets Supervision and Administration Commission of the State Council, No. 35] (hereafter Measures for Supervision of Overseas Investment 2017). ("The term "central enterprises" as mentioned in these Measures refers to the state-funded enterprises that . . . SASAC performs the investor's duties on behalf of the State Council." Ibid., art. 2).

44 SASAC, Reform, Development and Party Building of State-owned Assets Supervision and Administration Authorities and SOEs in the New Era, Material for Press Conference of the Publicity Department of the CPC Central Committee (June 17, 2022), available at www.scio.gov.cn/xwfbh/xwbfbh/wqfbh/47673/48373/48381/Document/1725838/1725838.htm (accessed 9 August 2023), p. 7. Authorities noted at that time the connection between consolidation and national political priorities.

We have launched special programs to strip non-core businesses and non-advantageous industries and dispose inefficient or invalid assets. By the end of 2021, 93% of central SOEs' subsidiaries were engaged in the core businesses, 97% of their investment went to such businesses, and more than 70% of their operating revenue came from important industries and key areas that have a vital bearing on state security, the lifeline of the national economy and people's livelihood. (Ibid.).

45 SOAEL, supra, art. 1 ("This Law is enacted for the purpose of safeguarding the basic economic system of China, consolidating and expanding the State-owned economic sector, strengthening protection of State-owned assets, giving play to the leading role of the State-owned economic sector in the national economy, and promoting the development of the socialist market economy.").

46 SOAEL, supra, arts. 3–4.

47 Lin, Li-Wen and Curtis J. Milhaupt (2013): "We are the (National) Champions: Understanding the Mechanisms of State Capitalism in China", *Stanford Law Review*, Vol. 65, No. 4: pp. 697–759 ("expand our focus beyond the usual corporate governance concern with agency

requires a framework for their operation, and that framework requires an administrative structure. In the modern era, productive assets (capital) are organized as a juridical person under a special law of making related sets of assets productive.[48] The legal personality of CSOEs is established in SOAEL[49] and includes "the rights to possess, use, benefit from and dispose of their movables, immovables and other property according to laws, administrative regulations and the articles of association of the enterprises."[50] While they act autonomously, they also must "accept the administration and supervision legally exercised by the people's governments and the relevant departments and institutions under them, accept supervision of the general public, shoulder their social responsibilities, and be responsible to the contributors"[51] to whom profits are distributed.[52] State-owned companies (other than enterprises) may be formed under the Company Law of the People's Republic of China[53] and subject to its internal governance rules (several of which focus exclusively on state-owned enterprises operating in corporate form, whether or not they are wholly owned by the state). This applies to CSOEs operating as limited liability companies[54] or as joint-stock companies.[55]

Nonetheless, implementation of these principles has been a dynamic process.[56] One commentator usefully divided the trajectory of CSOE reform in five stages: Stage 1, expanding SOEs' operating rights under the planned economic system (1978–1984); Stage 2, the contract responsibility system (CRS): separation of ownership and operating rights based on public ownership (1984–1992); Stage 3, establishing a modern enterprise system based on the market economy (1992–2002); Stage 4, the reform of the state-owned assets management system (2003–2012); and Stage 5, extensive SOE reform (consolidation and governance reforms to better align financial with political

---

relationships and try to understand the relational ecology that fosters production in a system where all roads eventually lead to the party-state." Ibid., p. 701).

48 Ibid., art 5 ("For the purposes of this Law, State-invested enterprises include wholly State-owned enterprises and companies, as well as State-owned-capital holding companies or State-owned-capital joint stock companies.").

49 Ibid., art 17 (which includes establishment of "systems for internal supervisory management and risk control").

50 Ibid., art. 16.

51 Ibid., art. 17.

52 Ibid., art. 18.

53 Company Law of the People's Republic of China [中华人民共和国公司法] 1993 (as amended through 2018) available at https://gkml.samr.gov.cn/nsjg/fgs/201906/t20190625_302790.html (accessed 9 August 2023); English translation available at www.npc.gov.cn/zgrdw/englishnpc/Law/2007-12/12/content_1383787.htm (accessed 9 August 2023) (hereafter China Company Law).

54 China Company Law, supra, Chapter II, §3.

55 Ibid., Chapter III.

56 Lin, Karen Jingrong, Xaioyan Lu, Junsheng Zhang and Ying Zheng (2020): "State-Owned Enterprises in China: A Review of 40 Years of Research and Practice", *China Journal of Accounting Research*, Vol. 13, No. 1: pp. 31–55.

objectives) (2012–present).[57] Others have usefully tied the evolution of CSOEs to the evolution of the relationship between the Vanguard Party and the state since the end of the cultural revolution.[58]

Those stages might be understood to serve as the outward evidence of the strong hand of direction undertaken through the state organs charged with giving CSOEs objectives and steering choices in the service of socialist modernization. In this sense, it is the state managerial and guidance structures, rather than the internal corporate governance of CSOPEs that give these enterprises their unique character and separate them from the normative framework built into the OECD-SOE. To that end, it is necessary to align the supervisory authority of SASAC with the corporate governance structures made available under the Company Law. This dual authority – operational in the CSOE (management and profit) and supervisory in SASAC (objectives, assessment, and approvals) – is built into the structure of SOAEL. This produces a dual set of objective maximization principles. At the micro level – the level of CSOE operations – the CSOE is expected to focus on objectives common to most enterprises: good governance, compliance, and bettering economic results, including social responsibilities.[59] Nonetheless, these objectives are to be realized under the "administration and supervision legally exercised by the people's government."[60] CSOEs administer state assets, but under the guidance and subject to the leadership of their public supervisory organs representing national ownership, which are, in turn, the organs established for the implementation of the political leadership of the CPC.[61] The administrative guidance is also tied to, and disciplined by, the personnel system overseen on the administrative side by SASAC and on the political side by the CPC.[62]

The model replicates the relationship between the vanguard CPC and the state apparatus organized through the State Constitution of China

57 Ibid.

58 Jin, Xiankun, Liping Xu, Yu Xin and Ajay Adhikari (2022): "Political Governance in China's State-Owned Enterprises", *China Journal of Accounting Research*, Vol. 15: p. 100236, 1–29, 3–5.

59 SOAEL, supra, art 17.

60 Ibid.

61 Jin, Xiankun et al. "Political Governance in China's State-Owned Enterprises," supra. The authors note their principal findings:

> 1) State ownership lays the foundation for the party's leadership. Ongoing ownership reforms will bring heterogeneity, new patterns, and challenges to SOE governance. 2) Under the principle of party cadre management, SOE executives prioritize political performance and strive for political promotions. 3) The involvement of party organizations in SOE decision-making facilitates political intervention and also mitigates agency problems. 4) Intra-party supervision benefits SOEs by conserving resources. 5) By 2019, most state-controlled listed firms had amended their corporate charters to endorse the party's leadership. (Ibid., p. 26).

62 See, Lin and Milhaupt, "We Are the (National) Champions", supra, pp. 737–743. The authors provide a useful illustration of the way the system operates in the cases of the China National Nonferrous Metals Industry Group, and the China Datang Group. Ibid., pp. 728–734.

(Xianfa).[63] Operational authority and micro-level discretionary authority are vested in the CSOE, but in macro matters it is in the state organs charged with exercising the rights of ownership that CSOE is vested, and it is to the effectuation of state policy that the operations of a CSOE are directed. The core of that alignment is what distinguishes the CSOE from other variations elsewhere. Under the OECD-SOE, the guiding ideology is based on the principle of separation of ownership from control and the protection of the autonomy of the SOE. This is a relationship of autonomous actors. The CSOE, on the other hand, cannot be understood as autonomous in the idealized sense put forward in the OECD-SOE and operationalized through OECD-MNE principles. Instead, the enterprise can be understood as part of an interactive relationship between SASAC and the CSOE. It is not that SASAC and CSOEs merge or that CSOEs are the alter ego of SASAC or that they are public bodies – the issue that emerges in the specific context of state subsidies.[64] Rather, it is the operation of enterprises, taken as a whole, that requires the operational capacity of the CSOE structure and the supervisory and managerial authority of SASAC, responsible for shaping and approving key CSOE discretionary decisions.

The state remains at the center, and at the center of the state are the leadership authority and guidance mechanisms of the CPC. That, at least, is the theory. Nonetheless, recent trends suggest that the principle of strict operational detachment between CSOE, state, and party has been rejected in favor of substantial interlinking among the three institutions – with the CPC at the center.[65] "Party building will be improved across the board in Party and state offices and will be advanced in public institutions. We will make sure that Party leadership in SOEs and financial firms is strengthened in the process of their improvements to corporate governance."[66] Thus, the model is

63 中华人民共和国宪法 (zhōnghuá rénmín gòng héguó xiànfǎ Constitution of the People's Republic of China (1982 as amended) (hereafter Xianfa)). Xianfa is to be distinguished from the autonomous political vanguard, the Communist Party of China, which is organized under its own constitution. Discussed in Catá Backer, Larry (2012): "Party, People, Government and State: On Constitutional Values and the Legitimacy of the Chinese State-Party Rule of Law System", *Boston University International Law Journal*, Vol. 30, No. 2: pp. 331–408. ("[T]he CCP serves as the institutionalization of the polity and the source of its substantive values. The government established under the Constitution serves as the institutionalization of State power, within which the people may more directly participate under the guidance of the Party." Ibid., 408).

64 See, Ding, Ru (2014): "'Public Body' or Not: Chinese State-Owned Enterprise", *Journal of World Trade*, Vol. 48: pp. 167–189 (governmental function versus governmental authority approaches). See also, Zhou, Weihuan, Henry Gao and Xue Bai (2019): "Building a Market Economy Through WTO-Inspired Reform of State-Owned Enterprises in China", *International and Comparative Law Quarterly*, Vol. 68: pp. 977–1022.

65 Wang, Jiangyu (2014): "The Political Logic of Corporate Governance in China's State-Owned Enterprises", *Cornell Journal of International Law*, Vol. 47: pp. 631–669 ("China seems to be developing a new model of SOE governance that combines universal elements of corporate law with communist political institutions" Ibid., p. 667).

66 Jinping, Xi, "Hold High the Great Banner of Socialism with Chinese Characteristics and Strive in Unity to Build a Modern Socialist Country in All Respects, Report to the 20th National

one in which there is formal operational detachment but effective personal interlinking forming a dense web of control-supervisory relationships, rather than a clean jurisdictionally structured system.[67] In addition to party building within CSOEs, implementing the deep networked project of putting the party at the center of the CSOE also focused on micro decision-making within the enterprise. For example to "strengthen the supervision and management of key positions and important personnel in state-owned enterprises, especially the top leaders, and highlight the supervision of project bidding, restructuring, property rights changes and transactions."[68] This intertwining affects both the domestic and foreign operations of a CSOE.[69] The interlinking, as a key policy principle, was further elaborated in 2022.[70] The focus is on data-driven high-quality development in line with political objectives that can be assessed against an indicator system.[71] Sometimes the indicators align Chinese political with international objectives.[72] Nonetheless, there is still some distance between formal alignment and perfect operationalization.[73]

This template is then repeated throughout the parallel structures of CPC guidance, state supervision, and institutional implementation. Within the structures of CSOE "owners," these are shorthanded through the politically normative concepts of whole process people's democracy, the leadership of

---

Congress of the Communist Party of China (16 October 2022) (hereafter Xi, Report 20th CPC Congress)); p. 59.

67 共产党员网 国企党建30项重点任务 [Communist Party Network, 30 key tasks of party building in state-owned enterprises] (2018–08–03); available at www.sohu.com/a/245023885_717281 (accessed 9 August 2023), drawn from "Notice on Printing and Distributing "Implementing the Key Tasks of the National State-owned Enterprise Party Construction Work Conference" (Zhongzufa [2016] No. 26) [《关于印发<贯彻落实全国国有企业党的建设工作会议精神重点任务>的通知》（中组发[2016]26号)].

68 Ibid., p. 5 [强化对国有企业关键岗位、重要人员特别是一把手的监督管理，突出工程招投标、改制重组、产权变更和交易等方面的监督].

69 Ibid. ("Conscientiously implement the guiding opinions on strengthening the party building work of overseas units of central enterprises, and flexibly set up party organizations to carry out party work according to local conditions." Ibid., p. 18 [认真贯彻落实关于加强中央企业境外单位党建工作的指导意见，因地制宜、灵活设置党的组织开展党的工作]).

70 SASAC, Reform, Development and Party Building of State-owned Assets Supervision and Administration Authorities and SOEs in the New Era, Material for Press Conference of the Publicity Department of the CPC Central Committee (17 June 2022), available at www.scio.gov.cn/xwfbh/xwbfbh/wqfbh/47673/48373/48381/Document/1725838/1725838.htm (accessed 9 August 2023).

71 Ibid., p. 5.

72 See, e.g., Qing, Xu and Christopher Wang (2020): *Technical Report on SDG Finance Taxonomy (China)* (New York: UNDP) ("Beyond China's own development progress, the country has a large and steadily growing role in promoting global development and attaining the SDGs in partner countries. This includes efforts to make the Belt and Road Initiative green and sustainable," Ibid., p. 133). See also "Green Industry Guidance Catalog (2023 Edition)" (draft for comments) [《绿色产业指导目录（2023年版）》的解释说明（征求意见稿）available at https://yyglxxbsgw.ndrc.gov.cn/htmls/article/article.html?articleId=2c97d16b-8678801b-0186-e9501f66-0000#iframeHeight=808 (accessed 9 August 2023).

73 See discussion infra.

the CPC as repository of effective political authority, and the role of the state as the instrument for the effectuation of that leadership and guidance suitable to the context and times. That leadership extends to all aspects of collective life and is bent to the perfection of the socialist model; the culmination of the process of perfection will be marked by the establishment of a communist society. In a like manner, between the structures of the CSOE and SASAC, the shorthand is similar. SASAC serves as the administrative and supervisory organ designated to ensure that the leadership and guidance of the CPC, articulated in rules, policies, objectives, and plans to be actualized through the appropriate state organs, is actually operationalized through the instruments created for the rationalization of national productive forces in the form of the CSOE. That is the pattern: grounding ideology, political leadership of the CPC, development of policy, and articulation of rule, plans, and objectives (through whole-process democracy and state administrative and legislative organs), the downward iteration of this pattern as between SASAC and CSOEs. Lastly, the market-driven environment in which CSOEs operate is understood differently in Marxist-Leninist theory. In liberal democracy, markets are spaces for non-public activity and the space where individual autonomy can be exercised subject to the protection of the integrity of markets (and their normative foundations) by public authorities. Current Chinese Marxist-Leninism suggests that markets are instruments; they are instruments of state policy necessary to move a society through its development stages to nudge it closer to its ideal final stage. The difference between markets terrains driven by private actors and markets as instruments of state direction towards a specified goal have substantial effects on the understanding of the role and purpose of CSOEs.[74]

To speak, then, about autonomy and separation, in the style of the OECD-SOE, is to miss the essential structuring ideology of the socialist CSOE within the current iterative framework of China's New Era theorization of Marxist-Leninism and its current policy manifestations. CSOEs certainly exercise autonomy in the implementation of their charges and for the protection of the integrity of their operations to achieve their goals. They exercise the autonomy of "how" but not of "what." Such autonomy is then exercised under the supervision of the party-state, which also sets the overall objectives and choices for activity (at a macro level, to be sure) that must be realized by the CSOE.[75] This is effectuated through systems of reporting, approvals, and the articulation of mission goals. The primary object is not necessarily the protection and promotion of the interests of the CSOE, but rather the effective use the CSOE form (and its control over productive assets) to achieve state goals under the

74 杨长鑫 列宁国家资本主义思想与中国的改革开放 [Changxin, Yang, "On Lenin's Ideology of State Capitalism and China's Reform and Opening Up,"], 常州大学学报(社会科学版) [*Journal of Changzhou University (Social Science Edition)*, pp. 28–32.

75 Consider Brødsgaard, Kjeld Erik (2012): "Politics and Business Group Formation in China: The Party in Control?", *China Quarterly*, Vol. 211, pp. 624–648.

guidance and direction of the vanguard. The relationship may be interactive but is bounded by hierarchical assumptions.[76]

Criticism of CSOEs as inefficient might be understood to emerge from the large conceptual gap between systems in which the economic integrity and autonomy of enterprises are foregrounded (OECD-SOE) and those in which the CSOE is understood as an instrument of party-state objectives.[77] What is efficient under an OECD-SOE conceptual framework may not be understood in the same terms under Chinese Marxist-Leninist structures of economic-political organization. A similar split underlies CSOE conceptual frameworks and the structural principles underlying the OECD-MNE. It is one that is anticipated in the OECD-MNE[78] and the UNGP.[79] In effect, CSOEs may be subject to NCP special instance procedures under the OECD-MNE in participating host states like everyone else when operating abroad, the way Chinese companies are amenable to action by the Norwegian SWF in applying their ethics guidelines to their investment strategies. It works the same from the Chinese side: compliance with local law for CSOEs operating outside China but compliance that seeks to honor Chinese law and governance principles and, to the extent possible, operate under the guidance of the state organs and the vanguard. At the center of that difference is the central role of the development of the socialist market economy,[80] within which CSOEs play an important role. The model becomes more interesting and has significant

76 Yo-Chong, Xu (2017): "China's Giant State-Owned Enterprises as Policy Advocates: The Case of the State Grid Corporation of China", *The China Journal*, Vol. 79: pp. 21–39.

77 For an early example from the time of anticipated convergence between the two models, see Lin, Juston Yifu, Fang Cai and Zhou Li (1998): "Competition, Policy Burdens, and State-Owned Enterprise Reform", *AEA Papers and Proceedings*, Vol. 88, No. 2: pp. 422–427; see also Huang, Philip C.C. (2012): "Profit-Making State Firms and China's Development Experience: 'State Capitalism' or 'Socialist Market Economy'?", *Modern China*, Vol. 38, No. 6: pp. 591–629, 594–598 (on the hegemonic discourse).

78 OECD-MNE is grounded in the principle of compliance with local law; "in countries where domestic laws and regulations conflict with the principles and standards of the Guidelines, enterprises should seek ways to honour such principles and standards to the fullest extent which does not place them in violation of domestic law." OECD-MNE, supra, Concepts & Principles 2, p. 17.

79 UNGP23 provides that businesses should comply with local law (UNGP, supra 23(a) & (c). "Seek ways to honour the principles of internationally recognized human rights when faced with conflicting requirements." (UNGP, supra, 23(b).

80 The socialist market economy is, effectively, grounded in the principles of socialist public ownership as a leading force in the economy, guided support of the private economy, and all under the leadership of the CPC. See earlier discussion on the nature of the CSOE. Xi, Report 20th CPC Congress, supra. ("We must uphold and improve China's basic socialist economic systems. We must unswervingly consolidate and develop the public sector and unswervingly encourage, support, and guide the development of the non-public sector. We will work to see that the market plays the decisive role in resource allocation and that the government better plays its role." Ibid., 23–24). For a useful discussion, see, Pelmans, Jacques (2018): "China's 'Socialist Market Economy': A Systemic Trade Issue," *Intereconomics*, Vol. 53, No. 5: pp. 268–273, 269–270.

consequences when it is projected beyond China's borders: that is, when the socialist market economy goes global. It is in the practice of honoring socialist market economy principles, even as CSOEs strictly comply with host state law, that the issues becomes acute, especially in the context of international human rights and sustainability principles. One sees this especially in the context, for example, of the UN Human Rights Council Universal Periodic Reviews of China.[81] That is the subject taken up next.

3 The outward projection of the CSOE national model

CSOEs serve as key instruments of outbound investment policy in the New Era – to bring the CPC back to the center and to develop and protect principles of Chinese internationalism as a principal narrative of trade, social, political, and economic relations.[82] "But what makes China's unique brand of market economy, or more broadly its developmentalism, a challenge to the LIO today is the extent to which the CCP has reminded us that markets can also be used to advance geopolitical goals."[83] This represents, as well, the internationalization of approaches to meet the contemporary challenge of what Leninist theorists label the current principal contradiction between the production of wealth and its fair distribution.[84]

That projection has grown significantly.[85] In a June 2022 press conference, Chinese authorities noted the extent of outbound CSOE activity. "We have

81 See discussion later in this chapter. See, generally Ahl, Björn (2015): "The Rise of China and International Human Rights Law", *Human Rights Quarterly*, Vol. 37, No. 3: pp. 637–661; and Heupel, Monika (2018): "How do States Perceive Extraterritorial Human Rights Obligations? Insights from the Universal Periodic Review", *Human Rights Quarterly*, Vol. 40, No. 3: pp. 521–554.

82 Cf., Ufimtseva, Anastasia (2020): "Investigating the Impact of State-Owned Enterprises (SOEs) on the Contemporary World Order: A Case of Chinese SOE Investment in the Canadian Hydrocarbon Sector", *Cambridge Review of International Affairs*, Vol. 33, No. 1: pp. 61–80.

83 Malkin, Anton (2020): "Challenging the Liberal International Order by Chipping Away at US Structural Power: China's State-Guided Investment in Technology and Finance in Russia", *Cambridge Review of International Affairs*, Vol. 33, No. 1: pp. 81–104, 87 ("Centrally controlled SOEs are also mandated to become globally competitive enterprises that are incentivized to carry out China's foreign economic policy goals by seeking out commercially viable foreign direct investment (FDI) destinations." Ibid., p. 83.)

84 See Wei, Xingua (2018): "The Principal Contradiction and Its Evolution in the New Era of the Socialism Society with Chinese Characteristics: From the Perspective of the Marxist Political Economy Methodology", *China Political Economy*, Vol. 1, No. 1: pp. 2–12.

85 It has been reported that, in Europe, Chinese FDI hovered at about €96 billion in 2021 while M&A activity dropped to about €25 billion, against a peak of €46 billion in 2016. Zenglein, Max J. and Gregor Sebastian (2022), "Chinese Foreign Direct Investment in Europe: The Downward Trend Continues", *Industrial Analytics Platform Newsletter* (2022), available at https://iap.unido.org/articles/chinese-foreign-direct-investment-europe-downward-trend-continues. On a comparative basis, investment in Latin America has grown substantially. "To put things in perspective, last year China invested $8.4 billion in the EU, $4.7 billion in the

further promoted the high-quality development of the Belt and Road Initiative, and the overseas assets of central enterprises have reached nearly 8 trillion yuan, distributed among more than 8,000 projects in over 180 countries and regions."[86] And it has had special consequences for the projection of Chinese power through its CSOE investments in Latin America.[87] In this way, of course, Chinese authorities may project outward the structures of national security concerns (especially with respect to the construction, protection, and exploitation of global production chains). "The development path of China's outbound foreign investment basically mirrors the process of its reform and opening up. In other words, it is directly tied to changes in China's economic system."[88] It serves, in other words, as the outward manifestation of the recently developed Chinese dual circulation economy principles.[89] This shift has important security concerns,[90] especially as the US and Chinese economies continued to decouple, and competition for resources and the productive forces necessary to fuel global supply chains intensified.[91]

The regulatory sources of CSOE investment and operation abroad are deeply embedded in a complex domestic and international legal order. The chapter has already touched on key legal sources that shape the character and operation of CSOEs in China. The legal structures of outbound investment carry forward a substantial amount of that domestic framework. Added to it

---

U.S. and $7–10 billion in LAC." Larraín, Felipe and Pepe Zhang (2023): "China's Evolving Presence in Latin America", *The Americas Quarterly* (3 January), available at www.americas-quarterly.org/article/china-is-here-to-stay-in-latin-america/. As much as almost $6 billion of that investment appears to have been directed toward Brazil. Ibid.

86 Jieming, Weng, (vice chairman of SASAC), Transcript of Press Conference (17 June 2022); available at http://english.scio.gov.cn/pressroom/node_8031542.htm (accessed 9 August 2023) (English translation).

87 Urdinez, Francisco, Fernando Mouron, Luis L. Schenoni and Amâncio J. de Oliveira (2016): "Chinese Economic Statecraft and U.S. Hegemony in Latin America: An Empirical Analysis, 2003–2014", *Latin American Politics and Society*, Vol. 58, No. 4: pp. 3–30.

88 Pei, Changhong and Wen Zheng (2015): *China's Outbound Foreign Direct Investment Promotion System* (Heidelberg: Springer), p. 14.

89 Lin, Justin Yifu (2021): "Dual Circulation and China's Development," *Frontiers of Economics in China*, Vol. 16, No. 1: pp. 30–34; Sul, Lijun and Junshang Liang (2021): "Understanding China's New Dual Circulation Development Strategy: A Marxian Input-Output Analysis", *Review of Radical Political Economics*, Vol. 53, No. 4: pp. 590–591.

90 See Slawatsky, Joel (2018): "The National Security Exception in US-China FDI and Trade: Lessons from Delaware Corporate Law", *The Chinese Journal of Comparative Law*, Vol. 6, No. 2: pp. 228–264 (on the broadening of the concept of national security to include technological and economic security); see, generally, Chaisse, Julien (2015): "Demystifying Public Security Exception and Limitations on Capital Movement," *University of Pennsylvania Journal of International Law*, Vol. 37: p. 583. The concept has been broadened to include other areas: for example, food security. See, e.g., Dogan, Berna (2022): "Does FDI in Agriculture Promote Food Security in Developing Countries? The Role of Land Governance", *Transnational Corporations: Investment & Development*, Vol. 29, No. 2: pp. 47–74.

91 Discussed in Javed, Saad Ahmed, Yu Bo, Liangyan Tao and Wenjie Dong (2023): "The 'Dual Circulation' Development Model of China: Background and Insights", *Rajagiri Management Journal*, Vol. 17, No. 1: pp. 2–20.

are the framing rules of Chinese bilateral investment treaties and related agreements.[92] In addition, Chinese authorities have enacted a number of measures designed to give a legal framework to the management of overseas investment by both public and private enterprises.[93] Among these, two measures merit some attention. The first is the 2017 NDRC Guiding Opinions on Overseas Investment Direction,[94] and the second and, for purposes of this chapter, more relevant provision is the Measures for the Supervision and Administration of Overseas Investment by Central Enterprises.[95]

The 2017 NDRC Guiding Opinions on Overseas Investment Direction seeks to rationalize supervision of overseas investment within the developing structures of Chinese outward projection of economic activity. That rationalization is meant to reduce overseas investment risk while taking full advantage of investment opportunities and promoting standardization.[96] The guidance reinforces the core principle of supervisory and operational level separation. While supervision and guidance rest with state organs, "enterprises make independent decisions under the guidance of the government and are responsible for their own profits and losses, and assume their own risk."[97] Decentralization is a regulatory objective, one that is focused on encouraging development and constraining it through the circulation of blacklists of discouraged investment.[98] At the same time, enterprises are to be guided to risk assessment based on local conditions in the host country and, in that context, to cultivate good relations with local officials and "create good economic and social benefits, and promote mutual benefit and win-win cooperation."[99] That risk assessment is based on a strategy of prevention (坚持防范风险), coordination of host relations with home state national economic and diplomatic strategies, and legal compliance, under the active supervision of state organs.[100]

92 Schneiderman, Tyler Cohenand David (2020): "The Political Economy of Chinese Bilateral Investment Treaty", *The Chinese Journal of Comparative Law*, Vol. 5, No. 1: pp. 110–128; Leutert, Wendy and Zachary Haver (2020): "From Cautious Interaction to Mature Influence: China's Evolving Engagement with the International Investment Regime", *Pacific Affairs*, Vol. 92, No. 1: pp. 59–87.

93 Briefly described in Pei and Zheng, *China's Outbound Foreign Direct Investment Promotion System*, supra, chapter 2.

94 国家发展改革委　商务部　人民银行　外交部关于进一步引导和规范　　境外投资方向的指导意见　投资方向指导意见的通知　国办发〔2017〕74号 [National Development and Reform Commission Ministry of Commerce People's Bank of China Ministry of Foreign Affairs, Regarding further Guidance and specification, Guiding Opinions on Overseas Investment Direction, Notice of investment direction guidance (2017) No. 74] (hereafter 2017 NDRC Guiding Opinions on Overseas Investment) Direction.

95 Measures for Supervision of Overseas Investment 2017, supra.

96 2017 NDRC Guiding Opinions on Overseas Investment Direction, supra, art. 1.

97 Ibid., art. 2 ("企业在政府引导下自主决策、自负盈亏、自担风险。").

98 Ibid. ("鼓励发展+负面清单").

99 Ibid. (坚持互利共赢。引导企业充分考虑投资目的国国情和实际需求，注重与当地政府和企业开展互利合作，创造良好的经济社会效益，促进互惠互利、合作共赢。).

100 Ibid.

A compliance and risk mitigation strategy forms part of the supervisory principles. The other then fosters a risk-sensitive plan of state interest–driven investment.[101] The idea is to coordinate and intertwine micro-investment decisions of CSOEs with the macro strategies for enhancing the comprehensive strategy for outward projection of Chinese economic, social, cultural, and political-ideological power influence.[102] Special attention is placed on the coordination of investment strategies and risk minimization with the strategic coordination of outbound investment that most efficiently and comprehensively advances the Belt and Road Initiative as a political, economic, and normative project.[103] The 2017 NDRC Guiding Opinions on Overseas Investment Direction also specify blacklisted investments. Here, there is a coordination between operational effects on CSEOEs of blacklists in article 2 and the more comprehensive supervisory and normative specifications that are the responsibility of overseeing state organs. The categories specified touch on "overseas investments that are inconsistent with the country's peaceful development foreign policy, mutually beneficial and win-win opening strategy, and macro-control policies."[104] More specifically, "[D]omestic enterprises are prohibited from participating in overseas investments that endanger or may endanger national interests and national security."[105]

In contrast, the Measures for Supervision of Overseas Investment 2017 focus more on the framework for supervisory discretionary decision-making respecting CSOEs. The focus is on central enterprises, described as

> pillars of the national economy. How to maintain and increase the value . . ., how to achieve sustainable development . . . how to promote the transformation and upgrading of industrial chains, how to better

101 Ibid., art. 3.

102 Ibid (支持境内有能力、有条件的企业积极稳妥开展境外投资活动，推进"一带一路"建设，深化国际产能合作，带动国内优势产能、优质装备、适用技术输出，提升我国技术研发和生产制造能力，弥补我国能源资源短缺，推动我国相关产业提质升级。["Support capable and qualified enterprises in China to actively and steadily carry out overseas investment activities, promote the construction of the 'Belt and Road,' deepen international production capacity cooperation, drive the export of domestic superior production capacity, high-quality equipment, and applicable technologies, improve my country's technology research and development and manufacturing capabilities, and make up for The shortage of domestic energy resources has promoted the upgrading of related national industries."]).

103 Ibid. Other sectors are identified, including the agriculture and tech sectors. These align the outward investment strategies with the enhancement of value-added domestic capacity under the principles of the dual circulation strategy.

104 Ibid., art. 4. These include investments in designated sensitive countries, investments in certain economic sectors (real estate, hotels, cinemas, and the like), investment funds not tied to industrial projects, projects using substandard equipment, and projects out of compliance with host state regulations.

105 Ibid., art. 5. These include a broadly specified spectrum of investments that might touch on national interests or national security concerns. The guidance is open ended, suggesting a broad discretionary flexibility vested in the supervisory organs under the leadership of the CPC.

> serve national strategies and social development . . . are questions worth pondering.[106]

These tend to be the vehicles that shape and drive the forms of Chinese outbound projections of economic activity, now framed within the normative and conceptual structures of the Belt and Road Initiative (BRI). Contemporary regulatory efforts might be best understood as focused on the refinement of structures of supervision of the interlinking between the regulatory structures and objectives of the BRI, a macro policy linking of CSOEs as instruments of BRI, with the cluster intermeshing of state, Party, and enterprise that shape the internal operations of CSOEs. That is, regulation must accommodate a double supervision, one that occurs both within the CSOE, and the other between the CSOE and outbound State projections of economic policy through BRI. First, the Measures for Supervision of Overseas Investment 2017 reinforces the role of SASAC as the primary coordinating organ for state-party oversight, direction, and assessment.[107] The distinction is between micro-level management by the central CSOE (which bears operational risk) and the supervisory guidance role of SASC.[108] Thus, central CSOEs are tasked with the establishment of overseas investment management systems; the basic principles under which they are developed and operated;[109] and the specifics of which[110] are specified, centered around the core elements of compliance, risk-based decision-making and the focus on the state-directed objectives of outbound operations. Macro-based supervision includes the establishment and enforcement of negative investment lists,[111] oversight of CSOE investment management systems, and integration of party and state presence in CSOE internal management and operations,[112] CSOE operational compliance with the thrust of national five-year development strategies,[113] and special rules for overseas projects in the negative investment lists.[114] Risk management strategies both drive investment and are managed at the enterprise, state, and party levels.[115] In that context,

106 Wei, Li, Remarks at Exchange Meeting of Central Enterprises (December 2022); *MENA Report* (London, 29 December 2022).

107 Measures for Supervision of Overseas Investment 2017, supra, art. 1 (referencing specifically the "Company Law of the People's Republic of China," "The Law of the People's Republic of China on State-owned Assets of Enterprises," and "Guiding Opinions on Deepening the Reform of State-owned Enterprises" (China [2015] No. 22) and "Several Opinions on Reforming and Improving the State-owned Assets Management System" (Guo Fa [2015] No. 63)).

108 Ibid., arts. 3–6, 8. SASAC supervision provisions are elaborated in Ibid., arts. 16–23. Enterprise accountability structures are specified Ibid., arts. 29–30.

109 Ibid., art. 6.

110 Ibid., art. 7.

111 Ibid., art. 9.

112 Ibid, art. 10.

113 Ibid., art. 11.

114 Ibid., art. 12.

115 Ibid., arts. 24–28.

CSOEs are encouraged to act responsibly with a sensitivity to local context. In that respect, they are required to "actively fulfill social responsibilities, and focus on cross-border investment, cultural integration, and the creation of a good external environment."[116]

The content of those risk-mitigating behaviors and the structures within which they are realized is, to some degree, shaped by the development of a key coordinated system for the projection of Chinese outbound investment – the Belt and Road Initiative.[117] BRI extends the core principle of strict legal compliance with host state law in and through which Chinese values and operations may be supplemented.[118] In effect, it mimics the principles of the UNGP and OECD-MNE of layering norm compliance responsibilities on enterprises beyond strict legal compliance, but starting from a Chinese Marxist-Leninist baseline. These efforts to re-orient the practice and character of global trade, along with the underlying principles of Chinese internationalism, including what the Chinese authorities call socialist human rights, are considered next.

4 Structuring projection of CSOEs abroad within a conceptual cage of policy objectives: The belt and road initiative and the rise of socialist human rights

What emerges from CSOE conceptualization and operational structuring are the core notions of the centrality of the CPC, the close alignment between the CPC and the administrative organs of the state, the central role of the SASAC apparatus in the management of state enterprises, and the manifestation of strategically aggregated state assets into CSOEs. Within China, that produces a close alignment of public (administrative) and private (market- and profit-driven) objectives in which CSOEs focus on value-enhancing deliverables that further the key interests and objectives of the public sector supervisory organs. The projection of that model abroad introduces an additional set of challenges. The first focuses on issues of normative transposition and the second

116 Ibid., art. 28.

117 Zhu, Jigao, Wang Yi and Tang Guliang (2020): "China's Central SOEs' Corporate Social Responsibility Performance under the BRI", *China Economist*, Vol. 15, No. 5: pp. 45–56. The article draws on three case studies: China Communications Construction Co., Ltd. (CCCC); Power Construction Corporation of China, Ltd. (PowerChina); China Three Gorges Corporation (CTG) to consider the expression and practice of what the authors call corporate social responsibility within a BRI framework. They divide CSR into three categories: 1) responsive CSR (compliance), 2) strategic CSR (cooperation and localized human resources management), and (3) social responsive CSR (environmental protection and contribution to local communities). Ibid., 54.

118 Some BRI countries are plagued by the lack of rule of law, frequent regime change, and political risks. In an unfamiliar and complex institutional context, all the case companies treaded carefully to comply with local laws and regulations. In the words of CCCC's executive director and CFO, "[U]nder the BRI, compliance is CCCC's lifeline, and ensures a project's approval and continuation despite political change in a host country." Ibid., p. 48.

on the development of coordinating structures for the better management of state objectives through economic and financial activities abroad. Normative transposition to host state environments might be most usefully considered through the lens of competing perspectives on human rights. The strategic framework within which that transposition is coordinated requires sensitivity to the emerging framework of the Belt and Road Initiative.

4.1 The emergence of socialist human rights and sustainability

Human rights and sustainability suggest a number of implications are the heart of much of the current global debate about human rights, the responsibilities of business with respect to its promotion, and the formal structures within which these normative values may be given either legal effect or social effects within markets. This basic approach to the challenge of human rights in economic activity is at the structural heart of the UNGP project.[119] Nonetheless, that framework leaves open a number of questions: Whose human rights? Whose regimes of prevention-mitigation-remedy: private or public law? Whose choices respecting alignments of norms, law, and practices sourced in the legal or societal sectors?[120] Resolution of these questions, much less the development of even a rough consensus, remains elusive within the liberal democratic vanguard that has been a primary driver of this project at the

119 UNGP, supra, especially the relationship between the first pillar state duty to protect human rights and the second pillar corporate responsibility to respect human rights. An added dimension is then supplied by the embedding within this framework of the operational goals and principles of the UN Sustainability Development Goals, (UNGA Resolution: Transforming our world: the 2030 Agenda for Sustainable Development (A/70/1, 25 September 2015), the connection between which was declared by the UN in 2022. See, UNGA, Resolution: The human right to a clean, healthy and sustainable environment (A/76/L.75, 26 July 2022).

120 Human rights might be understood here as a struggle toward rationalization and consensus that is always elusive because it is always historically and situationally contingent. See, e.g., Ibhawoh, Bonny (2013): "Commemorating Human Rights: Exploring Origins, Episodes, and Historicity in Constructing a Human Rights Timeline", *Peace & Conflict: Journal of Peace Psychology*, Vol. 19, No. 4: pp. 338–348; Taylor, Mark Roger (2022): "Inside the EU – China Human Rights Dialogue: Assessing the Practical Delivery of the EU's Normative Power in a Hostile Environment", *Journal of European Integration*, Vol. 44, No. 3: pp. 365–380. It may be worth recalling that framework efforts, like the UNGP, do not purport to create international law or change the constitutional traditions of states (UNGP; General Principles). They serve as a means of rationalizing the system of human rights as mandatory public (legal compliance) and responsibility-based private (aspirational and markets sensitive) around its three-pillar structure. UNGP 12 specifies that the scope of responsibility to respect extends only to "internationally recognized human rights." For a structural discussion, see, Catá Backer, Larry (2012): "From Institutional Misalignments to Socially Sustainable Governance: The Guiding Principles for the Implementation of the Governance: The Guiding Principles for the Implementation of the United Nations' 'Protect, Respect and Remedy' and the Construction of Inter-Systemic Global Governance", *McGeorge Global Business and Development Law Journal*, Vol. 25: pp. 69–171.

international level through the second decade of the 21st century,[121] even as the gaps are growing wider between liberal democratic and Marxist-Leninist approaches in some respects.[122]

Until the start of the leadership of Xi Jinping, it was generally believed that states were converging their approaches and understandings of human rights, as well as their applicability to all aspects of organized collective human activity, following the discursive trajectories founded on the consensus represented by the Universal Declaration of Human Rights. While human rights had been divided in the 1960s between social, economic, and cultural rights on the one hand[123] and civil and political rights on the other[124] that, from the end of the 20th century, a rough consensus sensitive to both would emerge.[125] That was an assumption that carried over into the endorsement of the UNGP in 2011[126] and then later into the development of the UN 2030 Plan and its sustainability development goals,[127] as well as into the efforts to develop consensus around issues touching on climate change.[128] This consensus was built on the primacy of the protection of the rights of autonomous individuals whose rights, grounded in human (individualized) dignity,[129] against actions of public and then private collectives (including governments, enterprises, and religious and social collectives). The principles were built around the sensibilities of liberal democracy and of a private market–driven economic model.

121 On emerging orthodoxies around human rights in economic activity, see U.N. Working Group on Business and Human Rights (2021): *UNGPs at 10+: A Roadmap for the Next Decade of Business and Human Rights* (Geneva: United Nations), available at www.ohchr.org/sites/default/files/documents/issues/business/ungps10/2022-11-08/UNGPS_ROADMAPPLUS10_EN.pdf (accessed 9 August 2023).

122 See, e.g., United Nations Office of the High Commissioner for Human Rights (2022): "OHCHR Assessment of Human Rights Concerns in the Xinjiang Uyghur Autonomous Region, People's Republic of China" (31 August), available at www.ohchr.org/sites/default/files/documents/countries/2022-08-31/22-08-31-final-assesment.pdf (accessed 9 August 2023), p. 46. Note Verbale of the Permanent Mission of the People's Republic of China to the United Nations in Geneva, dated 31 August 2022, and annex (No. GJ/56/2022); available at www.ohchr.org/sites/default/files/documents/countries/2022-08-31/ANNEX_A.pdf (accessed 9 August 2023).

123 United Nations (General Assembly). (1966). International Covenant on Economic, Social, and Cultural Rights. Treaty Series, 999, 171 (entry into force 1976).

124 United Nations (General Assembly). (1966). International Covenant on Civil and Political Rights. Treaty Series, 999, 171 (entry into force 1976).

125 Vienna Declaration and Programme of Action adopted by the World Council on Human Rights (25 June 1993) U.N. Doc. A/Conf. 157/23 (1993); available at www.ohchr.org/sites/default/files/vienna.pdf (accessed 9 August 2023) ("All human rights are universal, indivisible and interdependent and interrelated" Ibid., p. 5). See also, Convention on the Rights of the Child (adopted 20 November 1989, entered into force 2 September 1990) 1577 UNTS 3).

126 UNGP, supra.

127 UNGA, Resolution, Transforming our world: the 2030 Agenda for Sustainable Development (A/RES/70/1) (21 October 2015).

128 Conference of the Parties, Adoption of the Paris Agreement, (Dec. 12, 2015) U.N. Doc. FCCC/CP/2015/L.9/Rev/1 (Dec. 12, 2015).

129 Grundgesetz der Bundesrepublik Deutschland (Basic Law), art. 1.

The development of Chinese Marxist-Leninism, especially since 1989 and more consciously rationalized in and through text and policy since the start of the leadership of Xi Jinping, has sought to either enlarge the basis for consensus or prepare China (and like-minded states) to go their own way. The rupture points build on the old Cold War divide between the Soviet and American camps and the challenge to the notion of human rights universality,[130] now embedded within the discursive tropes of globalization development, and the territorialization of global production beyond the state. The divide manifests in the way the implications of liberal democratic and Marxist-Leninist ideologies produce substantially different orderings of the commonly recognized spectrum of human rights. China's legal commitments under international human rights treaties is limited, in line with its unwillingness to commit to treaty norms that are incompatible with its Marxist-Leninist human rights principles.[131]

Chinese approaches to human rights must first and foremost be read as undertaken in the service of the task of overcoming the principal contemporary contradiction. In contemporary China, the central contradiction is "What we now face is the contradiction between unbalanced and inadequate development and the people's ever-growing needs for a better life."[132] To overcome this principal contradiction, the vanguard must develop and governmentalize a series of policies that better distribute the fruits of prosperity and stability. And that challenge itself is focused on the forward movement along the "socialist path" – that is, on a path that is meant, eventually, to come closer

130 See, e.g., Goodale, Mark (2018): "The Myth of Universality: The UNESCO 'Philosophers' Committee' and the Making of Human Rights", *Law and Social Inquiry*, Vol. 43, No. 3: pp. 596–617 (on the construction and importance of human rights as mythos, "a cultural narrative that is meant to do important work in shaping the course of society in particular ways." Ibid., p. 599).

131 See European Parliamentary Research Service (2021): Briefing "China's Compliance with Selected Fields of International Law", available at www.europarl.europa.eu/RegData/etudes/BRIE/2021/696207/EPRS_BRI(2021)696207_EN.pdf (accessed 9 August 2023). The briefing notes, for example: "China has adopted a 'wary', tactical approach to human rights commitments, partly because of a perceived incompatibility between its own cultural and political traditions and those of the West. At the same time, it is motivated by a desire to burnish its international reputation, deflect criticism and encourage international economic integration, albeit on its own terms. . . . China has ratified only four of the eight core international labour conventions of the International Labour Organization (ILO): the Equal Remuneration Convention, the Discrimination (Employment and Occupation) Convention, the Minimum Age Convention, and the Worst Forms of Child Labour Convention, arguably because they are compatible with its own socialist legal tradition." Ibid., p. 5.

132 Xi Jinping, Secure a Decisive Victory in Building a Moderately Prosperous Society in All Respects and Strive for the Great Success of Socialism with Chinese Characteristics for a New Era, Report to the 19th Congress of the CPC (2018); available at www.chinadaily.com.cn/china/19thcpcnationalcongress/2017-11/04/content_34115212.htm (accessed 9 November 2023).

to the establishment of a communist society in China.[133] "BETTER LIFE," articulated by Xi Jinping:

> The needs to be met for the people to live a better life are increasingly broad. Not only have their material and cultural needs grown. And that final goal can only be reached when, as Deng Xiaoping once suggested, the nation is so rich and materially stable that issues of wealth become irrelevant in the operation and constitution of society. To that end the development of productive forces globally to enhance Chinese core political responsibility to the nation becomes important; and its articulation can serve multiple interests. That is especially the case where BRI objectives align with traditional policies of post-colonial and developing states to foreground development, prosperity and stability of the social and political collective, perhaps over the autonomous rights of individuals to express themselves in their own ways, or to dissent other than through the mechanism made available through law.[134]

Convergence is strongest in area of sustainability and environmental protection, but even the divergence in human rights lends itself to points of overlaps.[135] On the Chinese side, this is echoed, though from their own starting orientation, in the principle policy known as the "Community of Common Destiny."[136]

What emerges is a clash of interpretation emphasis.[137] In the Chinese New Era conceptual universe, collective development comes first. Chinese human

133 Cf., State Council Information Office of the People's Republic of China (2021, September): *Human Rights Action Plan of China (2021–2025)* (Beijing: State Council); available at http://english.www.gov.cn/news/topnews/202109/09/content_WS6139a111c6d0df57f98dfeec.html (accessed 9 August 2023).

134 This then foregrounds an important element of the discussion – the legitimacy of distinct mechanisms for ensuring democratic participation. China has developed a model and, in some respects, quite different approach – stressing structured consultation through representative bodies than on the election of representatives to state organs. Discussed in Larry Catá Backer, "Linking People to Governing Institutions Through Leninist Political Parties: 全过程民主 (Whole Process Democracy), Socialist Consultative Democracy, and 《中国新型政党制度》 (China's New Political Party System) (June 2022); available at https://papers.ssrn.com/sol3/papers.cfm?abstract_id=4134483 (accessed 9 August 2023).

135 Catá Backer, Larry, "Peaches and Plums Do Not Speak, but They Are So Attractive That a Path Is Formed Below the Trees" [桃李不言，下自成蹊]: China's Belt and Road Initiative and the United Nations Guiding Principles for Business and Human Rights," Remarks delivered at the 8th United Nations Forum for Business and Human Rights, 26 November 2019, available at https://lcbackerblog.blogspot.com/2019/11/full-text-of-remarks-delivered-at-8th.html#more (accessed 9 August 2023).

136 Jinping, Xi "Towards a Community of Common Destiny and A New Future for Asia, Keynote Speech at the Boao Forum for Asia Annual Conference" (28 March 2015), available at www.china.org.cn/business/2015-03/29/content_35185720.htm (accessed 9 August 2023).

137 Elaborated in Catá Backer, Larry, Brief Reflections on the Building of a Theory and Practice of Community with a Shared Future for Mankind and Global Human Rights Governance

rights combine the theory of reform and opening up with the fundamental premises of socialist modernization (the focus on the development of productive forces). Security is next. These are related to the discourse of stability and prosperity principles. These require an engagement in political work that then refocuses from productivity and development of the economic resources of the nation to a renewed focus on the development of the cultural and social position of the community within that productive culture. They have been manifested in the Chinese patriotic campaigns[138] and then in the policy projects of advancing values and shared culture.

These are also echoed, of course, generally in China's outbound foreign direct investment promotion system (operationalized through their CSOEs)[139] and, more specifically, in the BRI framework. Economics expresses values (aligns with liberal democracy's notion of responsibilities of enterprises for human rights and sustainability wrongs), and that expression is carried in the work of CSORs of this expression of what after 2020 is understood as socialist human rights. And it is in the context of CSOE engagement outside China that these differences can become challenging, as interpretations will risk clashing, especially in CSOE relations with local stakeholders. In the West, the focus is on the individual: individual autonomy and the constraint of the state respecting individual civil and political rights as the core from which decisions about economic, social, and cultural rights may be elaborated. Consequences follow: The process of developing a more or less consensus-based cultural signification of the words – human rights, development, environment – may continue to change substantially. In the West, this is effectuated through a merger between sustainability, bio-diversity, and human rights. In the Global South (including its Chinese Marxist variation, one which may drive the discussion), it emerges in the merger of development, environmentalism, and collective human rights.[140] The result requires a more sustained consideration of the human rights implications of this interactive system of law, policy, politics, and structural principles.

[建立具有人类共同未来的社区理论和实践以及全球人权治理的简 要思考], Remarks presented at a side event on the occasion of the 51st Session of the Human Rights Council: "Human Rights Development in the Perspective of Community with Shared Future for Mankind" hosted by the China Society for Human Rights Studies (29 September 2022), Geneva, Switzerland; available at https://lcbackerblog.blogspot.com/2022/09/larry-cata-backer-remarks-brief.html (accessed 9 August 2023).

138 For its development in the context of the Hing Kong protests of 2019, see Catá Backer, Larry (2021): *Hong Kong Between 'One Country' and 'Two Systems'* (Atlanta: Little Sir Press).

139 Described in Pei, Changhong and Wen Zheng (2015): *China's Outbound Foreign Direct Investment Promotion System* (Berlin: Springer), pp. 28–37 (component sub-systems: legal, supervision/administrative, tax/financing, IP/standards, risk prevention and control, overseas trade cooperation, overseas securities investment, service sector).

140 See, e.g., Qiang, Sun (2014): "Theoretical Innovations in the Marxist Theory of Human Rights in China Since Reform and Opening Up", *Human Rights*, Vol. 13, No. 1: pp. 10–14.

4.2 *The Belt and Road initiative*

In his report to the 20th Congress of the CPC, Xi Jinping set the tone for forward-looking outbound Chinese engagement.

> As a collaborative endeavor, the Belt and Road Initiative has been welcomed by the international community both as a public good and a cooperation platform. . . . Through these efforts, we have advanced a broader agenda of opening up across more areas and in greater depth.[141]

Like CSOEs with respect to specific clusters of state assets (micro lens), BRI represents the framework through which China and its vanguard, the Chinese Communist Party, rationalize its trade, security, cultural, and political policies (macro lens).[142] That rationalization seeks a framework for the seamless and coherent connection between China's internal and external relations. It is the expression of the state's "major country diplomacy" policy developed during the time of the leadership of Xi Jinping.[143] That policy, in turn, produces dissonance in home-host state expectations, at least at the conceptual level. Chinese policy is grounded in the primacy of collective development, political and economic stability, and collective prosperity – a set of principles that then informs the development of socialist human rights and Chinese internationalism;[144]

141 Xi, Report 20th CPC Congress, supra, p. 8 ("China has become a major trading partner for more than 140 countries and regions, it leads the world in total volume of trade in goods, and it is a major destination for global investment and a leading country in outbound investment." Ibid.).

142 Larry Catá Backer, At the ASIL 2019 Annual Meeting: Matthew Eric on the Belt and Road Initiative–Six Key Points (Plus One of My Own), Law at the End of the Day 30 March 2019; available at https://lcbackerblog.blogspot.com/2019/03/at-asil-2019-annual-meeting-matthew.html (accessed 9 August 2023). It serves, as well, the core-collective principle reflected in the party-state-enterprise relationship. In that respect, it serves one well to foreground consequences shaping the objectives and "personality" of the CSOE as 1) the outward expression of the core of the basic line of the Chinese Communist Party as the leadership collective of the nation, with China at the center, and 2) the current manifestation of that basic line as the principles of the New Era theory developed by the current leadership core of the Chinese state and its Communist Party collective, which, along with the elements of the United Front, represents the collective of the Chinese nation.

143 Smith, Stephen N. (2021): "China's 'Major Country Diplomacy': Legitimation and Foreign Policy Change", *Foreign Policy Analysis*, Vol. 17, No. 2: pp. 1–18.

144 National Development Reform Commission, Ministry of Foreign Affairs, and Ministry of Commerce of the People's Republic of China, with State Council authorization, Vision and actions on jointly building Belt and Road (10 April 2017), available at http://2017.beltandroadforum.org/english/n100/2017/0410/c22-45.html (accessed 9 August 2023); (hereafter NDRC et al., Vision and Action). See also Catá Backer, Larry, Brief Reflections on the Building of a Theory and Practice of Community with a Shared Future for Mankind and Global Human Rights Governance [建立具有人类共同未来的社区理论和实践以及全球人权治理的简要思考], Address at a side event to the 51st Session of the UN Human Rights Council organized by the China Society for Human Rights, "Human Rights Development in the Perspective of Community with Shared Future for Mankind" (29 September 2022),

liberal democratic normative orders tend to favor individual autonomy and civil and political rights as a framework for the realization of economic, social, and cultural rights.

Structurally, BRI can be understood as sourced in a comprehensive blending of four foundational pillars: 1) legal, 2) security, 3) culture, and 4) infrastructure development. The legal structures are built around an aggregation of bilateral, regional, and trade and friendship agreements. They are connected by the similarity of terms and as a means of defining and reducing legal and political risk. The legal structuring cements, as a formal matter, the hub and spoke structure of BRI. All agreements place China at the center and avoid the creation of a framework for collective legalities among BRI participants. More important, perhaps, than the treaties and related agreements are the memoranda of understanding that usually accompany BRI partnering. The terms of most of these remain undisclosed, but they appear to serve as a sort of letter of intent with respect to specific projects and collaborations. The security aspects of BRI are tied to the further development of the Shanghai Cooperation Organization (SCO).[145] The connection between the two is based on the notion that global production chains must be defended, and this security apparatus requires an institutional framework centered on the core of China's existing security architecture in Central Asia.[146] The complementarity is also synergistic. SCO relations may require the sort of infrastructure and socio-cultural connections that are at the heart of the BRI project.[147] U.S. analysts have recently focused on the alignment of economic, political, and military strategic interests in outbound Chinese foreign investment through its CSOEs.[148]

The cultural element of BRI focuses on government-to-government and people-to-people exchanges. The objective here is to build better relationships at the operational level. It also provides a space for political work.[149] Bringing

---

available at https://lcbackerblog.blogspot.com/2022/09/larry-cata-backer-remarks-brief.html (accessed 9 August 2023).

145 Chao, Wen-Chih (2022): "The Political Economy of China's Rising Role in the Shanghai Cooperation Organization (SCO): Leading with Balance", *The Chinese Economy*, Vol. 55, No. 4: pp. 293–302.

146 Pradhan, Ramakrushna and Siba Sankar Mohanty (2021); "Chinese Grand Strategies in Central Asia: The Role of Shanghai Cooperation Organization and Belt and Road Initiative", *Fudan Journal of the Humanities and Social Sciences*, Vol. 14: pp. 197–223.

147 Abajyan, Aram (2021): "Shanghai Cooperation Organization as a Platform for Promoting the Agenda of China's Belt and Road Initiative", *Banber Arevelagitut'yan Instituti*, Vol. 1, No. 2: pp. 144–154 ("The SCO serves as a multilateral platform and cooperative structure for Beijing to develop and upgrade infrastructures, strengthen China's bilateral ties in the region, improve institutions and drive much needed economic development." Ibid., p. 149).

148 Evan Ellis, R. (2023): "What China's Global Security Initiative Tells Us About Its Strategic Engagement with Latin America", *The Diplomat* (4 April), available at https://thediplomat.com/2023/04/what-chinas-global-security-initiative-tells-us-about-its-strategic-engagement-with-latin-america/ (accessed 9 August 2023) (noting the alignment between BRI investment and China's Global Security Initiative).

149 U.S. House of Representatives, Foreign Affairs Committee, "China Regional Snapshot: South America" (last updated 25 October 2022); available at https://foreignaffairs.house.

this all together was the infrastructure prong of BRI. It served as the framework for outward foreign investment and aligned that foreign investment with the construction of the great infrastructure projects that were meant to provide the physical connections among BRI partner states along the maritime and land-based "silk roads." This has proven to be an important element for European states, especially those without maritime access.[150] Infrastructure projects (and financing) are merely to be understood as the necessary first stage of the larger project of bringing like-minded groups of states together by solving the world's infrastructure gap. Nonetheless, they express, in concrete terms, the alignment of development, stability, and security for enhancing prosperity and stability that, as will become clear, now serve as the core principles of socialist human rights.

Taken together, one sees with some clarity the deep connections between the development of the BRI framework, the rise of a Chinese alternative to the functioning of globalization (based on development, prosperity, and stability principles), and the alignment between Chinese outbound investment and the socio-political-economic goals embedded in BRI. In this sense, BRI added another layer – and substantial investment guidance – to the supervisory responsibilities of SASAC with respect to CSOEs. Or, put differently, the SASAC guidance served to provide a foundation for the implementation of the objectives of BRI. The ordering does not matter; the tight intertwining does – suggesting the integration of the social, political, and economic in the construction of a comprehensive strategy for outbound investment tied to the projection of Chinese interests abroad. That projection can produce what the Chinese authorities called "win-win" strategies for all parties,[151] but they would not move forward in the absence of a sufficiently strong win on the Chinese side of that equation.[152]

---

gov/china-regional-snapshot-south-america/ (supporting Confucius Institutes, regional trade organizations from which the U.S. and Canada are excluded).

150 See Herrero, Alicia Garcia and Jianwei Xu (2017): "China's Belt and Road Initiative: Can Europe Expect Trade Gains?", *China and World Economy*, Vol. 25, No. 6: pp. 84–99.

151 Xi Jinping, Speech at the Meeting Commemorating the 50th Anniversary of the Restoration of the People's Republic of China's Legal Seat in the United Nations [习近平 依靠人民而发展，发展才有动力在中华人民共和国恢复联合国合法席位50周年纪念会议上的讲话] (25 October 2021; Xinhua News Agency); available at www.news.cn/politics/leaders/2021-10/25/c_1127992532.htm (accessed 9 August 2023); ("We should adhere to mutual benefit and win-win results, and jointly promote economic and social development to better benefit the people. The ancient Chinese said: 'The foundation of governance lies in the comfort of the people; the foundation of peace of the people is sufficient use.' Promoting development and living and working in peace are the common aspirations of people of all countries." [我们应该坚持互利共赢，共同推动经济社会发展更好造福人民。中国古人说："为治之本，务在于安民；安民之本，在于足用。"推动发展、安居乐业是各国人民共同愿望。为了人民而发展，发展才有意义].

152 This is particularly strongly felt in the context of Latin-American-China economic relations. See discussion in Paus, Eva (2020): "Innovation Strategies Matter: Latin America's Middle-Income Trap Meets China and Globalisation", *The Journal of Development Studies*, Vol. 56, No. 4: pp. 657–679.

Those structural considerations, then, shape the focus on hard and soft compliance factors, now understood as risk centers, where the risk is to the objectives of Chinese investment rather than the impact. BRI, in this sense, adds important balancing criteria, which, when assessed through the lens of Chinese socialist human rights principles, can suggest where on the risk continuum – prevention, mitigation, remediation, exit – a projected foreign investment falls. The tensions with host state (and especially host state civil society) perceptions of state duty and corporate responsibility then come into sharper focus. Tensions do not just produce conflicts around the identification and management of distinctive approaches to the interpretation and response to human rights and environmental wrongs; they also serve as challenges to Chinese outbound investment strategies. A May, 2023, report distributed by the Council on Geostrategy grouped these into four classes of challenges: "Civil unrest and local opposition to projects; Challenging local political and governance conditions; Rising environmental concerns; and, Poor strategic and financial planning."[153] Environmental issues suggest the nature of the challenge – here between the objectives of large infrastructure projects – against the recent development of a normative and regulatory sensitivity to environmental concerns with the Belt and Road Project itself through its "Green Belt and Road" framework.[154] The balancing of those objectives, for example, might be seen in the issue of deforestation in Brazil.[155] It is not clear how the adoption by the U.N. General Assembly of the principle of a human right to a clean, healthy, and sustainable environment may shape the calculus.[156]

The last layer in this self-reflexive construct focused on financing. That coordination between trade, development-oriented infrastructure investment, and

153 Ebel, Pippa, (2023): "Explainer: China's Belt & Road Initiative: Ten Years On," Council on Geostrategy Geopolitics Programme No. GPE 16 (May), p. 4.

154 See, e.g., National Development and Reform Commission, Ministry of Foreign Affairs, Ministry of Ecology and Environment, and Ministry of Commerce (2022), Opinions on the Joint Implementation of Green Development in the Belt and Road Initiative [国家发展改革委等部门 关于推进共建"一带一路"绿色发展的意见]; available at www.ndrc.gov.cn/xxgk/zcfb/tz/202203/t20220328_1320629.html (accessed 9 August 2023), See also Sun, Yixian and Bowen Yu, "Greening China's Belt and Road Initiative: From Norm Localisation to Norm Subsidiarity?", *Global Environmental Politics*, Vol. 23, No. 1: pp. 91–116 ("The ministry's 'Belt and Road Ecological and Environmental Cooperation Plan' identifies key areas of cooperation. While some are similar to Western practices (e.g., green finance, capacity building, safeguards), there are areas in line with China's long-lasting preferences in IDC (e.g., eco-friendly infrastructure, green demonstration parks, and province-led capacity-building and technology-transfer activities." Ibid., p. 106).

155 Fearnside, Philip M. and Adriano M. R. Figueiredo, "China's Influence on Deforestation in Brazilian Amazonia: A Growing Force in the State of Mato Grosso," Discussion Paper 2015-3 Boston University Global Economic and Governance Initiative, available at www.bu.edu/pardeeschool/files/2014/12/Brazil1.pdf (accessed 9 August 2023).

156 U.N. General Assembly, The Human Right to a Clean, Healthy, and Sustainable Environment A/76/L.75 (26 July 2022). That calculus as the document noted, "that the right to a clean, healthy, and sustainable environment is related to other rights and existing international law." Ibid.

a focus on natural resource and agricultural product export was underscored, for example, with the negotiation, in May 2023, of a China-Ecuador Free Trade Agreement.[157] And to those ends, Chinese authorities have also turned to the development of a lending facility that would better reflect the focus on Chinese global economic activity objectives – prosperity, stability and development. For that purpose, the Asian Infrastructure Investment Bank (AIIB) was established,[158] with strong backing from global partners.[159] "Though 2020 was a year of economic contraction around the world, it was also a year of continued growth and enlargement for the Belt and Road Initiative (BRI) and the Asian Infrastructure Investment Bank (AIIB) in Latin America."[160] AIIB was built on the narratives of responding to turbulent times in the wake of the financial crisis the end of the first decade of the 21st century along lines better aligned with the development and infrastructure needs of prospective client states. In that, the narrative paralleled the one on which BRI was founded.[161] In that sense, it serves as China's answer to what it saw as the flaws of post-1945 IFIs (World Bank Group and International Monetary Fund), with their increasingly frustrating, complex decision-making; failure to emphasize infrastructure projects; slow project preparation; and unacceptably risk-averse project evaluations.[162] AIIB was thus meant to be the next-generation version of post-1945 IFIs better suited for current conditions. It was also meant to value risk and reward along lines that aligned with the principles of the BRI and Chinese internationalism.[163] That has tended toward the production of

157 Daniels, Joe and Joe Leahy (2023); "China Deepens Ties in Latin America with Ecuador Free Trade Agreement: Beijing Is a Major Financial Backer in Andean Nation Despite US Efforts to Counter Its Influence," *Financial Times* (11 May), available at www.ft.com/content/b0cee143-1a38-4d93-b605-33e1cb91fc97 (accessed 9 August 2023).

158 See, e.g., Gu, Bin (2017): "Chinese Multilateralism in the AIIB", *Journal of International Economic Law*, Vol. 20: pp. 137–158.

159 According to the AIIB website, as of 2023, China's vote total was just over 26%; Asian reginal members accounted for about 72% of voting power (with no state member holding more than 9%), and non-regional members accounted for the rest, with Germany's 4.1% voting power the largest in that group. AIIB Website, "Members and Prospective Members of the Bank", available at www.aiib.org/en/about-aiib/governance/members-of-bank/index.html (accessed 9 August 2023).

160 Lang, Bridgette (2021): "Chart of the Week: Asian Infrastructure Investment Bank and Belt and Road Initiative Membership in Latin America," BU Global Development Policy Center (9 June), available at www.bu.edu/gdp/2021/06/09/chart-of-the-week-asian-infrastructure-investment-bank-and-belt-and-road-initiative-membership-in-latin-america/ (accessed 9 August 2023).

161 See, e.g., NDRC et al., Vision and Action, supra, Chapter I.

162 See, generally, Wang, Yu (2018): "The Political Economy of Joining the AIIB", *The Chinese Journal of International Politics*, pp. 105–130; Sondquist, James (2022): "Institutional Eclipse How Chinese Loans Substitute for IMF Assistance," Working Paper, Yale University (12 September), available at https://jamessundquist.github.io/website/docs/Sundquist_JMP.pdf (accessed 9 August 2023).

163 These have been recognized, at least in the world of the UN Human Rights Council. "On promoting mutually beneficial cooperation in the field of human rights" (A/HRC/37/L.36; 19 March 2018).

greater alignment in the context of sustainability and climate change issues than in the context of traditional human rights.[164]

AIIB adds a layer of coordination to a pattern of Chinese lending that is already significant.[165] There is some joint work, though, between IFIs. Projects are co-financed with either the Asian Development Bank or World Bank and others.[166] In Latin America, joint work under the "green financing" strategy has been effective, at least formally.[167] But there is also competition, around which the ideological function of risk and cost plays a role, though it may be at its most intense as traditional state borrowers seek to shift the locus of debt from one class of lender to another for strategic advantage.[168]

The operationalization of these coordinated layers tends to be targeted to regions. For Latin America, hints of the management of these layers can be discerned in the 16th China-LAC Business Summit (中国 – 拉美企业家高峰会), held in November 2023 for the first time in Beijing.[169] The agenda described the areas of inbound LAC investment at the center of the relationship – digital economies, agricultural technologies, cultural /tourism cooperation, and green economy cooperation.[170] Equally important was what was called

164 Considered in Thomas Hirsch (Lead author), Bartosch, Sophie, Yao Anqi, Guo Hongyu, Yulia Menshova, Ajita Tiwari Padhi, and Md Shamsuddoha (2019):, *Report: "Aligning the Asian Infrastructure Investment Bank (AIIB) with the Paris Agreement and the SDGs: Challenges and Opportunities. A Civil Society Perspective from: Bangladesh, China, India, Russia & Germany* (Bonn: Germanwatch), available at https://germanwatch.org/sites/default/files/AIIB_Report_web_0.pdf (accessed 9 August 2023).

165 "Since 2005, China's state-owned banks including the China Development Bank and the Export-Import Bank of China, have distributed 117 loans throughout the region – totaling $138 billion. The three recipients of these were Brazil, Ecuador, and Venezuela, where the terms were drafted to provide the PRC favorable access to each country's natural resources." US House of Representatives (Republicans), Foreign Affairs Committee, China Regional Snapshot: South America (25 October 2022); available at https://foreignaffairs.house.gov/china-regional-snapshot-south-america/ (accessed 9 August 2023).

166 AIIB website, "Partnerships [nd]", available at www.aiib.org/en/about-aiib/who-we-are/partnership/index.html (accessed 9 August 2023).

167 AIIB, Press Release (2022): "AIIB, CAF Enhance Collaboration on Green Projects in Latin America, the Caribbean: To Cofinance Sustainable Development Initiatives on Strategic Sectors Like Climate Change, Renewable Energy" (Washington, DC, 14 October); available at www.aiib.org/en/news-events/news/2022/AIIB-CAF-Enhance-Collaboration-on-Green-Projects-in-Latin-America-the-Caribbean.html (accessed 9 August 2023).

168 Demetri Sevastopulo, and Gideon Long, "US development bank strikes deal to help Ecuador pay China loans. The US International Development Finance Corporation has struck a deal that will help Ecuador repay billions of dollars in loans to China and boost development in exchange for excluding Chinese companies from its telecom networks." *Financial Times* (14 January 2021).

169 See "The 16th China-LAC Business Summit/XVI Cumbre Empresarial China-LAC," Homepage, available at www.clasummit.net/16th/en/index (accessed 9 November 2023). "Last year, President Xi Jinping delivered a written speech at the opening ceremony of the 15th China-LAC Business Summit, highly praising the important role played by the Summit in promoting economic and trade cooperation and deepening cultural exchanges between China and LAC countries over the past 15 years since its establishment." Ibid.

170 Ibid, Agenda, available at www.clasummit.net/16th/en/agenda (accessed 9 November 2023).

"think tank cooperation and, of course, "business matchmaking."[171] From the Chinese side, however, the relationship, built around the BRI memoranda of understanding focus, as in the case of Chile, "in areas such as mining, agriculture, connectivity technology, and economic integration, with an aim to create a regional hub along the 'Belt and Road' economic belt, thereby expanding trade and investment services."[172] That descriptive range then provides the framework within which the investment calculus of the CSOEs are to be made.

In contrast, the trading and investment climate has become far riskier for CSOEs in Europe. BRI has become an object of the EU policy of de-risking relations with China[173] but under conditions of growing suspicion and connection with Chinese engagement with human rights sanctions–targeted states, particularly Iran and Russia. The risk for CSOEs follows from growing monitoring aimed at exposing and isolating CSOE involvement in the development of EU policy through their investment presence in the EU. For example, some EU lawmakers became concerned and raised questions[174] when it was reported that some corporate advisors to the EU's own infrastructure alternative to the Chinese BRI, the "Global Gateway," were either controlled by CSOEs or had significant investment by CSOEs.[175]

5 The CSOE and human rights when operating abroad

It is only in the complex interplay of these layers of law, principle, regulation, and guidance that one can begin to see the outline of the normative cage in which human rights can be understood and practiced by CSOEs. In ways that have relevance to CSOE extraterritorial activities, the domestic cage has not been one in which CSOEs are easily confined.[176] One can also see that this

171 Ibid.

172 "Boost China-Chile Trade and Economic Ties for Win-Win Cooperation – Beijing-Chile Economic and Trade Cooperation Promotion Fair successfully held", China-LAC Business Summit (6 July 2023) (Ignacio Fernandez, Director General of ProChile (the Chilean Exports Promotion Bureau)), available at www.clasummit.net/16th/articles/335/detail?lang=en&col=news (accessed 9 November 2023).

173 Ashbee, Edward (2024): "The United Kingdom, the Belt and Road Initiative, and Policy Amalgams", *Asia Europe Journal*, Vol. 22: pp. 63–83; "What Does 'De-Risking' Trade With China Mean?: Europe Wants to Reduce its Exposure to, But Note Decouple From, the Country" *The Economist* (31 May 2023), available at https://www.economist.com/the-economist-explains/2023/05/31/what-does-de-risking-trade-with-china-mean (accessed 10 June 2024).

174 "EU lawmakers demand answers on Chinese firms' links to Brussels' response to belt and road," Yahoo! Finance (10 November 2023), available at https://finance.yahoo.com/news/eu-lawmakers-demand-answers-chinese-093000327.html (accessed 12 November 2023).

175 Bermngham, Finbarr (2023): "EU Includes Companies Linked to Beijing on Board of Global Gateway, Its Alternative to China's Belt and Road Initiative", *South China Morning Post* (25 October), available at www.scmp.com/news/china/diplomacy/article/3239057/eu-includes-companies-linked-beijing-its-global-gateway-board?module=hard_link&pgtype=article (accessed 9 November 2023).

176 See, e.g., Eatin, Sarah and Genia Kostka (2017): "Central Protectionism in China: The 'Central SOE Problem' in Environmental Governance", *The China Quarterly*, Vol. 231, pp. 685–704 ("We argue that a combination of "central protectionism" of state-owned national champions paired with insufficient regulatory capacity in the environmental bureaucracy

practice will differ, perhaps materially, between the domestic and foreign operations of CSOEs. And lastly, one can see that the central challenge (and thus the regulatory-supervisory risk) will be where CSOE human rights–implicating practices domestically and internationally may be difficult to reconcile.

The 2008 SASAC Guidelines to the State-owned Enterprises Directly Under the Central Government on Fulfilling Corporate Social Responsibilities[177] provides a window on the incorporation of Chinese-driven CSR for its enterprises.[178] The guidelines first align CSR with the political line of the CPC, then with the social requirements reflected in the implementation of that line, and then with the fulfilment of sustainable development goals.[179] It is also viewed as a prerequisite for successful outbound activity.[180] The context of CSR aligns well with the conceptual orientation of CSOEs as partitioned state assets assigned a role in contributing toward Chinese socialist modernization, either within or outside the state. The first focuses on compliance.[181] The second targets profitability.[182] The third touches on product quality and service.[183] The fourth focuses on resource conservation and environmentalism.[184] The fifth targets tech innovation.[185] The sixth foregrounds safety in

have provided central SOEs with both ample incentives and opportunities to shirk on environmental regulations." Ibid., p. 686).

177 Guidelines to the State-owned Enterprises Directly under the Central Government on Fulfilling Corporate Social Responsibilities (2008) [hereafter 2008 CSR Guidelines]; available at www.sasac.gov.cn/n2963340/n2964712/4891623.html (accessed 9 August 2023).

178 See also Lifeng, Wang (2014): "Analysis of Human Rights Policies of Chinese-Funded Overseas Enterprises", *Human Rights*, Vol. 13, No. 1: pp. 25–27.

179 2008 CSR Guidelines, supra., 1.3.

180 Ibid., p. 4. That provides: "Fulfilling CSR is the need for the CSOEs to participate in international economic cooperation. As the progress of economic globalization, the international community concerns more and more on the performance of an enterprise in social responsibilities. By fulfilling CSR, it is either helpful in establishing a 'responsible' public image by Chinese enterprises and more internationally influential, or significant for China to spread an image as a responsible nation." This resonates with the SASAC guidance on CSOE outbound investment supervision discussed earlier.

181 Ibid., p. 8. ("Insisting on a legal and honest way in business operation. The CSOEs are asked to comply with regulations and laws, public ethnics and commercial conventions, and trade rules.")

182 Ibid., p. 9. ("Constantly improving ability of making sustainable profits. They should improve corporate governance, and advocate scientific and democratic decision-making. They should optimize their development strategy, focus on and strengthen their core businesses, reduce management layers and distribute resources in a reasonable way.")

183 Ibid., p. 10. ("Improve product quality and service. CSOEs should try to ensure the safety of products and quality of services, update product performance and service system aiming at providing well-qualified products and service to consumers.")

184 Ibid., p. 11. ("Strengthening resource conservation and environment protection. The large State-own enterprises should take their responsibilities and lead in energy saving and emission reduction. So the enterprises have to upgrade their technology and equipment, and engage in the recycling economy, so as to develop energy-conserving products and improve resource utilization efficiency.")

185 Ibid., p. 12. ("Promoting independent innovation and technological advancement. CSOEs are required to complete mechanisms of technological innovation, increase investment in research and development so as to enforce independent innovation capability.")

production.[186] The seventh focuses on certain labor rights.[187] And the last aligns enterprise activity with state-directed philanthropic and social aid projects.[188] The guidance suggests the institutionalization of CSR objectives within the institutional organs of the enterprise, built to generate and produce useful data for the evaluation of CSR efforts,[189] and some transparency.[190] Benchmarking is also encouraged.[191] But at the center is the CPC and the core policy of its leadership. "The CSOEs should give full play to the political core role of the Communist Party of China (CPC) branches in the enterprise; encourage CPC members to take the lead in performing CSR."[192]

These quite distinct starting points, then, suggest the way that the corporate social responsibility of CSOEs, including human rights and sustainability, is framed and incorporated into the working style of enterprises. At the end of the historical period of reform and opening up (c. 2012), commentators suggested that the core CSR duty of entities was to "further implement the scientific development concept and to build harmonious society."[193] In the current era, development, risk mitigation, compliance, state aligned philanthropy, and some worker protection appear to define fundamental CSR principles. These are applied in specific context under the guidance of administrative and vanguard supervisory organs, described earlier. Human rights grounded in autonomy of individuals and expressive rights – civil and political – beyond those that are mandated through law play little role. International law and norms play no role other than to the extent they are incorporated into the risk parameters of engagement in a foreign jurisdiction.[194] As a briefing issued by

186 Ibid., p. 13. ("Ensuring production safety. Responsibility System for Safe Production should be established and more investment in production safety. Serious safety accidents ought be strictly prevented and forbidden.")

187 Ibid., p. 14. ("Protecting legal rights of employees. Employment contract with employees should be signed and respected, adhere to the principle equal pay for equal work, build up the mechanism of pay raises, and buy social insurance regulated by the government.")

188 2008 CSR Guidelines, supra, 15. ("Participating in social public welfare programs. CSOEs ought to encourage their employees to volunteer for social services, and actively participate in community and social welfare program, such as charity, donations, and giving support to schools, cultural or hygiene activities.")

189 Ibid., p. 17.

190 Ibid., p. 18. ("Enterprises having experienced in CSR work, should establish an information releasing mechanism, providing update and regular information about CSR performance and sustainable development, plans and measures in carrying out CSR.")

191 Ibid., p. 19.

192 Ibid., p. 20.

193 Qi, Dianwei, Chunhua Feng and Meina Jin (2012): "Research on the Social Responsibility of Corporations in China", *Asian Social Science*, Vol. 8, No. 15: pp. 184–188. ("All in all, corporations bear the responsibility for compliance laws and offer excellent quality products and services; customers, consumers, employees, supply chain partners, local communities, private welfare organizations and the government are the same as shareholders which are our stakeholders, corporate actions will have an impact on the surrounding environment and social development concerned the interests of all stakeholders." Ibid., p. 188.)

194 2008 CSR Guidelines, supra, This aligns with the emerging Chinese position on the supremacy of international law that effectively recognizes an obligation to strictly perform

the European Parliament noted, respecting China's international legal commitments, "China is typically careful to limit its commitments so that it does not formally breach them."[195] International law may be of some concern to the supervisory organs as state instrumentalities, but they would be incorporated only in the context of supervisory governance. The disjunctions then are readily apparent in the way in which CSOEs interact with the local environments into which they project economic power.[196] That dissonance is augmented by localized interpretation of rights, even where the general normative standards are undisputed; the case of work suspensions at Peru's Las Bambas copper mine provides a good example.[197]

But in practical terms, the conceptual dissonances are muted by operational convergence and the way CSOE risk analysis tends to steer outbound activity to those places and within those economic fields that tend to minimize risk (as that may be evaluated) by CSOEs and their supervisory organs in the state. That effectively operationalizes the Chinese policy of "win-win" internationalism through projects of compliance-based localization of practices, including human rights.[198] The problem comes when the expectations of host state stakeholders and CSOE managers do not align; the resulting conflict

all international legal obligations See, generally, Chen, Yifeng (2017): "International Law as Mere Obligations: Supremacy of International Law and Chinese Conception", *Peking University Law Journal*, Vol. 5, No. 2: pp. 285–308. ("For treaties of regulating public law issues, such as human rights treaties and international labour conventions, the obligations concerned are often fulfilled through enactment of domestic laws." Ibid., p. 300.) For some allegations made during the Third Universal Periodic Review of China, touching on the nonalignment of international norms with Chinese human rights related actions, cf., The Mekong Legal Network The International Service for Human Rights, "The Human Right Impacts of Chinese Overseas Investments and Other Business Operations in Third Countries," Submission to Human Rights Council (2018). ("States should recommend that China: incorporate protections for international human rights standards into new legislation addressing outbound investment and overseas development assistance" Ibid., p. 8.)

195 European Parliamentary Research Service, Briefing "China's compliance with selected fields of international law" (2021), supra ("China has been careful to avoid making commitments in two areas in particular: questions of national security and sovereignty, . . . and human rights, where its political and cultural traditions differ considerably from those of Western democracies." pp. 1, 5).

196 For a discussion of the example of Chinses CSR practices in connection with the Standard Gauge Railway in Kenya, see Liu, Bingyu (2021): "China's State-Centric Approach to Corporate Social Responsibility Overseas: A Case Study in Africa", *Transnational Environmental Law*, Vol. 10, No. 1: pp. 57–84, 75–80. A commentator noted: "Some BRI countries are plagued by the lack of rule of law, frequent regime change, and political risks. In an unfamiliar and complex institutional context, all the case companies treaded carefully to comply with local laws and regulations." Zhu, Jigao, Wang Yi, Guliang Tang, "China's Central SOEs' Corporate Social Responsibility Performance under the BRI," supra, at 48.

197 Merino, Roger (2022): "The Politics of Localizing Human Rights: Chinese Policies and Corporate Practices in Latin America", *Business and Human Rights Journal*, Vol. 7: pp. 439–460 (analysis of social conflicts around Las Bambas mine, one of the largest copper mines in the region).

198 Merino, Roger (2022): "The Politics of Localizing Human Rights: Chinese Policies and Corporate Practices in Latin America", *Business and Human Rights Journal*, Vol. 7: pp. 439–460

between local stakeholders and the CSOE manifests much like conflicts with local operations of companies from OECD states (for example), which look to human rights and sustainability breaches in enterprise practices.[199] That failure of alignment is, in turn, a function of risk tolerances and expectations about preferences for prevention versus mitigation or remedy that tend to make the differing calculus of home and host state actors around the calculus of activity that has human rights and environmental degradation effects.[200]

This disjunction, however, is not a small matter. The extent to which it has generated host state controversy is one way to measure its effects.[201] The CICDHA 2022 Report provides a recent snapshot assessed from the perspective of Western civil society.[202] On one hand, the CICDHA 2022 Report

---

(case study of Las Bambas, led by the Chinese Minerals and Metals Group (MMG) and located in the central highlands of Peru).

199 See Colectivo sobre Financiamiento e Inversiones Chinas, Derechos Humanos y Ambiente (CICDHA), Derechos humanos y actividades empresariales Chinas en Latinoamérica: Casos de Argentina, Bolivia, Brasil, Chile, Colombia, Ecuador, México, Perú y Venezuela; Informe de mitad de período del Examen Periódico Universal de la República Popular de China (February 2022), available at: https://amazonwatch.org/assets/files/2022-derechos-humanos-y-actividades-empresariales-chinas-en-latinoamerica.pdf (accessed 9 August 2023), (hereafter CICDHA 2022 Report), and discussion infra.

200 Ibid. These are explored in a number of writings referenced by Merino (Ibid., notes 7, 8). They include Lowe, Louise (2017): "La dimensión ambiental de las inversiones directas de China en América Latina y el Caribe", in: Pastrana, E. and H. Gehring (eds), *La proyección de China en America Latina y el Caribe* (Bogotá: Pontificia Universidad Javeriana); Mukete, Dynamic (2017): "China as Environmental Footprint: The Zambian Example", in Jaivin, L. and L. Tomba (eds), *Control* (Australia: ANU Press in China Story Yearbook); Po, Sovida and Kimkong Heng (2019): "Assessing the Impacts of Chinese Investments in Cambodia: The Case of Preah Sihanoukville Province", *Issues & Insights*, Vol. 19: pp. 1–19; Ballon, E. et al. (2019) "La Agenda de la Sociedad Civil frente a las Industrias Extractivas en América Latina", *Natural Resource Governance Institute* (May), available at https://resourcegovernance.org/sites/default/files/documents/reporte-regional.pdf (accessed 26 March 2021). International Federation for Human Rights (FIDH), "Universal Periodic Review, Third Cycle of the Civil Society's Evaluation of the Extraterritorial Obligations of the People's Republic of China: Case Studies from Argentina, Bolivia, Brazil, Ecuador and Peru No. 724", available at http://cdes.org.ec/web/wp-content/uploads/2018/10/Regional-Report.pdf (accessed 26 March 2021).

201 CICDHA 2022 Report, supra. The report had its genesis in efforts by the CICDHA collective to produce a series of shadow reports on China's extraterritorial responsibilities for its outbound investment aligned with the 2018 Universal Periodic Review under the auspices of the UN Human Rights Council. The CICDHA 2022 Report was meant to provide a midterm evaluation of progress based on the Universal Periodic Review and the recommendations set out in the shadow reports. CICDHA, "Executive Summary (English): Human Rights and Chinese Business Activities in Latin America" (2022); available at http://chinaambienteyderechos.lat/wp-content/uploads/2022/03/Resumen-Ejecutivo-Ejecutivo-EPU-Ingles.pdf (accessed 9 August 2023), p. 1.

202 In the CICDHA 2022 Report, supra, 60 civil society organizations evaluated 26 Chinese projects in nine Latin American countries that involved 20 mostly CSOEs involved in the mining, hydroelectricity, hydrocarbon, and other infrastructure sectors. It also focused on Chinese funding institutions with the greatest amount of investment in those projects, including the Industrial and Commercial Bank of China (8 projects), Export-Import Bank

noted that China assumed several commitments in the last UPR by accepting 284 recommendations, 6 of which relate to compliance with its extraterritorial obligations to guarantee that its economic activities respect and protect human rights and the environment outside China.[203] That, in turn, suggests a willingness to negotiate with host country stakeholders in ways that would be impossible within China. On the other hand, the report concluded that "the Chinese State has made insufficient effort to comply with the commitments it assumed in the UPR to guarantee human rights beyond its national territory. Evidence demonstrates that the pattern of human rights violations described in 2018 continues to be systematic."[204]

Operational failures were identified in six categories. First were breaches of environmental rights.[205] Second was failure to respect the right of participation in free, informed and prior consent.[206] Third were breaches of rights to land and adequate housing.[207] Fourth were impediments to exercise of civil and political rights.[208] Fifth were labor rights violations.[209] Last were COVID-related breaches.[210] The nature of the Chinese response might be gleaned from its submission to the 2018 Universal Periodic Review.[211] That would have framed the approach within the principles of human rights with Chinese characteristics:[212] "China gives due regard to both the universality and the particularity of human rights, combines promotion of democracy and people's livelihood, coordinates the pursuit of peace and development, and promotes and protects human rights in the process of development."[213] The emphasis on development and poverty alleviation as a function of national conditions might

of China (7), China Development Bank (7), and Bank of China (5). CICDHA, "Executive Summary (English)", pp. 1–2.

203 CICDHA, "Executive Summary (English)", supra, p. 2.

204 Ibid., p. 2.

205 Ibid. In 24 cases, "[i]rregularities were confirmed in the environmental impact studies: the lack of prior studies, conflicts of interest in the approvals, and improper modifications after approval." Ibid.

206 Ibid. A number of different forms of violations were identified, including failure to deliver complete information or to use the local language to communicate, strategies to fragment target communities, and failure to deliver guarantees.

207 Ibid., p. 3. These included forced displacement, pressure to sell land, inadequate compensation, use of police, and restrictions on movement.

208 Ibid., These centered on the protection of human rights defenders and the use of irregular forces.

209 Ibid. These violations were exacerbated by admittedly weak institutional capacity. They included prohibitions on joining labor unions and coercion against individuals to stymie labor unionization.

210 Ibid. These centered on inadequate biosecurity measures on one hand and labor exploitation with liability carve-outs for pandemic-related consequences on the other.

211 People's Republic of China, National report submitted in accordance with paragraph 5 of the annex to Human Rights Council resolution 16/21 (A/HRC/WG.6/31/CHN/1 (18 October 2018).

212 Ibid., pp. 4–10.

213 Ibid., p. 5.

nudge China toward a human rights risk assessment that favors the collective benefits of development and poverty alleviation (however measured) against breaches of human rights (including environmental rights) with respect to which compensation (post facto remedy) would be available – at least, as permitted by local law.[214] In the process, one can see how the two sides might be speaking past each other – liberal democratic civil society emphasizing the prevention principle in "prevent, mitigate, remedy" approaches to human rights violations while the Chinese side might emphasize remedy where the overall benefit of development is greater than the aggregate value of human rights breaches (a possible application of the so-called people-centered development approach at the heart of Chinese socialist human rights and, thus, a driver of risk assessment and decision-making by CSOEs). Nonetheless, there are studies that suggest that there may be little substantive difference in performance between CSOEs and non-Chinese overseas enterprises.[215]

Another and perhaps far more telling marker of difference may be found in the investment decisions for CSOEs or, rather, the regulatory climate in which CSOE outbound investment decisions are made. In Latin America, investment choices, as to both location and sector, are intimately tied to a risk calculus in which reduction of potential conflict with host states may be valued more than risk of conflict with local stakeholders.[216] Thus, there appears to be a connection between the structural approaches to outbound investment and the specific consequences to breaches of human and environmental rights.[217] These are tied to the policy priorities of the BRI.[218]

214 One gets a sense of this from a summary of the Chinese presentation during the course of its 2018 UPR. See Report of the Working Group on the Universal Periodic Review – China, A/HRC/40/06 (28 December 2018). The report noted: "China shared its experience . . . which included always giving top priority to development and promoting and protecting human rights in the process of development, prioritizing issues concerning the fundamental interests of the people and safeguarding social fairness and justice, formulating national plans and establishing coordination mechanisms to promote the integrated progress of various endeavours and fostering a peaceful and stable environment conducive to development while following a development path suited to its national conditions." Ibid., 22.

Note here the emphasis on development, state-to-state coordination, and fostering stability as the core of the human rights approaches for the state and, of course, as operationalized by its CSOEs.

215 Roger Merino, "The Politics of Localizing Human Rights", supra, pp. 453–455.

216 See Shapiro, Daniel M., Carlos Vecino and Jing Li (2018); "Exploring China's State-Led FDI Model: Evidence from the Extractive Sectors in Latin America", *Asia Pacific Journal of Management*, Vol. 35: pp. 11–37. (Noting the gap between CSOE legal license to operate versus success of obtaining a social license to operate, "[W]e find evidence suggesting that Chinese firms are more likely than non-Chinese firms to have conflicts with local communities and other nongovernment stakeholders." Ibid., p. 13.)

217 See, Gerlak, Andrea K., Marcelo Saguier, Megan Mills-Novoa, Philip M. Fearnside, Tamee R. Albrecht (2020): "Dams, Chinese Investments, and EIAs: A Race to the Bottom in South America?", *Ambio*, Vol. 49, No. 1: pp. 156–164.

218 Consider for example, Tritto, Angela and Alvin Caba (2023): "The Belt and Road Initiative in Southeast Asia: A Mixed Methods Examination", *Journal of Contemporary China*,

In Latin America, for example, CSOE-focused concentration in energy infrastructure has caused concern about energy security though, for the moment, regulators continue to approve Chinese acquisitions of local power generators.[219] Investment decisions follow two primary patterns; one touches on Chinese rejection of certain environmental and other standards and the other on the acquisition of local entities that are already alleged to be engaging in human rights or sustainability-based breaches.[220] But, at the same time, market-penetration strategies, especially within the larger states in Latin America, have produced market-driven strategies.[221] These emerging disquiets have converged with the trend in liberal democratic states to align human rights legalization with sanctions-based policies and the protection of key economic sectors from foreign control (sometimes over a certain threshold).

In Europe and North America, national security issues play a larger role.[222] Indeed, by May 2023, the European Commission appeared to be advancing a sanctions program against Chinese enterprises deemed to be evading anti-Russia sanctions.[223] Selected areas where CSOEs afford leading technologies and efficiencies, however, remain strong areas of inbound investment.[224] "From a geopolitical-regulatory perspective, Chinese investors see LAC

Vol. 32: pp. 436–454, whose research suggests that BRI appears to be a framework for outbound CSOE investment with a heavy focus on infrastructure and connectivity sectors, and substantial government guidance in choices (and places) of investment grounded in a preference for BRI states. It might be possible to posit that such preferences are based on risk mitigating analysis in which human rights considerations play a role.

219 Myers, Margaret (2023): "'It's Electric!': China's Power Play in Latin America", *Weekly Asado* (31 March), available at www.wilsoncenter.org/blog-post/its-electric-chinas-power-play-latin-america (accessed 9 August 2023).

220 Gerlak et al., "Dams, Chinese Investments, and EIAs," supra. ("China and other emerging countries offer lower-cost investment options to developing countries with fewer social and environmental safeguards that are often seen by borrowers as limiting what national governments perceive as their right to cause social and environmental impacts as they please." Ibid., p. 159.)

221 See, e.g., Busilli, Virginia Soledad and María Belén Jaime, "Chinese Investments in Brazil: Economic Diplomacy in Bilateral Relations", *Contexto International*, Vol. 43, No. 3: pp. 541–563 (automobile, telecommunications, and auto parts sectors, coupled with financial sector penetration to facilitate raw material exports).

222 See, e.g., Bartz, Diane (2022): "U.S. Bans New Huawei, ZTE Equipment Sales, Citing National Security Risk", *Reuters* (30 November), available at www.reuters.com/business/media-telecom/us-fcc-bans-equipment-sales-imports-zte-huawei-over-national-security-risk-2022-11-25/ (accessed 9 August 2023); Schmitz, Rob (2023): "Germany Moves Toward Restrictions on Huawei, as Europe Sours on China", *NPR* (8 March), available at www.npr.org/2023/03/08/1154315168/germany-china-huawei-restrictions (accessed 9 August 2023).

223 Spivak, Vika (2023): "How Sanctions Have Changed the Face of Chinese Companies in Russia", *Carneghie Politika* (18 May), available at https://carnegieendowment.org/politika/89785 (accessed 9 August 2023).

224 Doll, Scooter (2023): "Chinese State-Owned Automaker Shares Plans to Expand and Build Its EVs in Europe", *Electrek* (5 July), available at https://electrek.co/2023/07/05/chinese-state-owned-automaker-plans-build-evs-europe-china/ (accessed 12 November 2023).

as a friendly market, at a time when investment screening has significantly tightened – on grounds of national security concerns – against Chinese investment in the U.S. and the EU."[225] The price, as noted earlier, is a greater probability of conflict with host state non-state actors along human rights and sustainability fault lines.

The North American and European responses are themselves meant to be politically driven but normatively protective. These responsive regulatory and sanctions regimes use export controls "to help stem the tide of authoritarian government misuse of technology and promote a positive vision for technologies anchored by democratic values."[226] States are also augmenting a power to more deeply scrutinizing inbound investment. The United States, Canada, and European Union member states are active in this respect.[227] In the United States, President Joseph Biden, by executive order, effectively broadened the scope and factors to be considered in the review process of the Committee on Foreign Investment in the United States (CFIUS).[228] The cautionary response of Canada, for example, to CSOE investment in its hydrocarbon sector suggests that the predicate effect of outbound CSOE activity in core OECD states focuses on investment, and these cations are understood as liberal-democratic norm protective (including human rights and sustainability).[229] Increasingly,

225 Larraín and Zhang, "China's Evolving Presence in Latin America," supra.

226 The White House (2021): Fact Sheet: Export Controls and Human Rights Initiative Launched at the Summit for Democracy (10 December), available at www.whitehouse.gov/briefing-room/statements-releases/2021/12/10/fact-sheet-export-controls-and-human-rights-initiative-launched-at-the-summit-for-democracy/ (accessed 9 August 2023). See Code of Conduct for Enhancing Export Controls of Goods and Technology That Could be Misused and Lead to Serious Violations or Abuses of Human Rights (March 2023); available at www.state.gov/wp-content/uploads/2023/03/230303-Updated-ECHRI-Code-of-Conduct-FINAL.pdf (accessed 9 August 2023).

227 Orion Berg et al. (2022): Germany prohibits sale of two companies to Chinese investors – FDI scrutiny in full swing, White & Case (16 November), available at www.whitecase.com/insight-alert/germany-prohibits-sale-two-companies-chinese-investors-fdi-scrutiny-full-swing (accessed 9 August 2023).

228 White House, FACT SHEET: President Biden Signs Executive Order to Ensure Robust Reviews of Evolving National Security Risks by the Committee on Foreign Investment in the United States (15 September 2022), available at www.whitehouse.gov/briefing-room/statements-releases/2022/09/15/fact-sheet-president-biden-signs-executive-order-to-ensure-robust-reviews-of-evolving-national-security-risks-by-the-committee-on-foreign-investment-in-the-united-states/ (accessed 9 August 2023). (The criteria include effects on critical US supply chains, effects on US tech leadership, investment trends with effects on national security, cybersecurity risks, and risks to US persons' sensitive data.)

229 See, e.g., Ufimtseva, Anastasia (2020): "Investigating the Impact of State-Owned Enterprises (SOEs) on the Contemporary World Order: A Case of Chinese SOE Investment in the Canadian Hydrocarbon Sector", *Cambridge Review of International Affairs*, Vol. 33, No. 1: pp. 61–80, esp. 70–75. Ufimsteva notes the unique character of China's energy diplomacy that "combines political and economic factors. The economic side of energy diplomacy relies on the 'going out' strategy that combines trade, aid, and investment . . . while the political side, as noted earlier, supports a close relationship between SOEs and the Chinese government." Ibid., p. 68.

concern about Chinese investment in data-generating businesses has also produced efforts either to ban the investment or to prevent data from being delivered to public authorities in China. TikTok provides a current case in point.[230] These issues have little weight in Latin America, where TikTok has proven to be a useful political tool.[231]

Those sites of conflict on the ground, then, appear to underline the importance of conceptual starting points for approaching issues of human rights and environmentally sensitive investments abroad. It is also grounded in the political relations between China and its trading partners – more adversarial with OECD states, much less so with Latin American states. That drives human rights frameworks between home and host states and defines the human rights and environmental context in which CSOEs may operate. At its core, perhaps, are the very different approaches to risk that is generated as the end product of the principles, assumptions, and underlying objectives of liberal democratic market-driven systems on one hand and Marxist-Leninist development-driven systems on the other. For liberal democratic systems, human rights and environmental risk are increasingly understood as a set of normative choices within the structural-administrative framework of "prevent-mitigate-remedy" principles. These are embedded deeply in core international human rights and sustainability soft and hard law instruments.[232] They also reflect the transposition of the sensibilities of public administrative organs onto the model of appropriate business approaches to risk – at least to compliance- and disclosure-based human rights and sustainability risk. The current debate about the political-normative consequences of environmental, social, and governance (ESG) risk disclosure regimes in liberal democratic states is emblematic.[233]

For Marxist-Leninist systems operating within the framework examined in this chapter, risk is driven by development objectives and legal compliance. The focus is not on the value of economic production as a function of human rights or sustainability, but rather the risks of human rights (or their costs) as a function of the value added to specific economic activities the value of which is measured by their contribution to advancing socialist modernization, international relations, and the political objectives of home (China) and host (other)

230 See Maheshwari, Sapna and Amanda Holpuch (2023): "Why Countries Are Trying to Ban TikTok: Governments Have Expressed Concerns That TikTok, Which Is Owned by the Chinese Company ByteDance, May Endanger Sensitive User Data", *The New York Times* (26 April), available at www.nytimes.com/article/tiktok-ban.html (accessed 9 August 2023).

231 See Bergengruen, Vera (2023): "Why Latin American Leaders Are Obsessed With TikTok", *Time* (13 April), available at https://time.com/6270952/latin-american-leaders-tiktok/ (accessed 9 August 2023).

232 See, e.g., UNGP, supra.

233 Discussed in Catá Backer, Larry, "The Conundrums of Current Iterations of ESG in Market Economies – Utah et al v. Walsh: Challenging the Biden Administration's Rulemaking Incorporating of Certain ESG Factors in Pension Investment Decisions, Law at the End of the Day (28 January 2023), available at https://lcbackerblog.blogspot.com/2023/01/the-conundrums-of-current-iterations-of.html (accessed 9 August 2023).

states. In that environment, the automatic preference (and valuation skewing) is not toward or from prevention (and its risk parameters) but on the weighing of the cost and benefit of prevention, mitigation, or remedy strategies as a function of the value of the project itself. And, in that context, the value of human rights or the measure of their violation is undertaken from a socialist human rights perspective rather than one identified with liberal democratic regimes. The rest follows.

6 Conclusion

At this point, it would not be unexpected to think about the Chinse human rights CSOE environment in the same way as the confused characters at the first act finale of Rossini's *L'Italiana in Algeri*, a cacophony of bells gonging, cannons booming, crows cawing, and hammers pounding simultaneously.[234] The sonority produced can be hard on the ears, but at least everyone is onstage. That is the point here. And it reflects the age – a reflection that reveals a movement away from a global consensus about the overarching objective of deep normative convergence, conceptual and operational, to one marked by fracture and dissonance conceptually, though one that may also be marked by pragmatic convergence at the operational level.

This exploration of human rights and environmental sustainability in the CSOEs drives home that conclusion. Conceptually, the CSOE emerges from the foundational concepts of property in Chinese Marxist-Leninist theory. They are vessels within and through which the state organs, under the leadership and guidance of the vanguard CPC, may better manage the utilization of the means of production for the accomplishment of the important project of socialist modernization. Socialist modernization, in turn, is itself a conceptual vessel within which the party-state develops policy, the object of which is the perfection of the material, social, cultural, and political to prepare the way for the fulfilment of the core objectives of the revolutionary social leading forces – the establishment of a communist society.

Those vessels, then, are operated in a constant iterative state of engagement between their operations, with respect to which they are vested with a certain degree of autonomy in meeting their goals, and supervision by state and CPC organs, which are meant to ensure that macro choices and policies are aligned and further short-, medium-, and long-term policy. The relationship between CSOEs and state organs is formal and institutional. The relations between the state organs, the enterprise, and the CPC are far more interlinked at all levels of operation. In this way, the CPC can assert a deep supervisory role directed

234 Angelo Anelli, L'Italiana in Algeri (music of Gioachino Rossini (premiere Venice, 22 May 1813) ("Sabella, Elvira E Zulma: Nella testa ho un campanello che suonando fa din din. MUSTAFÀ Come scoppio di cannone la mia testa fa bum bum. TADDEO Sono come una cornacchia che spennata fa crà crà. LINDORO E HALY Nella testa un gran martello mi percuote e fa tac tà." Ibid., Scena tredicesima).

both toward the enterprise at all levels of its operation and toward state organs at all levels of their supervisory and guidance responsibilities. In this sense, then, the constructs for evaluating and developing policy with respect to SOEs relevant to non-Marxist Leninist SOEs are either profoundly irrelevant or incomprehensible. And it is at this juncture that one encounters the substantial dissonance in the area of trade and trade relations between liberal democratic and Marxist Leninist systems, usually articulated in the so-called level playing field discussions.

But the dissonance affects other core normative and operational concepts as well. The first touch on the role and character of markets. Here again, a fundamental difference: Liberal democratic systems start with the proposition that economic policy is driven by markets, and the role of the state is to ensure the integrity and good operation of those markets. Chinese Marxist-Leninist systems start with the proposition that markets are instruments that may be used to more efficiently realize state-based normative projects. Markets, in this sense, are the means through which asset vessels (CSOEs) may exercise autonomy to best extract value from their activities, but only for and constrained by the overarching (macro) political-policy objectives specified by state and party supervisory organs.

The second touches on human rights and sustainability issues, including climate change. Again, liberal democratic states start from the proposition that individual human autonomy must be privileged and that human rights are driven (in the marketplace of ideas) through civil and political rights regimes. Chinese Marxist-Leninism starts from the fundamental notion of the centrality of collective rights, driven by the need to realize socialist modernization in the quest to bring the nation closer to the perfection represented by an ideal communist society. If human rights are both collective and driven by development (socialist modernization), then both state and enterprise organs must privilege those objectives over the possible adverse effects of the resulting operations against the rights of individuals. Better put, such rights are understood as a function of the need for collective effort to make the lives of all people better through development strategies. Here one finds the dissonance between Marxist-Leninist and liberal democratic states at their apogee. The mediation between the individual and the collective in this context is possible only through law – thus, the focus of CSOE human rights on compliance with local law. It can also be mediated through palliative measures – thus, a focus on charitable work targeting populations affected by CSOE operations. Again, in this latter case, some convergence is possible, but by focusing on the remedial and mitigative effects of philanthropy rather than the conceptual basis for the action. On the other hand, the collectivity and production enhancement embedded in sustainability, environmental principles, and climate change provide a space where, at least at the level of operational behavior, the possibility for substantial alignment may be realized. But even here, the possible gap between systems that focus on rights and individuals and those that focus on collectives, development and, legality may sometimes produce deviation that may be hard to bridge, especially when the conflict occurs between CSOEs and host states.

Consequently, one might usefully think about CSOEs as vigorous actors in the global market – actors sensitive to human rights and sustainability concerns. At the same time, they are not actors detached from their state "owners" in the way that is understood in OECD- and OECD-embracing jurisdictions.[235] That dual character of the CSOE – as vigorous actors in markets with a sensitivity to human rights, and as a vigorously supervised amalgam of State assets directed toward the achievement of State policy objectives – can suggest to host states that the CSOE ought to be treated as a political instrumentality of the CSOE home state. The inference that a home state might use the cover of economic relations and markets as spheres of operations for projecting political objectives beyond their borders might be especially enhanced where a host state comes to believe that state supervision significantly embeds political objectives using markets as a means toward those ends. At the same time, there is a space in which it may be possible to develop systems and expectations of operations that satisfy the conceptual and practical objectives of both systems. The conversation about the construction and operation of that space, however, has barely begun.

235 See, e.g., Diana Roy, "China's Growing Influence in Latin America," *Council on Foreign Relations* (12 April 2022); available at www.cfr.org/backgrounder/china-influence-latin-america-argentina-brazil-venezuela-security-energy-bri (accessed 9 August 2023). ("China's role in Latin America has grown rapidly since 2000, promising economic opportunity even while raising concerns over Beijing's influence. . . . But the United States and its allies fear that Beijing is using these relationships to pursue its geopolitical goals, including the further isolation of Taiwan, and to bolster authoritarian regimes.")

10 Preliminary conclusions and prospects for further research

Judith Schönsteiner and Markus Krajewski

This book assembled a series of case studies on SOEs operating in Latin America and Europe in order to examine their human rights performance. Authors discussed how their state owners regulate and incentivize by governance tools and the respect for human rights in line with the UN Guiding Principles on Business and Human Rights and, thereby, manage to "lead by example" in terms of the recommendation issued by the UN Working Group in 2016. Overall, we found a meagre outcome, and despite exceptions in certain countries, and with regard to specific human rights obligations, states were lacking leadership in relation to the human rights performance of their companies. These preliminary conclusions summarize key findings of the chapters and attempt to draw some comparative conclusions that could be specified or confirmed in future research.

The Mexican oil and gas giant PEMEX has made timid steps towards adopting a human rights policy and a kind of human rights compliance regarding providers and contractors, argued Humberto Cantú Rivera. While the company is not carrying out human rights due diligence procedures and has insufficient remedy mechanisms, in both governance and administrative oversight structures, it does incorporate some human rights–relevant issues into its compliance procedures. Furthermore, several cases have been successfully brought in Mexican courts to hold PEMEX to account for human rights violations that were foreseeable. The Mexican Human Rights Commission recently asserted competence with regard to the topic and could provide another venue for victims to look for remedy.

In Ecuador, as María José Luque Macías showed in the chapter on Ecuador, victims tend to have fewer possibilities and less success in addressing human rights violations in domestic courts. There are, however, exceptions, such as a finally successful litigation on intimidation and false criminal suits against a human rights defender who denounced harmful activities by the national mining company ENAMI. The author identified weak governance structures generally and a weak human rights framework for Ecuadorian SOEs. In the mining company that the author selected for a more detailed study, for example, there is no human rights policy, and prosecution of human rights defenders protesting ENAMI's projects has been reported. However, several CSR

DOI: 10.4324/9781003291428-10

issues address human rights. The author recommends using the GRI reporting scheme and carrying out human rights due diligence, with a special focus on participation. In the future, as one of the projects is co-owned by the Chilean SOE Codelco, research might look at projects jointly carried out by SOEs from different countries, in order to analyze whether the foreign state investor in a South-South relationship can raise standards.

Another debate arises with regard to attribution: ENAMI does not carry out government functions, and, as the author argues, no attribution should be derived from the fact of operating mines; however, we would think, in turn, that the administration of concessions seems to be a public function, and, on this ground, acts and omissions of ENAMI should be considered attributable to the Ecuadorian state. The Inter-American Court of Human Rights took this approach years ago in the Sarayaku case; however, the court did not justify its approach, as was common for cases that involved SOEs until recently.[1] Overall, while the state exercises direct control over the board of directors and, furthermore, through the National Planning Secretariat that oversees the company and the concessions, the state is reluctant to use this position in favour of human rights policies in its companies. This is true despite the recent adoption of a national action plan and joining the EITI initiative. Certainly, this debate would be interesting regarding any SOE with functions in administrative law. Many Latin American SOEs have abandoned this model, in which SOEs have explicit regulatory functions,[2] in order to comply with OECD entry requirements, as happened, for example, in Chile before the country entered the OECD as a member in January 2010.

The Brazilian analysis took place in the context of massive privatization of SOEs; still, Eletrobras is a state-owned company and inserted in international markets. Victória Vitti de Laurentiz and Danielle Anne Pamplona showed that, while the company is able to evidence some positive human rights impacts and considerable efforts in anti-corruption measures that also can be expected to have a positive bearing on human rights enjoyment, Eletrobras has difficulty demonstrating how it addresses negative human rights impacts in its projects and governance structures; furthermore, the authors highlight the fact that the company's governance mechanisms do not provide sufficiently robust access to remedies, as the Belo Monte hydroelectric dam project showed. Current regulatory and governance mechanisms have not significantly improved the historical situation that became apparent in that case, which ended up before the Inter-American Commission of Human Rights. Based on the evidence compiled in the chapter, the authors suggested that state action is needed in order to take the measures necessary to improve and implement Pillar II and Pillar III tools that will improve the company's human rights performance.

1 Schönsteiner 2022, 6.

2 Musacchio, Aldo and Emilio Pineda (eds) (2019): *Fixing State-Owned Enterprises. New Policy Solutions to Old Problems* (Washington, DC: Inter-American Development Bank).

In particular, human rights reporting – still not required by law or governance instructions – and human rights due diligence would be necessary. While labour and environmental regulations do exist, they do not have a preventative focus and are not based on materiality and risk assessment. Furthermore, the authors highlight, reporting metrics do not correspond to a human rights approach. In that sense, we might add, potential and actual victims of Electrobras's negative human rights impact can only fall back on general environmental and labour regulation that has shown inefficient in several cases before the Inter-American Court of Human Rights, such as Hacienda Brasil Verde[3] and Fireworks Factory.[4]

The case study for Chile showed that Banco Estado fulfils a public function, although its governance is less influenced by ministries than other Chilean SOEs like Codelco or ENAP. Macarena Contreras Soto, Francisco Sánchez Lay, and Judith Schönsteiner highlighted that this public function consists in carrying out a public policy fostering accessibility of financial services for clients whom private banks, at least up until 2021–2022, would not even have considered eligible for a checking account and less so for a mortgage. This policy constitutes important evidence of the non-discriminatory, affirmative action approach the bank is taking when administering its products. In terms of formal human rights governance regarding negative impact on employees or communities, as well as the loan policies, Banco Estado is committed to implementing the UNGP but has not done so yet; as the authors showed, the bank is committed to carrying out human rights due diligence and has an environmental due diligence process for financing larger projects and awarding loans. It has also designed several mechanisms for inclusion of women in the financial market. Like all Chilean SOEs, it uses affirmative action to achieve gender balance on its board and in its leadership. By law, the bank is furthermore subject to the transparency requirements of the Chilean state organs; Banco Estado also reports human rights issues under norm 461 of the Financial Market Commission, a transparency norm for listed companies. Remedies for potential and actual victims, however, just as in all companies studied for this book, are relatively weak, although governance-based grievance mechanisms do exist, and courts usually respond favourably to discrimination claims by clients.

Overall, in Latin America, companies might have to bridge, through governance mechanisms, a larger gap between UNGP standards and the human and environmental rights reality for different reasons: first, labour and environmental regulation, as well as access to justice, is, in general, weaker than in European countries; second, oversight is less stringent, particularly in countries with deficient rule of law and higher levels of corruption; and third, no specific human rights due diligence or reporting legislation is usually in place.

3 *Hacienda Brasil Verde v Brazil*, IACtHR Series C 318 (2016).

4 *Fábrica de Fuegos v Brazil*, IACtHR Series C 407 (2020).

If this is correct, with the introduction of bills and norms regarding these issues, SOE performance should improve generally while the adoption of governance measures (company based or based in the ownership agency states have created) should be able to improve specific SOE performance. Future research could provide insights regarding specific incentives that work in fragile rule of law contexts.

In Europe, as country studies showed, challenges arise regarding crucial points that also constitute issues for private companies and for regulation in general: companies are inserted into transnational supply chains and need to attend to overseas impact. In terms of governance, companies that are not exposed to due diligence regulation or international markets, however, lag behind in scaling up to the UNGP standards.

Finland does not have a due diligence law or national regulation on business and human rights, and legislation does not include any specific human rights obligations for SOEs. However, as Mikko Rajavuori and Juho Saloranta showed, human rights issues have been incorporated into the national governance policy for SOEs in recent years. This human rights policy extends to supply chains. In this context, the authors systematically evaluated the SOEs' human rights and sustainability policies and found that, despite a common policy framework, there are considerable differences between the six companies. Particularly, Solidium, the company that exercises state ownership rights in several companies, does not have human rights policies, due diligence procedures, or remedy mechanisms. The authors detect "marked differences between publicly listed companies that operate in global markets and the closely held special assignment companies" and find that climate change–related policy goals outweighed human rights issues in the 2021 policy instruments. They conclude that the "weak state of independent human rights policies and reporting data in some of the largest financial SOEs – especially the state holding company Solidium – raises questions as to the effectiveness of ownership policy-based human rights integration in Finland".

For France, Mihaela Maria Barnes also focused on the extraterritorial application of company policies and the Due Diligence Law, revising EDF and Air France-KLM. She highlighted a judicialized case – the Hidalgo project in Mexico – and a Chinese project that EDF abandoned due to the social impact it would have created through resettlement needs. It is interesting to see that the risk of judicialization was not the determinant factor in going forward with the projects; judicialization risks in Mexico are much higher than in the People's Republic of China. The author furthermore showed how EDFs' own activities are at the centre of its due diligence exercise while suppliers and contractors are not included in the exercise, despite the French Vigilance Law. In that sense, the company's strategy is exactly contrary to PEMEX's policy that, according to Humberto Cantú Rivera's chapter, considers supplier risks but neglects its own activities. For Air France-KLM, Barnes highlighted that suppliers, highly relevant in the air transport industry, are included in the human rights due diligence processes; however, the company adopts CSR rather than human rights discourse, that, together with the chapter's author, we consider problematic. Overall, she considers that the due diligence legislation helps achieve greater consciousness of human rights issues in SOEs.

Even though SOEs in Germany are typically not engaged in the production of goods, extraction of minerals, or petroleum or other high-risk activities, they may rely on imported goods and services which could be connected with human rights abuses in global supply chains and production networks. Furthermore, human rights responsibilities of SOEs are specifically relevant if these entities engage in activities outside Germany. Markus Krajewski and Tina Brosi, therefore, took a closer look at GIZ and KfW, two SOEs which operate in the field of development cooperation and financing. They showed that both entities and their public owners (i.e., the Federation and partly the Länder) are aware of the human rights responsibilities of GIZ and KfW. However, the assessment of the complaint mechanisms of both entities and of the La Salonga case study showed that SOEs may be faced with challenges similar to those of private law companies. The authors therefore suggested that both GIZ and KfW need to improve their strategies and policies concerning access to remedies and to complaint mechanisms and with regards to the transparency of the relevant procedures and their outcomes. As a consequence, the authors also called for further empirical research concerning the human rights obligations and responsibilities of SOEs in Germany, including following up the cases which reached the complaint procedures of SOEs as well as the exact mode and scope of attribution of the activities of SOEs under German law.

While in both Latin America and Europe, states at least partly privatized their SOEs, one increasingly important economic actor on both continents carries out projects, investment, trade, and economic policy through SOEs: the People's Republic of China. This is why the editors decided to complement the case studies with an analysis of Chinese SOEs abroad – in particular, in Europe and Latin America. As Larry Catá Backer showed, the Chinese government and Chinese transnational SOEs are adapting their extraterritorial performance to national – rather than international – legal standards. This means that if a country's laws do not require human rights due diligence or human rights performance or is, de facto, not implementing its laws, Chinese companies will not address human rights issues.

To compare, the scores of the largest Chinese companies show this rift in the comprehension of human rights accountability; in particular, the lack of transparency lowers the score of Chinese companies in many cases to an outright 0.0, as the CHRB does not award points if the information is not publicly available and would not engage in contacting the company in order to obtain relevant information. ANTA International, a Chinese apparel company with the highest score, lies at 8.3, followed by Sinopec at 4.8, China National Offshore Oil with 2.7. Shenzhou International with 2.5, Anhui Conch Cement at 0.7, and CHN Energy and apparel companies Youngor Group, Heilan, and Semir at 0.0.

As Backer argued in his chapter on human rights in Chinese SOEs' overseas activities, the Chinese government is redefining the UN human rights discourse and obligations, with consequences for the extraterritorial activities of Chinese SOEs. This discourse, more familiar with SDGs than with human rights issues, explains how Chinese SOEs operate in Latin America and Europe. In that sense, the author showed how SOEs operating abroad will comply with local law but otherwise be vehicles for the implementation of economic state objectives, leading to SOEs favouring collective (development-oriented) readings of human rights, omitting individualized analysis of impact. Thus, as Backer highlighted, PRC's SOEs use a conceptual starting point on human rights that is very different to the UN approach that partly contradicts the human rights definitions established in the respective treaties. We might add that if host countries do not abide by their own treaty obligations in regulating and overseeing these companies, their governance will not close but rather widen the gap with the UNGPs.

Overall, and despite the relatively small sample of country studies in this book, it is possible to draw some preliminary conclusions and identify questions for future research.

Latin American and European state-owned companies engage in some type of sustainability and human rights reporting and have a policy commitment to respect at least some aspects of human rights. However, very few carry out human rights due diligence, and if they do, the process is likely to be distant from the international human rights standards. Even SOEs with a particular development or sustainability mission, such as the German KfW and GIZ, do not serve as model examples in this regard. It can be concluded that, in many countries, the standard of UNGP 4 is not met. National action plans included in our study – designed, adopted, and implemented from 2014 onwards in most countries – do not seem to have made a significant difference in that regard. To the contrary, countries with due diligence laws seem to fare better than countries that do not have them, although the quality of the due diligence process does not automatically come with the legal obligation. Such laws, however, cannot explain the fact that a Colombian SOE – although not subject to any due diligence law where headquartered – scores nearly as high as a Norwegian SOE that we identified as the best among the 100 largest companies worldwide in the extractive, automotive, textile, and agribusiness sectors that responds to a due diligence law since its adoption in June 2021. This opens up the question of sector-related differences and larger comparisons of state-owned and private companies within certain sectors and drivers that are – for some companies – equivalent to local due diligence laws.

The implementation of Pillar III of the UNGP remains weak, even for those SOEs incorporated in countries that do impose due diligence obligations by law. Overall, concerning grievance mechanisms, we found the largest gaps. This result is consistent for all case studies, independent of where the company is incorporated and which continent it operates on. In this respect, states could clearly do more in order to "lead by example". Future research might examine whether this phenomenon might be due to the fact that the OECD Guidelines and Guidances do not have a particularly strong development of Pillar III, a weakness that might have led companies to overlook access to remedies or whether other variables provide stronger explanations. It is plausible, however, that due diligence processes are oriented by OECD standards – SOEs tend to look to the OECD even more than some private companies as many must implement the governance standards for SOEs that the organization has issued, and the measures on Pillar III tend to remain weak. The next OECD Compendium on SOEs could gather evidence on human rights policies, human rights due diligence, and transparency as well as, in particular, the functioning of company-based and state-sponsored grievance mechanisms in order to gain a clearer picture of what SOEs are doing to implement respect for human rights throughout their activities, especially regarding Pillar III.

Generally, companies with activities abroad respond more swiftly to implement reporting and human rights policies due to overseas requirements; this might even be true for European companies that do not have foreign activities or investors as the conclusions in the Finnish case study suggest. The absence of a due diligence law in combination with the absence of foreign or industry-wide incentives might be worth exploring as additional reasons for not living up to the international standard. The adoption of the EU Directive on Corporate Sustainability Due Diligence can be expected to bring changes in this aspect; the impact of the EU Green finance policy, requiring minimum environmental, labour, and human rights safeguards, has to be seen as well, as those minimum safeguards are not explicitly aligned with the requirement to carry out human rights due diligence.

In future research, Chinese SOEs should be analyzed as vehicles of PRC's foreign policy and economic policy, and therefore, we consider, based on the evidence provided in Backer's contribution, that their actions and omissions are to be considered attributable to the state rather than belonging to the private remit. From the victims' and rightsholders' perspectives, the redefinition of human rights makes those rights insignificant insofar as their individual prong is concerned. In addition, distribution and non-discriminatory access to the fruits of Chinese economic growth, one of the overarching goals for Chinese economic activity abroad, does not seem to be an issue either. If China subordinates rights to party and state, rather than engaging in balancing rights and competing interests as mandated by international human rights law, the obvious way forward for host states seems to be ensuring that human rights protection is enforced by their own public bodies and the respective governance procedures – due diligence, transparency, grievance mechanisms – required by law. Overall, if host states do not regulate all foreign companies on human rights issues, reducing carve-outs in bilateral investment treaties (BITs) or free trade agreements (FTAs), Chinese investment through SOEs is very likely not to adopt standards required by international human rights treaties or suggested in the UNGPs. This reinforces the need for states to regulate all companies and not just "lead by example" through their own companies. If a state led by example through its SOEs, this would leave completely unaffected the business and governance models of Chinese SOEs and their operations in the respective host states.

It is in this context that it becomes even more important that SOEs – and, indeed, all businesses, independent of their owner, national or foreign, public or private – are bound not only by efficient regulations on environmental labour and climate issues but also by fundamental rights. Case studies showed that, for example, in Germany, fundamental rights are directly applicable against SOEs; in Chile, there is a constitutional clause that makes constitutional rights enforceable against all actors, public and private. In Mexico, SOEs have had to respond to constitutional law remedies. But in other countries, even when carrying out public functions, SOEs cannot be sued for the violation of fundamental rights, opening a gap of accountability. It is conceded that it depends very much on the quality of access to justice in a country generally whether SOEs – foreign or national – have to effectively respect human rights, but if SOEs were not bound by fundamental rights or not subject to constitutional remedies, there is certainly a gap regarding the implementation of the UNGPs.

While constitutional law has thus a crucial function and shows the relevance of debates on the direct applicability of international human rights law in domestic courts, an important limit of public law appeared in the country studies: Extraterritorial violations cannot be covered due to jurisdictional rules. Specific legislation, as in France, can cover some of the gaps but uses civil law and only focuses on ex post remedies. Certainly, more research is needed on the jurisdictional construction of preventative constitutional action for the extraterritorial activities of SOEs. The cases of the Chilean Codelco in Ecuador, the German KfW in Africa, and Chinese companies overseas, among others, point to this need.

Overall, strong state control or incentives regarding SOE governance decisions regarding sustainability, environmental, and human rights still seem to be quite usual among European SOEs and even among Latin American SOEs, which are generally seen as closer to government. However, the country studies in this volume show that human rights policy and human rights governance by SOEs remain hesitant rather than exemplary, without a strong political decision by the state to implement due diligence and respect for human rights in companies generally.

In Latin America, activities of state-owned enterprises tend to be strongly linked to state budgets and the financing of social policies as well as the functioning of state institutions. This rent seeking might be posing a limitation in terms of the willingness of states to regulate their SOEs from an environmental and human rights perspective.

Further research might want to explore these hypotheses in a bigger sample and search for determining variables regarding access to justice: for example, corruption, revenue dependence, and the relevance of overseas activities and financing. Furthermore, it would be interesting to explore the relevance of OECD governance standards and their usefulness to streamline human rights due diligence in SOEs. Finally, it might be useful to ask whether chapters on SOEs in FTAs or BITs constitute positive or negative incentives regarding the adoption of human rights due diligence in SOEs.

Index

Note: Page numbers in **bold** indicate tables in the text

Access to Information Law 44, 69, 71
access to remedies 193, 196, 198; Chile 77–78; Finland 97, **100–101**, 103–104; Germany 126, 127
accountability 2, 5, 196, 199; Brazil 53, 58, 60; Chile 72, 75, 82; Ecuador 27, 31, 36, 37n95, 38–39, 43; Finland 97; Germany 126, 145; Mexico 17
Agencia Nacional de Energia Eletrica (ANEEL) 54–55
Air France-KLM case 134, 142–145, 146, 195
Aktiengesellschaft 108, 109
American Convention on Human Rights 23, 29, 63
amparo procedure 23n44
Anstalt des öffentlichen Rechts (AoR) 109, 120
ANTA International 196
Anti-discrimination Law 64
Asian Infrastructure Investment Bank (AIIB) 152, 177–178
attribution 4–7, 13, 30, 54, 92, 128, 193, 196

B3 (Brazil) 59
Banco Estado 62–63, 81–82, 194; access to remedies 77–78; board of directors 68–69; due diligence 72–73; environmental norms 66–67; gender equality 76–77; green and sustainable finance 73–76; human rights in 66–67, 70–72; investment 64; regulation and actors in 65; risk and impact assessment 72–73; special rules for 68; state control over 67–68; strategy of financial inclusion 78–81; transparency policy 69–70
Banco Estado Microempresas subsidiary 77, 80
Belo Monte hydroelectric dam project 50–52, 60, 193
Belt and Road initiative (BRI) 152, 165n102, 166–167, 171n135, 172–179, 174n147, 185–186
Biden, J. 187
bilateral investment treaties (BITs) 152n26, 164, 198
board of directors (BODs) 193; Brazil 46, 55; Chile 68–69; Ecuador 32, 32n43, 34–36; France 136, 137, 144; Germany 121; Mexico 15–16
Bottini, F. 131
Brazil 2, 44–45, 48n13, 61, 135, 178n165, 193; accountability 53, 58, 60; B3 59; bidding law 57; board of directors 46, 55; corporate governance 45–46, 55–59, 60; corporate responsibility 60; deforestation in 176; due diligence 49–52, 53n31, 58, 61; environmental sustainability 57; human rights 44–50, 52–61; land sales in 104; national action plan 53, 61; New Market 53; public law 54; ratification of Convention in 2002 51; recovery of river basins 52; regulation applicable to state-owned and private companies 59–60; regulations on human rights and business activity 53; regulations on theme of human rights in energy sector 54–55; regulatory agencies 54; rise of SOEs in 45–48; risk management 60; social and environmental governance 59, 60–61; state-owned enterprises

regulations on human rights and business 55–59; transparency policy 54n36, 55–56, 58n48, 59–60; UN Global Compact in 52; *see also* Eletrobras
Brazilian Institute of Corporate Governance (IBGC) 60
Brazilian Securities Commission (CVM) 60

Cardenas Doctrine 12
Central Government on Fulfilling Corporate Social Responsibilities 180
child labour 19, 49, 71, 102, 140
Chile 2, 29n17, 135, 179, 193–194, 199; access to remedies 77–78; accountability 72, 75, 82; banks in (*see* Banco Estado); board of directors 68–69; complaint mechanism 82; Constitution 70; corporate governance 66; due diligence 62–64, 66, 69–75, 82–83; environmental sustainability 66; financial inclusion 70, 78–80, 82; human rights 62–67, 69–77, 80–83; international human rights law 63, 72, 83; laws on discrimination and harassment 75; risk assessment 66, 72; risk management 67, 71; social and environmental governance 66, 71, 74, 82; structural socio-economic discrimination 78; transparency policy 69–70, 71, 75, 82
China 165n102, 167n117, 170n131; Belt and Road initiative 152, 165n102, 166–167, 171n135, 172–179, 174n147, 185–186; Eastern Airlines 142; international human rights law 162n81; legal commitments 170; Marxist-Leninism 149, 150n21, 151, 153, 160, 170, 190; New Political Party System 171n134; social and environmental governance 188, 188n233; socialist economic systems 161n80, 163; socialist modernization 150, 155, 157, 172, 180, 188–189, 190; transparency policy 181; wind turbine project in 140; *see also* Chinese state-owned enterprise (CSOE)
Chinese state-owned enterprise (CSOE) 2, 104, 147, 189–191, 195–196, 198; corporate governance 148n5, 155, 157–158, 180n182; corporate responsibility 148, 168, 176; corporate social responsibility 167n117, 180–181, 182n196; criticism of 161; discretionary decisions 158; domestic and foreign operations of 159; engagement outside China 172; environmental laws 148; environmental sustainability 147n1, 189; establishment of communist society in 170–171; extraterritorial activities 179–180; -focused concentration in energy infrastructure 186; foreign economic policy goals 162n83; foreign operations 179–189; human rights 147–152, 161–162, 167–173, 176–191; internal and external relations 173; investment decisions for 185; in legal-normative context 153–162; legal personality of 156; limited liability 156; national model 162–167; nature of 161n80; operational compliance 166; reform 156; risk assessment 147, 164, 179, 182, 185; risk management 166; SASAC and 147n2, 154, 157–158, 160, 175, 180, 180n180; socialist human rights 150, 167, 168, 172–173, 175–176, 185, 189; sovereignty 151, 182; state ownership policy 157n61; structuring projection of 167
Code of Ethical Conduct and Integrity 48
Colbert, J.-B. 129
Colectivo sobre Financiamiento e Inversiones Chinas, Derechos Humanos y Ambiente (CICDHA) 183–184
Committee on Foreign Investment in the United States (CFIUS) 187
Community of Common Destiny 171, 171n136
complaint mechanism: Chile 82; Germany 113, 118–119, 123–124, 126–128, 196; *see also* grievance mechanism
comply or explain approach 60
contract responsibility system (CRS) 156
corporate governance: Brazil 45–46, 55–59, 60; Chile 66; China 148n5, 155, 157–158, 180n182; Finland

86n7, 88–89; German 110–111, 118; Mexico 13–16, 17
Corporate Human Rights Benchmark (CHRB) 102, 196
corporate responsibility: Brazil 60; China 148, 168, 176; Ecuador 28; Finland 96; Germany 112, 116–117, 122
corporate social responsibility (CSR) 74n80, 192; China 167n117, 180–181, 182n196; Ecuador 27, 36–37, 37n89, 37n92, 37n94; Finland 90, 93–94, 93n23, **95**, 96; France 139n62, 140n67, 143, 143n84, 144, 146; Germany 106n2
Corporate Sustainability Due Diligence Directive (EU CSDDD) 106, 113
Corporate Sustainability Index 59
Crece Mujer Emprendedora programme 76
Criminal Organisations Law 44

democratic internationalism 147, 149
disclosure 27–28, 69, 97; based human rights and sustainability risk 188; of information 30; requirements, Non-compliance with 67; standards 65; of subsidiaries 146
discrimination 75; accessibility of financial services without 63; allegations of 141; claims 194; ethnic 64, 74–75; freedom from 118; laws on 75; non-discrimination 18–20, 64, 71, 73–75, 77, 81; prevention 138; risk 81; socio-economic 64, 78
due diligence 2, 4, 192–200; Brazil 49–52, 53n31, 58, 61; Chile 62–64, 66, 69–75, 82–83; Ecuador 38, 43; Finland 91, 93, 96–97, **99**, 102–105; France 132, 138n52, 140, 142n82, 145; Germany 106, 112–114, 116–119, 122–128; Mexico 12, 20–21, 26
duty of care: France 130n12, 132–134, 138–139, 141–142; Mexico 24
Duty of Vigilance Law 130–134, 135n31, 137–138, 140–146, 195

Ecuador 2, 27–29, 40, 43, 192–193; accountability 27, 31, 36, 37n95, 38–39, 43; attribution of human rights abuses to 30; board of directors 32, 32n43, 34–36; Chilean Codelco case in 199; China-Ecuador Free Trade Agreement 177; corporate responsibility 28; corporate social responsibility 27, 36–37, 37n89, 37n92, 37n94; due diligence 38, 43; environmental laws 42n133; environmental sustainability 27, 30; human rights 27–31, 33, 35–43; international human rights law 30, 40; national action plan 28, 28n8, 28n9, 37, 43; transparency policy 33n53; typology, sectors and governance of 31–32; *see also* Empresa Nacional Minera
Electoral Mini Reform of 2015 44
Électricité de France (EDF) 130, 135–141, 144, 146, 195
Eletrobras 47, 60–61, 193; commitment of 48–52; in energy sector 54; joint ventures 50–52; role ambassador of UN Ambition Net Zero Movement 52
Empresa Coordinadora de Empresas Públicas (EMCO EP) 32
Empresa Nacional Minera (ENAMI EP) 27n1, 33n51; compliance 34; creation of 29n16; criminal complaint against Ramirez Piedra, Darwin 40–41; disclosure of information 30; due diligence by 38; environmental-related human rights record of 39; exploration activities 29, 42–43; failure to establish joint venture 39n109; failure to evaluate adverse human rights 38–39; governance-based accountability mechanism 36; HSE policy 36–38; human rights' abuses by 35–36, 39–43; limited integration of non-economic concerns 34–36; mining concessions of 29n18, 33n54; non–human rights focus of 38; policies and processes 31n29; regulatory-based accountability mechanism to 31; responsibilities of 32n48; right to water and RTHE 42; role in mining sector 32–34; social responsibility 38n104, 38n105
Enso Gutzeit 85, 92
environmental damage 22, 23–24, 33n55, 114
environmental degradation 12–13, 22–23, 26, 183
environmental impact: Brazil 58; Chile 73; Ecuador 38, 42, 50–51; France 132, 143n84, 144–145; Mexico 20, 24–25

environmental laws: Chinese state-owned enterprise 148; Ecuador 42n133; Germany 119; Mexico 23
environmental liability 22–24
environmental management plans (EMPs) 35, 39–40, 42n133
environmental remediation 24
environmental risks 17, 22, 63, 66, 72–73, 113–114, 188
environmental standards 21
environmental sustainability: Brazil 57; Chile 66; China 147n1, 189; Ecuador 27, 30; France 130
Europe *see specific countries*
European Convention of Human Rights (ECHR) 91, 92
European Court of Human Rights (ECtHR) 3, 6, 92
Extractive Industries Transparency Initiative (EITI) 27, 27n5, 28n6, 193
extraterritorial obligations (ETOs) 107, 114–115, 149, 179, 183n201, 184, 195–197, 199

Federal Law on Environmental Liability 22, 23
financial inclusion: Chile 70, 78–80, 82; strategy of 78–80
Financial Market Commission (CMF) 65–66, 69, 74, 82, 194
Finland 2, 92n20, 195; access to remedies 97, **100–101**, 103–104; accountability 97; composition and size of SOE sector 86–87; Constitution 88, 91; corporate governance 86n7, 88–89; corporate responsibility 96; corporate social responsibility 90, 93–94, 93n23, **95**, 96; developmental model 86; due diligence 91, 93, 96–97, **99**, 102–105; human rights 84–85, 87, 90–93, 96–105; industry stake **98**; key public debates **101**, 104–105; law and policy 87–90; limited liability 87; national action plan 97, 97n24; ownership rationale **98**; risk assessment 97, **99–100**, 103; risk management 103; social and environmental governance 93, 96, 105; state ownership policy 84–86, 87–98, 102, 104–105; transparency policy 96, 103
Finnair 86, 97, **98–101**, 102–104
Finnvera 87, 91, 97, **98–101**, 102–103
forced labour 20, 71–72, 102, 114, 118, 140
Fortum 86, 97, **98–101**, 102–104
France 2, 129–132, 195, 199; Air France-KLM case 134, 142–145, 146, 195; board of directors 136, 137, 144; corporate social responsibility 139n62, 140n67, 143, 143n84, 144, 146; due diligence 132, 138n52, 140, 142n82, 145; duty of care 130n12, 132–134, 138–139, 141–142; Duty of Vigilance Law 130–134, 135n31, 137–138, 140–146, 195; *Électricité de France* 130, 135–141, 144, 146, 195; environmental sustainability 130; human rights 130, 132–133, 134, 137, 139–141, 143–146; limited liability 134, 136, 145; risk assessment 141; risk management 139n61, 144; state ownership policy 130n6
free, prior and informed consent (FPIC) 51, 124, 140
freedom of association 30n26, 71
free trade agreements (FTAs) 177, 198

gender 38; balance 77, 194; diversity 76; empowerment 72, 82; equality 59, 71n66, 76–77, 93; equity 76; gap 77; identity 64; inequality 104; pay gap 64; policy 82; – sensitive innovative finance and investments 76; violence 76
General Law for the Prevention and Integral Management of Waste 22–23
German Institute for Human Rights 125–126
German Supply Chain Due Diligence Law 106, 113, 118, 126
Germany 107–108, 127–128; access to remedies 126, 127; accountability 126, 145; agency for international cooperation 115; board of directors 121; Commercial Code 110; complaint mechanism 113, 118–119, 123–124, 126–128, 196; Constitution 107, 108; corporate governance 110–111, 118; Corporate Governance Code 110; corporate responsibility 112, 116–117, 122; corporate social responsibility

106n2; due diligence 106, 112–114, 116–119, 122–128; environmental laws 119; governance 110–111; Government's Public Corporate Governance Code 118; human rights 106–107, 110–128; Human rights risks of 113–115; international human rights law 127–128; legal forms 108–109; limited liability 109–110, 116; national action plan 106, 111–112, 116, 127; risk assessment 113; risk management 113, 117, 123; security management 123; Supply Chain Due Diligence Act of 2021 112, 117–119, 122–123, 126; Sustainability Code 112; transparency policy 126–128; types and sectors of SOEs 107–108; *see also Gesellschaft für Internationale Zusammenarbeit*; *Kreditanstalt für Wiederaufbau*
Gesellschaft für Internationale Zusammenarbeit (GIZ) 107–108, 115–116, 196–197; complaint mechanism 118–119; Compliance and Integrity Case Management Process 119; corporate responsibility and human rights due diligence 117–118; financial and non-financial information 118; legal status and governance 116; risk management system 117
Gesellschaft mit beschränkter Haftung (GmbH) 109–110, 115, 116, 121
Global Reporting Initiative (GRI) 43, 140n63
green finance 73, 76, 82, 178
green funds 74, 75
green-washing 70, 76
grievance mechanism 26, 70, 73, 77–78, **100**, 103, 126, 135, 145, 146, 194, 197–198; *see also* complaint mechanism
group ethics and compliance division (GECD) 137–138

harassment 75; judicial 40; labor 19; moral 49; sexual 19, 64; workplace 64
health, safety and environmental issues (HSE) policy 36–38
Hidalgo project, Mexico 195
Human Capital Standard 66
human rights 66–67, 70–72; Banco Estado 66–67, 70–72; Brazil 44–50, 52–61; Chile 62–67, 69–77, 80–83; Ecuador 27–31, 33, 35–43; Finland 84–85, 87, 90–93, 96–105; France 130, 132–133, 134, 137, 139–141, 143–146; Germany 106–107, 110–128; Mexico 11–13, 17–26; socialist 150, 167, 168, 172–173, 175–176, 185, 189
Human Rights Declaration 20, 127
Human Rights Strategy Policy Statement 117

IG-SEST instrument 55–56
ILO Declaration on Fundamental Principles and Rights at Work 20
Institut Congolais pour la Conservation de la Nature (ICCN) 125
Inter-American Court of Human Rights 58n47, 69, 193, 194
Inter-American Commission of Human Rights 8, 193
Interministerial Commission of Corporate Governance and Administration of Corporate Holdings of the Union (CGPAR) 55
International Covenant on Economic, Social and Cultural Rights 5, 29, 63, 122, 169
international human rights law (IHRL) 2, 198–199; Chile 63, 72, 83; China 162n81; Ecuador 30, 40; Germany 127–128
IPEX Bank 121, 123, 124

KfW Capital 121, 123
KfW DEG 121, 123
KfW Development Bank 121, 123
Kreditanstalt für Wiederaufbau (KfW) 120, 128, 196–197, 199; complaint mechanism 123–124; corporate responsibility and human rights due diligence 122–123; Development Bank 121, 123; human rights policy statement 123; La Salonga National Park case 125–127; legal status and governance 120–123; risk management system 123

La Salonga National Park case 125–127
Lasso, G. 37

liberal democracy 148–152, 160, 168–170, 172–174, 185–190
limited liability: Chinese state-owned enterprise 156; Finland 87; France 134, 136, 145; Germany 109–110, 116; Mexico 24
Limited Liability Companies Act 87–88
Lopez, G. 58n48
Los Cedros case 41–42

major country diplomacy policy (China) 173
Marxist-Leninism, Chinese 149, 150n21, 151, 153, 160, 170, 190
Measures for Supervision and Administration of Overseas Investment 147n2, 155n43, 164–166
Mexican Human Rights Commission 192
Mexico 2, 11–12, 23, 135, 140, 199; accountability 17; board of directors 15–16; Constitution 13; economy 11, 13, 21; energetic reform in 17n25; environmental laws 23; freed 12; GDP 17; Hidalgo project in 195; human rights 11–13, 17–26; Hydrocarbon Law 20; judicialization risks in 195; limited liability 24; major sources of revenue 14; National Human Rights Commission 25; national identity 13n8; political discourse 21; risk management 17–18; sovereignty 16–17; state ownership policy 22; sustainability 17, 21; transparency policy 17; *see also* PEMEX
Ministry for Women and Gender Equity 76
mixed-economy company 45, 45n6, 48
Monkey Forest Consulting (MFC) 125

national action plan (NAP) 3, 193, 197; Brazil 53, 61; Ecuador 28, 28n8, 28n9, 37, 43; Finland 97, 97n24; Germany 106, 111–112, 116, 127
National Bank for Economic and Social Development (BNDES) 52
National Consumer Protection Service (SERNAC) 77–78
National Human Rights Commission (CNDH) 25
National Planning Secretariat (NPS) 34, 193
NDRC Guiding Opinions on Overseas Investment Direction 164, 165
Neste 87, 97, **98–101**, 103–104
Netherlands 24n47, 135, 144
New Market (*Novo Mercado*) (NM) (Brazil) 59
non-discrimination: Chile 64, 71, 73–75, 77, 81; Mexico 18–20
Norges Bank 50
Norway 50, 85, 92, 161, 197

Operation Lava Jato 46, 58
Organisation for Economic Cooperation and Development (OECD) 2–4, 47, 56, 62; Compendium on SOEs 103, 198; Due Diligence Guidance 70, 82; governance standards 200; Guidance of 2017 2, 5; Guidance on Due Diligence for Responsible Business Conduct 21; guidances for finance institutions 83; Guidelines for Multinational Enterprises 4, 21, 48, 53, 96, 102, 105, 110, 117, 123, 139, 143, 148; Guidelines on Corporate Governance of State-owned Enterprises 89; Guidelines on Governance of SOEs 4; non-OECD countries 139n57; OECD countries 139n57; OECD-MNE principle 148, 155, 158, 161, 161n78, 167; OECD-SOE principle 148, 154, 157–158, 160–161; Principles of Corporate Governance 60, 89; standards 4, 198
oversight 2, 5, 63, 82–83, 85, 153; administrative structures, 192; criteria for, 53; of CSOE investment management systems, 166; of disclosure standards, 65; forms of, 45, 154; functions for SERNAC, 77–78; judicial, 113; from political influence, 54; state-party, 166; state power of, 33n57, 34n63; stringent, 67, 194

parastatal entity 14, 14n12
PEMEX 11–12, 26, 192; activities and operations 15; administrative procedure against 23; adoption of Organic Statute 19–20; appointment of director 15; business plan 15; corporate governance approach of 13–16, 17; duty of care 24; environmental liability 24;

governance of 13; human rights considerations 17–22, 195; Law 13, 18, 22; liability for environmental and human rights violations 22–25; limited liability 24; private parties and 14; receiving recommendations 25n51; role of 13–14, 16–17; security management 25n51; strategic goals and objectives 15; transformation of 16; as transnational conglomerate 16–17
Petróleos de Mexico (PETROMEX/PEMEX) *see* PEMEX
policy debates 97, 104
prevent-mitigate-remedy principles 188
protect, obligation to 1, 3, 5–6; Brazil 45, 46n7, 47, 48n14, 52–55, 57–61; Chile 70, 73, 75, 77–78; China 150n21, 151–153, 154n36, 155n45, 158, 160, 162–163, 167–169, 171, 180–187; Ecuador 28, 28n9, 40–43; Finland 88, 90–92; France 138, 141, 142n76, 143n84, 144; Germany 111, 113–114, 117–118, 122–123, 126–127; Mexico 12, 17, 19–20
private market–driven economic model 169
Public and Industrial Commercial Establishment (EPIC) 135–136
public company 45, 45n5, 52
Public Corporate Governance Code (PCGC) 111, 118
public procurement (PP policy) 33n53, 36–37, 47

Ramirez Piedra, D. 40–41
respect, obligation to 2–5, 192, 197–199; Brazil 45, 47–49, 52, 57–58, 60–61; Chile 62, 72, 83; China 147–148, 150n21, 152, 163, 165–169, 171–175, 184–185, 187, 189–190; Ecuador 27n3, 28–29, 35, 37, 39, 43; Finland 96, 102; France 137, 140, 143, 144; Germany 106, 108, 110–111, 114, 116–117, 122–123, 126; Mexico 12, 18–20, 25–26
remedy 12n5, 28n10, 83, 192, 195; access to (*see* access to remedies); commitment to 102; post facto 185; prevent-mitigate-remedy principles 152, 168, 183, 185, 188–189
right to a healthy environment (RTHE) 23, 24, 29, 48, 64, 83
risk assessment 194; Chile 66, 72; China 147, 164, 185; Finland 97, **99–100**, 103; France 141; Germany 113
risk management: Brazil 60; Chile 67, 71; China 166; environmental 17; Finland 103; France 139n61, 144; Germany 113, 117, 123; Mexico 17–18
Rossini, G. 189
RUT account 80, 82

Sao Paulo Stock Exchange 47
Secretariat of Coordination and Governance of State Enterprises (SEST) 55–56
security management: Germany 123; Mexico 25
Shanghai Cooperation Organization (SCO) 174
Smaller Enterprise Empathy Programme (EMT) 79
social and environmental governance (ESG); Brazil 59, 60–61; Chile 66, 71, 74, 82; China 188, 188n233; Finland 93, 96, 105
socialization process 38, 38n105, 43
Social Responsibility Policy 48, 49, 52
Solidium 87, 97, **98–101**, 102, 103–105, 195
State-Owned Assets in Enterprises Law (SOAEL) 154n41, 154–155, 155n45, 157
State-Owned Assets Supervision and Administration Commission (SASAC) 147n2, 154, 157–158, 160, 175, 180, 180n180
state-owned enterprises (SOEs) *see specific countries*
State Ownership Act 88–89, 90
state ownership policy 1n2, 195; China 157n61; evolution of **94–95**; Finland 84–86, 87–98, 102, 104–105; France 130n6; human rights in 90–97; law and policy of 87–90; Mexico 22
Stora Enso 85, 87, 92, 97, **98–101**, 102–104
Supreme Federal Tribunal (STF) (ADI 4650) 44
Sustainability Accounting Standards Board (SASB) 66, 67

Sustainable Development Goals (SDGs) 48, 52, 66, 71, 75, 76, 79, 116, 120, 180
Sustainable Industry Classification System (SICS) 67

transnational conglomerate 16–17
transparency policy 194, 196, 198; Brazil 54n36, 55–56, 58n48, 59–60; Chile 69–70, 71, 75, 82; China 181; Ecuador 33n53; Finland 96, 103; Germany 126–128; Mexico 17

undue interference 90
UN Human Rights Council 27n3
United Nations Conference on Climate Change (COP28) 52
United Nations Guiding Principles on Business and Human Rights (UNGPs) 1, 3, 4, 25, 28, 45, 57, 62, 71, 84, 97n24, 111n33, 117, 122, 133n24, 139, 148, 152n27, 192
United Nations Working Group on Business and Human Rights 1, 58, 70, 122, 192
Universal Declaration of Human Rights 71, 102, 117, 122, 137n48, 143, 169
UN Treaty 27, 28, 92n20
UN Women's Empowerment Principles (WEPs) 76

white-washing 70
win-win cooperation 164
win-win equality initiative 76
win-win internationalism 182
win-win opening strategy 165, 175
World Wildlife Fund (WWF) 125

Xi Jinping 150n22, 152, 169, 170–171, 173, 175n151, 178n169

For Product Safety Concerns and Information please contact our EU
representative GPSR@taylorandfrancis.com
Taylor & Francis Verlag GmbH, Kaufingerstraße 24, 80331 München, Germany

www.ingramcontent.com/pod-product-compliance
Lightning Source LLC
LaVergne TN
LVHW021127300926
849160LV00010B/891

* 9 7 8 1 0 3 2 2 7 1 1 6 3 *